P9-CFX-553

STEFAN GEORGE

by

Michael M. Metzger and
Erika A. Metzger

Stefan George played a unique role in European cultural life between 1890 and 1930 through his critical attitude, his poetry, and the other artists he influenced. He was among the first to understand the significance of the French Symbolist movement and to translate poems of Baudelaire, Rimbaud, and Verlaine into German. Almost alone in the increasingly chauvinistic context of Wilhelmine Germany, George attempted to extend the horizon of his countrymen to an awareness of literary developments elsewhere through his translations of contemporary European poets. His anthology, *Deutsche Dichtung,* opposed the image of a sublimely rational humanity cherished by Goethe, Schiller, and Hölderlin to the deterministic materialism and nationalism which George encountered in his time.

In George's own poetry, from the *Hymnen* (1890) through *Das Neue Reich* (1928), the poet gradually adopts a "vatic", culturally critical stance which evolves from an initially problematic relationship to reality. The austere eloquence and striking imagery of George's poetic language influenced strongly such poets as Trakl, Heym, and Benn. In the present monograph, Stefan George's life and times are described and critical interpretations offered for his major works.

S SERIES

rature

ersity

ersity

TWAYNE'S WORLD AUTHORS SERIES (TWAS)

The purpose of TWAS is to survey the major writers —novelists, dramatists, historians, poets, philosophers, and critics—of the nations of the world. Among the national literatures covered are those of Australia, Canada, China, Eastern Europe, France, Germany, Greece, India, Italy, Japan, Latin America, New Zealand, Poland, Russia, Scandinavia, Spain, and the African nations, as well as Hebrew, Yiddish, and Latin Classical literatures. This survey is complemented by Twayne's United States Authors Series and English Authors Series.

The intent of each volume in these series is to present a critical-analytical study of the works of the writer; to include biographical and historical material that may be necessary for understanding, appreciation, and critical appraisal of the writer; and to present all material in clear, concise English—but not to vitiate the scholarly content of the work by doing so.

permission from R. Boehringer

STEFAN GEORGE

Stefan George

By MICHAEL M. METZGER AND
ERIKA A. METZGER
State University of New York at Buffalo

Twayne Publishers, Inc. :: New York

Library of Congress Catalog Card Number: 75-153453

MANUFACTURED IN THE UNITED STATES OF AMERICA

Preface

The authors of this book intend to concentrate on Stefan George, the poet. The changing perspectives of German political life and literary criticism since 1933 have long made it difficult to evaluate the poetry of Stefan George as art in its time and in terms of its relevance to our contemporary situation. For many years, George's work was known to a relatively small group of people, whose lives were deeply influenced by it. George always shunned the broader "literary" public and initially permitted his work to appear only in privately circulated editions. Especially in later years, an atmosphere of almost sacerdotal mystery surrounded him, which he did little to encourage or dispel, in order to let his ever younger "disciples" feel the full personal impact and commitment implied in his poetic statements. On the other hand, Stefan George was highly conscious of his literary reputation and did not choose to leave its fate in the hands of the popular literary critics of his time. He refused to become identified with any ism or literary movement. He entrusted the explanation of his literary and cultural intentions and the explication of his works only to the gifted scholars and critics of his circle. With these, such as Karl Wolfskehl, Friedrich Gundolf, Robert Boehringer, Friedrich Wolters, Ernst Morwitz, and Edith Landmann, George communicated frankly and freely. He disdained the literary interviews so typical of a journalistic age, which demands of a poet not only that he reveal himself in his works, but also that he be a public personality. In later years, George's refusal to play such a role gave rise to a paradoxical phenomenon: both by virtue of his translations of Baudelaire and of contemporary European poets, as well as of Shakespeare and Dante, his anthologies of relatively neglected German authors, and a growing appreciation of his own works, George's literary reputation increased. As his fame grew, however, he withdrew more and more from the public eye, preferring to exert his influence upon a select circle of young men in the manner of a latter-day Socrates, rather than solely through the mediation of his austere and demanding poetry.

The growth of George's audience was stunted by the advent of National Socialism in Germany, which George had anticipated with dread. Ironically, sharing the fate of the work of so many German poets, such as Schiller and Hölderlin, some of George's poems were distorted in interpretation to suit the ends of the new regime. Accordingly, those unfortunate studies which claim Stefan George as a prophet of the Third Reich and which falsify his statements, usually by taking them out of their proper context, are virtually devoid of value. Because of his uncompromising stand and open contempt for the Hitler regime during the last year of his life, and the ever more obvious disparity between the ideals propounded in his works and the actions of the regime in every sector of national life, literary attention was soon forcibly shifted from George to those writers whose works better fitted the pseudoethos of "blood and earth." After the war, the cultural officials of the occupying powers in Germany also saw in George a politician rather than a poet and confiscated his last collection, *Das Neue Reich* (1928), forbidding his works to be printed for several years after 1945. Ironically, Friedrich Nietzsche and Stefan George alike seemed to stand indicted of having helped to cause no less than the ideological upheaval in Germany which had led to the war. On the other hand, it soon was revealed that the only direct attempt to depose the Nazi dictators had been undertaken on July 20, 1944, by one of George's youngest friends, Claus Schenk Graf von Stauffenberg. While the image of the poet thus remained veiled as before, and neither the harsh labels "mystagogue" (E. M. Butler) or "idler" (Bertolt Brecht), nor the attempts to identify him with pure estheticism, could resolve such an enigma, Stauffenberg's attempt to assassinate Hitler played a major role in motivating a reconsideration of Stefan George's personal and literary stature. Although a political failure, Stauffenberg's act has been termed by the French critic Claude David, "*the* gesture which puts George's thought into perspective."

After the war, the task of describing Stefan George as he really had been was undertaken by those who had known him most intimately. The groundwork was laid by Robert Boehringer and Edgar Salin, who realized that the testimony of friends was necessary now to dispel the impression of ritual secrecy and autocracy which had been associated with George by those who were distant from him and his range of ideas. Other memoirs (a form which seemed most appropriate to "trace the poet's silhouette," as Robert Boehringer termed it), letters, and diaries were published, which have added considerably to our knowledge of Stefan George as a man and as a poet. Especially valuable are the conversations with George reported by Edith Landmann and his correspondence with Friedrich Gundolf. Karl Wolfskehl, who had fled from Germany in 1933, continued to pay poetic tribute to the poet until his death in

New Zealand in 1948. In his poem, "To the Germans," he still called George his "Master." A new edition of George's complete works was published in 1958 (and reprinted in 1968). Together with the word concordance by Claus Victor Bock and the series *Castrum Peregrini,* which is published in Holland by German immigrants, this is an indispensable contribution to the critical evaluation of George's achievement.

In France and England, the appreciation of George, particularly by other poets, had come more quickly than in his native Germany. The earliest translations in the major European languages date from the 1890's, coinciding with George's own efforts at bringing the works of non-German authors to the attention of his public. Among others, English and American critics, such as C. M. Bowra, E. K. Bennett, U. K. Goldsmith, and G. R. Urban, opened new avenues for a literary appreciation of George as a "good European," very much in harmony with other major poetic manifestations of his time. A significant step toward a wider reception of George in the English-speaking world was the translation of almost all of his poems into English undertaken by Olga Marx and Ernst Morwitz. Ernst Morwitz has also written a detailed commentary on the whole body of George's works based, to a large extent, on conversations with the poet. The authors are indebted to him for his interpretations and explanations. Therefore, writing an introductory monograph on Stefan George today is a different task than it was twenty or even ten years ago.

This book is written in the hope that the time might be ripe for a new interest in the work and personality of Stefan George and for an understanding of his *poetic* relevance beyond his own time. Klaus Mann once said that the poetry of Stefan George—like other phenomena, such as the German youth movement—was so specifically German that it could not be comprehended outside the country of its origin. Our understanding of other cultures has been so broadened of late, however, that such pessimism is no longer entirely justified. The present aversion of youth toward the values of the established mass society, the quest for personal meaning in life beyond material well-being, definitely encourage such a hope, as does the revival of interest in *Art Nouveau,* and the renewed esteem for the literature of the turn of the century.

In the first chapter of our monograph we will discuss the life and times of the poet, whose works will be treated in the four following chapters. The various cycles of poems have been discussed as to their basic ideas and background, but it is, of course, impossible for an introduction to do more than indicate the conceptual scope of George's poetry and the variety and depth of the latest critical approaches to it. All translations in the text are by the authors, unless otherwise indicated. We attempt to give as literal a rendering as possible, retaining the metric scheme, but sacrificing rhyme.

In closing, we wish to express our thanks to: Dr. Robert Boehringer and Mrs. Ursula Küpper of the Küpper-Bondi-Verlag for their encouragement and generous permission to quote the texts essential to this study; the Research Foundation of the State University of New York for financial support during the summers of 1966 and 1968; Professor Peter Heller and the Department of German and Slavic of the State University of New York at Buffalo for aid in securing research funds; Mrs. Roisin Marcus, who typed parts of the manuscript. Special thanks are due to Professor Ulrich Weisstein of Indiana University and Mr. Frank Kirk of Twayne Publishers for their patience and many constructive suggestions. Dr. Georg Peter Landmann improved our chronology and answered several questions. Through conversations over the years, Professors Momme and Katharina Mommsen helped this book grow.

MICHAEL M. METZGER
ERIKA A. METZGER

Contents

ABOUT THE AUTHORS

The authors teach German Literature at the State University of New York at Buffalo. Together, they have written two German Cultural Readers, *Clara und Robert Schumann* and *Paul Klee.* Erika A. Metzger has published articles on Klopstock and the Stefan George *Kreis,* Kafka, and Günter Grass. She co-edited the third volume of the critical edition of Benjamin Neukirch's anthology of German Baroque poetry and edited a facsimile edition of the works of the 17th century poet, Hans Aßmann von Abschatz. Michael M. Metzger's publications include *Lessing and the Language of Comedy* and, with Gerard F. Schmidt, *Der Hofmeister und die Gouvernante.*

Contents

Chronology

1868 July 12; Stefan George born in Büdesheim near Bingen/Rhein. Father: Stephan George (1841-1907); Mother: Eva George, née Schmitt (1841-1913).

1882-1888 George attends the Ludwig-Georgs-Gymnasium in Darmstadt; first poems.

1888-1892 Travels to England, Switzerland, Italy, France, Spain, and Denmark. In Paris, George meets Albert Saint-Paul, Stéphane Mallarmé, Paul Verlaine, Albert Mockel, Waclaw Rolicz-Lieder, and in Brussels Paul Gérardy.

1890-1891 Berlin. Student of Romance philology and literature.

1890 First volume of poetry: *Hymnen.*

1891 Translation of 37 poems by Baudelaire circulated in handwritten copies. Carl August Klein. December: Vienna, Hugo von Hofmannsthal. *Pilgerfahrten.*

1892 *Algabal. Blätter für die Kunst,* I, 1; I, 2. Beginning of friendship with Ida Coblenz.

1893 *Blätter für die Kunst,* I, 3-5. Karl Wolfskehl.

1894 *Blätter für die Kunst,* II, 1-4. Melchior Lechter.

1895 *Die Bücher der Hirten-und Preisgedichte, der Sagen und Sänge und der Hängenden Gärten. Blätter für die Kunst,* II, 5. Albert Verwey.

1896 *Blätter für die Kunst,* III, 1-5. End of friendship with Ida Coblenz.

1897 *Das Jahr der Seele. Blätter für die Kunst,* IV, 1-2.

1899 Beginning of friendship with Friedrich Gundolf. *Der Teppich des Lebens und die Lieder von Traum und Tod, mit einem Vorspiel. Blätter für die Kunst,* IV, 3-4.

1899-1903 Period of most intensive friendship with the "Cosmics," Alfred Schuler, Ludwig Klages, and Karl Wolfskehl.

1900-1902 *Deutsche Dichtung,* vols. I-III, edited by George and Wolfskehl. *Blätter für die Kunst,* IV, 5; V. *Die Fibel,* a selection of George's earliest poems. Translation: *Baudelaire, Die Blumen des Bösen.*

1903 *Tage und Taten, Aufzeichnungen und Skizzen. Blätter für die Kunst,* VI.

1904 Munich. Break with the "Cosmics." Friendship with Karl Wolfskehl continues. Maximin's death. *Blätter für die Kunst,* VII.

1905 Translation: *Zeitgenössische Dichter,* vols. I, II. Robert Boehringer, Ernst Morwitz, Walter Wenghöfer, Friedrich Wolters, Berthold Vallentin, Kurt Hildebrandt.

1906 *Maximin. Ein Gedenkbuch.* Last letter to Hofmannsthal.

1907 *Der Siebente Ring.*

1908	Last trip to Paris. George visits Auguste Rodin.
1909	Translations: *Shakespeare, Sonnette; Dante, Göttliche Komödie. Blätter für die Kunst,* VIII.
1910	*Blätter für die Kunst,* IX. *Jahrbuch für die geistige Bewegung.* Friedrich Wolters.
1911	Gundolf professor in Heidelberg, where George often visits him. Max Weber. Circle of younger friends, among them Norbert von Hellingrath and Edgar Salin.
1913	Julius and Edith Landmann.
1914	*Der Stern des Bundes. Blätter für die Kunst,* X.
1917	*Der Krieg.*
1919	*Blätter für die Kunst,* XI/XII.
1920	Severe illness. Estrangement from Gundolf.
1921	*Drei Gesänge.*
1923	Max Kommerell. Johann Anton.
1926	Final break with Gundolf.
1927	Goethe-Preis of the city of Frankfurt am Main.
1928	*Das Neue Reich.*
1927-1934	Publication of the *Collected Works.*
1933	Summer: George leaves Germany but does not return from his summer vacation. December 4: death in Locarno, Switzerland.

CHAPTER 1

Stefan George: Pilgrim and Poet

Ihr sehet wechsel· doch ich tat das gleiche.

NOVALIS describes the poets as "rare nomads" who renew the ancient reverence of men for humanity and their first gods, for the stars, spring, love, fortune, fertility, health, and joy. "Possessed here already of heavenly repose, they are not driven by foolish desires. They inhale only the aroma of earthly fruits without eating of them and becoming irrevocably bound to the nether world."[1] Essentially, this was also Stefan George's image of the poet, the ideal on which he modeled his life and work. George viewed his personal being as utterly subordinate to the service of his art and thus of men and their "first gods." His life was simple in the extreme, "nomadic" indeed. Its contours fully coincide with the gradual emergence of his poetic achievement. To many of his contemporaries, his life itself, his bearing, his most occasional and offhand remarks, had something of the work of art about them by capturing both the immediate moment and the universal, poetic significance. Hence there exists a large body of reminiscences of George which have relatively little relevance to his poetry. In this introduction to the life of the poet and his works—and especially in relating his biography—we restrict the scope of our description to those details which have a bearing on his work.

Stefan Anton George was born on July 12, 1868, in the village of Büdesheim near Bingen. He was the second child of a well-to-do wine merchant who moved to Bingen when the boy was five years old. George's ancestors had lived in the area for several generations and had gradually improved their lot, rising from farmers and millers to small-town merchants. Bingen, set among the vineyard-covered hills where the Nahe River flows into the Rhine, had a deep influence on the child's imagination and was to be the landscape of many of his later poems. Being situated on the Rhine, historically a main artery of travel and commerce, Bingen lies in that area of Germany where Western civilization has its deepest roots, *Germania Romana,* the region within the *Limes,* beyond which, in Roman times, the barbarians lived. Actually, a Roman fortress had stood at that point of the Rhine. Later, too, the area achieved a rich cultural and religious heritage. The mystic Hildegard von Bingen (1098-1179) had lived there as the abbess of a convent. The earthy and spontaneous religious fervor of the local population was recorded by Goethe in *St. Rochus's Feast-day in Bingen* (1817). Roman antiquity and medieval Christianity have left their traces everywhere in and around the city, which also possesses great natural beauty and a gentle climate.

George describes his earliest impressions of the landscape and the people in various poems and in the two prose pieces, *Sonntage auf meinem Land* (*Sundays at Home*) and *Der kindliche Kalender* (*The Child's Calendar*). Eastertime, especially, brought out for George the strong link with the dignity of primal paganism, which still survived, he felt, in the religious customs of the area:

> Holy Week came with its shrouded altars, the silent organ, and the sounding of the rattles instead of the handbells and church bells. On Good Friday, after the priest and the sexton had done so, we prostrated ourselves in the choir and kissed the Holy Cross which had been laid there. In the twilight one could hear the ancient lays of mourning for the downfall of the City. Then came Saturday with the unveiling of the Cross and the trumpets of Easter joy. On Low Sunday the chorales from the spires wakened us and we stood to see the procession of little white bridegrooms and brides who were going to the Table of the Lord for the first time. All of them had on their brows the pallor of awe and reverence, and this was the only day on which even the awkward children of the simple folk became graceful.[2]

The Catholic faith and its ritual played an important part in the life of Bingen and that of George's family. When George's mother died, the oleander trees she had planted when she married were presented to the nuns on the nearby Rochusberg, an act symbolizing a returning of His gifts to God.

George seems to have had no significant conflict with his family about the direction his life was to take. His parents were willing to let their son do exactly as he pleased without serious financial worries. This contributed in no small measure to George's self-confidence and balanced, harmonious personality. Despite the highly peripatetic life which George led from his earliest years onward, his home was Bingen and he brought his many friends to the hospitable house, where his room and his books were always ready. Like George himself, neither his sister, Anna Maria Ottilie (1866-1938), nor his brother, Friedrich Johann Baptist (1870-1925), ever married.

George's intellectual gifts early became apparent. After attending primary school in Bingen, he was sent, at the age of thirteen, to one of the best secondary schools in the duchy of Hesse, the Ludwig-Georgs-Gymnasium in Darmstadt. Here, in the years 1882-88, he received a humanistic education in which Greek, Latin, and French were stressed. He excelled in French[3] and acquired a thorough knowledge of modern European literature, as well as of the Greek and Roman authors. The ducal residence of Darmstadt was a revelation to the youth from the small Rhenish town. Although generally described as a "loner," he assembled his first small circle of friends; and he had access to libraries, and especially to the theater, whose literary possibilities fascinated him at this time, although he later chose other means of artistic expression.[4] George was particularly fond of the works of Henrik Ibsen. He taught himself Norwegian and translated from Ibsen's *Catilina* and *The Vikings of Helgeland*—a fact which indicates that he was not interested in Ibsen as a "realist," but strictly in the traditional poetic drama. George's generation was the *Ibsen-Jugend* ("Ibsen-Youth"), as Karl Wolfskehl was later to characterize it.[5] In those days, Nietzsche was still almost completely unknown to the reading public of provincial cities, and for the younger generation, Ibsen represented the striving for truth, originality, and thorough and scrupulous self-examination. In Ibsen one experienced the heroic glorification of the ego instead of the hypocritical values of middle-class society. Spontaneity and naturalness were the watchwords, and insincere gestures were disdained.

A trait that George had displayed even in his early childhood became even more marked in Darmstadt. This was the need for companions to help him achieve his goals and accept his leadership. As a boy, he had created a mythical kingdom, "Amhara," whose ruler he was. His playmates were his subjects, conversing with him in a secret language. Now, at the age of nineteen, together with a few other students at the Gymnasium, he founded a literary journal, *Rosen und Disteln* (*Roses and Thistles*), in which he published his earliest poems under the pseudonym of Edmund Delorme. George's first poetic exercises consisted of copying and translating poems of Petrarch and Tasso rather than of the German "Olympians," whose works constituted the accepted literary "course" at the Gymnasium. He taught himself Italian in order to be able to read and translate the Italian Renaissance poets he revered.

George had begun writing poems at the age of eighteen. Aside from those appearing in *Rosen und Disteln,* he later published some of these early lyrics in the *Blätter für die Kunst* (*Leaves,* i.e., *Journal for the Arts*)[6] and a large selection in 1901 in a volume entitled *Die Fibel* (*The Primer*). These poems have, as their common themes, the struggle between reason and feeling, change as the underlying force of all life, unhappy love, and death. Although they reflect genuinely felt emotions and perceptions, the poems of *Die Fibel* are still "within the framework of traditional idealism."[7] Striking, however, is the melancholy about the transitoriness of life, and the insight that he who is loved by the gods is destroyed early: "Heaven soon calls/ To its glorious throne/ Him who enjoys its highest grace" (II, 483). As in the play *Manuel*, written at the same time, George strikes a note of despair stronger than the mere melancholy so common to young poets. Where love is concerned we find more than a touch of Petrarchism, as in the poem "Die Sirene" ("The Siren") (II, 477). The closeness of love, life's highest expression, to death is poignantly expressed in "Abendbetrachtung" ("Evening Meditation") (II, 472). Walking in the evening, the time when "lips are opened to kiss, arms to embrace," the poet follows a path that leads him to the wall of a graveyard, "Where so many now decay,/ Who once to radiance/ Inflamed human passion/ Where into eternal night/ Those we revere/ Sink away with never another sign to us."

To a remarkable extent, the young poet declined the easy equation of the personal and the poetic self typical of German lyrical poetry of the late nineteenth century, which strove to imitate the *Erlebnisdichtung* of Goethe long after other poetic principles had gained dominance elsewhere. George later said that "the deepest impression, the strongest feelings are no guarantee for a good poem. . . . Art is neither torment nor ecstasy, but rather a triumph over the one and a transfiguration of the other" (I, 531-32). He called for the objectification of passion into a musical, poetic form: "Can you not express all of your silent longing in the whispering of flowers or a gentle May rain, . . . carry the struggle for the impossible to dizzying mountain peaks which are still far enough from the clouds? Express the futility of being and procreation through that aimless, grey, foggy street, and proud, unavoidable despair through the blood-red and purple of a sunset?" (I, 529). This kind of awareness, anticipating the direction George was to follow during the coming years, is already evident in the following poem from *Die Fibel*:

Drunten zieht mit bunten wimpeln
Schnell ein schiff den strom entlang–
Saiten-klingen und gesang.

An dem abhang steht der winzer

In der sonne siedend heiss–
Schwere arbeit saurer schweiss.

Droben senkt man auf dem friedhof
Einen in die frische gruft–
Klagetöne moderduft.

Freude mühsal tod birgt in sich
EINE zeit EIN himmelsstrich–
Keiner findets wunderlich. (II, 481)

Below there moves with colored pennants
Swift on the stream a ship along–
Strum of strings and song.

On the hillside stands the vintner,
In the sun's blazing heat–
Hard work, sour sweat.

Above they lower in the churchyard
Someone into the fresh-dug grave–
Sounds of mourning, smells of decay.

Joy, work and death are embraced
By ONE time, ONE place–
No one is amazed.

The complete suppression of the speaker's self, the austere musicality created by alliteration and vowel color, and the striking visual sweep of the poem indicate how originally even the very young George could write, especially compared with the effusive and self-centered productions of his older German contemporaries. "No one is amazed"—except the poet, whose presence is all the more compelling through its not being mentioned.

"L'Allemagne commence à me dégoûter"[8] ("Germany is starting to disgust me"), George wrote to a friend some years after leaving school. There is evidence that he felt this way far earlier, for he found little echo or approval of his writing in his immediate surroundings or in the German literary world of the late nineteenth century. An observation which appeared in the *Blätter* could also be applied to the situation prevailing in his youth: "The poetic personality seems to have become lost to Germany. Now there is only the educated bureaucratic subject of the state who makes poems, and worse yet, the German man of letters who makes poems."[9] At the time he graduated from the Gymnasium in 1888, it must have been evident to George that he was not to follow the conventional path of education which would have led into one branch or another of German civil service or commerce. Instead of entering the university, he began to travel. As he confided to a friend many years later, his mood was explosive: "Germany was intolerable then; just think of Nietzsche! I would have thrown a bomb if they had kept me here; or I would have perished like Nietzsche. My father was glad to get rid of me, for he sensed the danger."[10] Partly to improve his command of the English language, George visited England from May until October, 1888. In London, which at that time was still the capital of the all-powerful British Empire, he perceived "an expansive sense of life, borne by great political tasks and goals, an ancient cultural unity which carefully preserved traditions, a firmly molded way of life for all classes of the populace, a decorous politeness among all the people, phenomena which were no longer to be found in the Germany of those years, or which were just beginning to emerge."[11] "You must know that I am becoming more and more cosmopolitan,"[12] George wrote to a friend, indicating the impact which London had on him. It is likely that here he became familiar with the works of the "honored masters," Dante Gabriel Rossetti, Algernon Charles Swinburne, and Ernest Dowson, whose poems he was later to translate and publish in Germany. In one of the poems he wrote on this journey, George describes his stay in England as "a long summer's morning/ Half earnest dream, half game and farce" (II, 493).

One "earnest dream" that was beginning to materialize at this juncture was George's idea that by the force of his personality and poetry he might influence the course of men's lives. Austerity, self-denial, the ethical imperative of the spirit over material life—traits which were to characterize George in later life—are lucidly expounded in a letter to one of his friends written from London: "The sybarites [*Genussmenschen*] are the apparently happy ones, and yet I would not like to trade places with them. Let the sybarites laugh at us; reforms for the good of mankind, all good that prevails (for we must not say that everything is bad), everything good that has come about and all the evil that has been eliminated—all of this was not done by sybarites, but by those whose example we follow."[13] Upon his return to Germany, George wished to convene a "Congress" of like-minded young poets and publish a collection of their works, and he began to realize the power of his inward urge to write. The "reforms" mentioned above are clearly of a spiritual or cultural nature, far from any social goals. As he wrote, "a silent hope inspires me that I might provide for my fellow men a gentle trace of refreshment or delight."[14] In the "Congress" and the publication plan, however, we see foreshadowed the later circle of the *Blätter für die Kunst.*

After his return from England and a short stay in Bingen, George visited Montreux, Switzerland, and northern Italy; and, after another sojourn in Montreux, he arrived in Paris in May, 1889. This seems to have been a time of turmoil for the poet, of youthful exaltation alternating with periods of almost cynical melancholy. Clearly he was striking various poses, trying on various masks with which he might confront the world and himself, ultimately to reject all of them. At Montreux he had played the title role in Molière's *Le Misanthrope,* and his depiction of himself is revealing in the extremeness with which George saw himself at the time: "Can you imagine anything more contradictory than that I, the socialist, communard, atheist, should play in a comedy with a German baron in the house of a professor of theology surrounded by a whole bevy of society ladies?"[15] Surely George termed himself "socialist" and "communard" in order to make the contrast more drastic and interesting. The term "atheist," however, contains a glimmer of truth, although the word is far too extreme. Unquestionably, George was turning away from the conventions of the Catholic Church in which he had grown up. Throughout his life, however, an essential religiosity was never to leave him and plays a central role in his ethical and poetic attitudes. His ambivalence is evident in a poem written on this journey, "Seefahrt" ("Voyage on the Lake"), which describes how he and his friends rowed to a small town on a winter evening. The church door stands open, and they enter as the litany is being sung and the mothers are reciting the prayers of the rosary. The poem closes: "My friends laugh—we hurry away./ The time has passed! the darkness looms!/ But I am hurt by their mocking words/ Though I am not much better than they—/ Lost in thought I climb into the boat" (II, 496-97).

In these years, too, George began to suffer a sense of loneliness, of isolation brought about through his vision of the world and the demanding medium with which he chose to express it. This spell was, if only temporarily, broken for him in Paris. On his first day there, he met the young French poet Albert Saint-Paul (1861-1946), through whom he became acquainted with the Paris he had so long been seeking—the artistic, intellectual, and spiritual atmosphere in which he felt himself spontaneously accepted by his peers. Among others, he met Paul Verlaine (1844-96), Francis Vielé-Griffin (1863-1937), the Belgian writer Albert Mockel (1866-1944), and the Polish poet Waclaw Rolicz-Lieder (1866-1912). Through Saint-Paul he was finally introduced to Stéphane Mallarmé (1842-98), who during those years welcomed selected guests once a week. As

Arthur Symons described him: "Every Tuesday for the last twenty years he has talked more fascinatingly, more suggestively, than any one else has ever done, in that little room in the Rue de Rome, to that little group of eager young poets. 'A seeker after something in the world, that there is in no satisfying measure, or not at all,' he has carried his contempt for the usual, the conventional, beyond the point of literary expression, into the domain of practical affairs."[16] Mallarmé received George warmly, especially when he heard that he had begun translating Baudelaire's *Les Fleurs du Mal* into German. George had been described to Mallarmé as resembling "le jeune Goethe d'avant *Werther*,"[17] conveying something of the impression of troubled genius George must have made at the time. In Mallarmé's circle, the young George impressed his French friends as a poet of unusual promise. Later they were to note his apparently contradictory qualities of pride and shyness, graciousness and awkwardness. Rarely did he participate in their discussions, preferring to listen and learn. The intensity with which George approached the works of these poets, however, is attested by the 365 pages of poems of French and other European authors which he copied down at this time, and some of which he was later to translate.

Stefan George's early progress is not comprehensible without a consideration of the influence which Stéphane Mallarmé and his circle exerted upon him, Symbolism being not only a "style" but suggesting a specific attitude towards life. According to Mallarmé's poetic concepts, the world of phenomena exists in order to be transformed into the world of art, into poetry. The poet, therefore, is the mediator, the alchemist who alone knows the secret of this metamorphosis. He communicates his perceptions and the responses of his being to inward and outward phenomena in terms of highly personal symbols, in words charged with a meaning fully understood only by the poet himself, if at all. Words themselves are symbols, which, in the hands of the poet, achieve a meaning beyond their commonly understood definitions. Thus, "the poem is a mystery to which the reader must find the key" ("un mystère dont le lecteur doit chercher la clef").[18] The language of the Symbolist poem should consist of allusions, avoiding all direct expressions used in everyday language and thought. The poet should achieve a highly musical effect, create a mood, a certain *état de l'âme* within which the symbol's meaning can be felt most felicitously, since to perceive it rationally is impossible. "Man lives in a forest of symbols," Baudelaire had said. The visible world and its objects are symbols for the eternal and invisible, as the German Romantics and especially Novalis had already asserted. The poet merely "suggests" their meaning beyond the apparent reality. This power of mediation is restricted entirely to the poet, giving him an almost priestly office. For the Symbolists, the pursuit of "art for art's sake" was a highly serious—nearly a sacred—function, since beauty, in and of itself, stood for a higher meaning beyond itself.

In their ultimate striving, the French Symbolists are not far from the Platonic ideals of the Good, the True, and the Beautiful, and this idealistic aspect was undoubtedly what appealed to George far more than the estheticism, the Bohemianism, and the apparent nihilism so often superficially associated with this group. "His ideal of style, even before he knew the 'Fleurs du Mal,' was directed towards a verse saturated with perception and maximally compressed in its expression."[19] George had come to Paris with a predisposed affinity to the ideas and the works of the men he encountered there. He was ready to accept Verlaine's admonition: "Que ton vers soit la bonne aventure/ Éparse au vent crispé du matin/ Qui va fleurant la menthe et le thym . . ./ Et tout le reste est littérature"[20] ("Let your verse be a good-luck charm/ Scattered on the brisk morning wind/ That passes smelling of mint and thyme . . ./ And everything else is mere literature") (Tr. Muriel Kittel).

Paul Verlaine and Stéphane Mallarmé were the only living poets whom George ever acknowledged as his "masters" and whose apprentice he ever wanted to be. Mallarmé was referred to as "*le maître*" by his circle, solemnly evoking the sense of poetry as a craft. As his eulogy on Mallarmé indicates, George endowed this concept with even greater mystery, seeing Mallarmé, and thus the poet *per se,* as a sort of master sorcerer, almost a priest:

> The sage who knows of the miraculous powers and distills the elixir of life from them must not be accused when the apprentice, who has peeped through a crack, clumsily imitates the sacred motions and causes exhaustion and death with his brew. Therefore, o poet, do companions and disciples gladly call you master, because you least of all can be imitated and yet have such power over them, because all of them strive for the highest perfection in sense and melody to find approval in your eyes, because you perpetually retain for them a secret, and grant us the faith in that beauteous Eden which alone is eternal. (I, 508)

In Paris, George found a circle of congenial and productive intellects gathered around a single dominant "master" who exerted his influence over them by virtue not only of his intellect and his gift of expression, but also through an ineffable, almost magical mystique of personality, or through charisma. George was predisposed to affirm the idea of such a relationship, which is an archetypal component of all intellectual activity. The idea of the thinker or poet as a social being, teaching and being taught by his peers, has as valid a tradition in the history of Western thought as does the view that eremitical seclusion is the *sine qua non* of spiritual productivity. The idea of interaction between minds and souls, of dialectic and dispute, is at the root of the Platonic Academy, the Stoa, and the medieval university. In Germany, poetry has always had a strong pedagogical and didactic bent; and poets, such as Goethe (especially in his younger days), Schiller, and the Romantics had circles of adherents who gathered around them, even if not in the atmosphere of solemnity of the Paris circle around Mallarmé as described by George. An earlier analogue to George's sense of the "circle" (*Kreis*) surrounding a poet and teacher was Friedrich Gottlieb Klopstock's cultivation of his friends, "the noble few" (*die wenigen Edlen*) and his detailed plan of the "Republic of Scholars" (*Die Gelehrtenrepublik*), which was to embrace all spheres of spiritual activity. The later *Kreis* which George attracted and influenced thus had its most direct lineage from the French literary circle of the Symbolists but derived its pedagogical aura from a venerable Western heritage.

For the period around 1890, there is ample evidence that George's enthusiasm for his Parisian friends was not one-sided: numerous letters, including eleven by Mallarmé, indicate that the young German poet was regarded by his older colleagues as their peer, an impression reinforced by the memoirs of many of them appearing in an issue of the *Revue d'Allemagne* devoted to George which appeared in 1928 on the occasion of his sixtieth birthday. "Paris, the only place where I have found and still possess true friends,"[21] George wrote in 1896, at a point in his life when he was beginning to command the admiration of his own group of friends and literary allies in Germany. This indicates that George found in Paris, where he later returned several times, the most intense experience of the fusion of poetry and friendship. Much as George would have desired it, such a constellation never recurred, because he never again found a comparable meeting of equal minds. Most importantly, Paris had finally freed George from the haunting fear of being altogether alone in his artistic striving. The poem "Franken" ("Frankish Lands") (I, 235), whose title recalls the original unity of Germany and France under Charlemagne, is the most eloquent statement of what the Parisian experience meant to George:

> It was the direst crossroad of my path:
> There from the abyss poisonous flames did writhe,
> Here were the zones I shunned sick with disgust
> I felt for all things men there praised and did.

Their gods were mocked by me and mine by them.
Where is your bard, you poor and boastful race?
Not one is here: the one lives in exile,
The other's tortured head is touched by frost. (I, 235)

Thus George describes the spiritual situation in which he saw the Bismarckian-Wilhelmine Germany of his day. Dominated by the imperialistic goals of Prussia and the complacent materialism of the German middle classes, this society had, in effect, sent the painter Arnold Böcklin into exile (line 7, above), Nietzsche to madness (line 8, above). The poet is drawn by a magical call to the West, to France, "the Mother of the alien, the despised and persecuted." The last two strophes, a hymn to Paris and the strength George drew from the spiritual unity of "the Frankish lands," require no further commentary:

And in the town of festive grace, its gardens'
Melancholy charm where 'midst night-bright spires,
O'er vaults, enchanted youth itself enthralled me,
In ecstasy of all things dear and sacred.
There, bard and hero had preserved the Secret:
VILLIERS in his mind worthy of a throne,
VERLAINE in fall and penance meek and childlike,
And for his ideal bleeding, MALLARMÉ.

May dream and distance strengthen us and nourish,
Only what lives can bring us the air we breathe.
Thus I thank you, my friends, who still sing there,
And fathers at whose graveside I have stood
How often, even since I have gained ground,
Battling in dismal homeland, of victory
Still unsure, has this whispering strengthened me:
RETURNENT FRANC EN FRANCE DULCE TERRE. (I, 235-36)

After his first stay in Paris, which had been interrupted by a brief trip to Spain, George returned to Germany. Following plans he had made earlier, he began to study Romance literature at the University of Berlin, where he stayed for three semesters. At this time, George had severe doubts about the capability of the German language to express what he wanted to say in the musical form he desired. For a time he actually preferred to speak and write French and Spanish and even invented a "Lingua Romana," which combined Spanish and Latin vocabulary with German syntactical patterns.[22] At one point, he seriously considered emigrating to Mexico, at the behest of a Mexican father and his two sons whom he had met in Paris and who had followed him to Berlin. Evidently George overcame this profound personal and cultural crisis, for when he brought his friends to their ship for their return to the New World, he presented them with a copy of his first book of poems, *Hymnen* (*Odes*), which had been printed privately in 1890, in a limited edition of 100 copies, an event emblematic of his resolve to remain in Germany and practice his craft as a poet in the German language, to be, above and beyond all else, a poet.

While at Berlin, George, together with Carl August Klein (1867-1952), a fellow student and friend, founded the *Blätter für die Kunst*, the journal which was to be the principal organ for his ideas and works and those of his associates for the next twenty-seven years. It appeared at a time when, in Germany, the poet had been reduced to being either a provider of pleasant diversion—"a lilac-sweet Spring rhapsode," as Arno Holz called him—or a social critic in the naturalistic mode, "an apostle of reality," as George ironically said. George intended to present a "new art" designed to overcome and supersede both these directions. If the period before 1892 is characterized by George's search for a wider circle of like-minded friends and affirmation of his artistic aims, the next decade was to bring the first manifestations of this "new art," which was inspired by the program of the Symbolists he had encountered in Paris. George was not the first German writer to discover the possibilities inherent in Symbolism, but he was surely the most gifted, eloquent, and productive exponent of the poetic aspects of the movement in his homeland. He did not slavishly follow any masters but set his own personal stamp upon those elements of Symbolism which he found appropriate for his ambitious program of revitalizing German culture through art; he reasserted the primacy of the artist, especially of the poet, in this effort.[23]

The first issue (probably consisting of about 100 copies) of the *Blätter* was published in Berlin. The initial contributors bore the costs of publication, restricting the distribution of the journal to a small circle of carefully selected readers. A limited number of copies was at first offered in one bookstore each in Berlin, Paris, and Vienna. Considering its slenderness, the first issue, which was thirty-two pages long, contained works which more than justified the claims of its editors that they were laying the foundations for a new standard of poetic art. The issue contained poems by George from *Hymnen, Pilgerfahrten,* (*Pilgrimages*, printed privately in 1891), *Algabal* (1892), and the early poem "Legende" ("Legend") published under the pen name of Edmund Lorm, which George had used in his youth; the first printing of Hugo von Hofmannsthal's *Der Tod des Tizian* (*The Death of Titian*); and poems by the Belgian Paul Gérardy (1870-1933) and by Carl Rouge, a friend of George's since his schooldays. The cover illustration of the first issue is a line drawing of a young shepherd in Greek attire pensively playing a flute and lightly holding his staff. In its simplicity and directness, this cover itself is in strong contrast to the rather more pretentious decoration of other literary publications of the day. The program of the journal made the break with current literary trends in Germany even more explicit:

> The name of this publication already partially indicates its intention: to serve art, and particularly lyric poetry and prose, eliminating all that is of a political or social nature.
> [The journal] demands a SPIRITUAL ART based on the new mode of feeling and new means of execution—an art for art—and thus stands in opposition to that obsolescent and mediocre school which originated from a misconception of reality. It also cannot occupy itself with improving the world or with utopian dreams of universal felicity in which is seen nowadays the seed of everything new. These ideas may be quite good, but belong in another realm than that of poetry. . . .
> We believe in a glorious renascence within the arts.[24]

Despite the high level of quality and the ambitiousness of this program, the *Blätter* were ignored at the time, largely owing to the obscurity of the authors and their lack of connections within the accepted literary circles of Germany, which they would have disdained to cultivate. All the more surprising is the universally favorable comment the publication received in French and Belgian journals, which welcomed the *Blätter für die Kunst* as a valued ally in the pan-European effort to raise the arts to a new dignity. George was the only German poet elected to a committee soliciting subscriptions to a book, *Le tombeau de Ch. Baudelaire,* the proceeds of which were to go toward erecting a monument to the French poet. As an emblem of the internationalism of its intentions, the first issue of the *Blätter* carried an announcement of the project.

By virtue of its high standards and the growing prestige of its contributors—among whom were Karl Wolfskehl, Ludwig Klages, Max Dauthendey, Karl Gustav Vollmöller, Friedrich Gundolf, Henry von Heiseler, and the Dutch poet Albert Verwey—the *Blätter für die Kunst* remained one of the most important media for the realization of George's ideas and the education of the younger artists around him. Only in 1919, when George was fifty-one years old, was its publication suspended. The names and reputations of his contributors mattered less to George than their willingness to accept the rigorous principles set forth by him. He personally invited possible contributors to the journal and weighed each of their works carefully as to its fitness to be published. He did not hesitate to reject the works of fairly established writers if he found them wanting; on the other hand, he could cultivate even a slender talent if he felt that its possessor was worthy of being considered a poet, if his spirit and attitude were sound.

During the twenty-seven years of its existence, twelve volumes of the journal appeared. These were published fairly regularly at the rate of one a year from 1892 until 1904, the first four volumes being divided into four or five issues each. After 1904, with the publication of books of excerpts from earlier volumes, they appeared more sporadically: VIII in 1908-9; IX in 1910; X in 1914; and a book containing the last two volumes, XI, and XII, in 1919. During the early years of its existence, George wanted the journal to present the works of European poets in as unified a manner as possible, believing that they all belonged to one cultural entity. George desired to be only one voice in their chorus. Hence, the first five volumes contained works not only by George and Hofmannsthal but also translations from the works of Mallarmé, Verlaine, Moréas, de Régnier, Swinburne, d'Annunzio, Vielé-Griffin, Stuart Merrill, Saint-Paul, Jens Peter Jacobsen, Verwey, and Waclaw Rolicz-Lieder. Over the years, the nature of the *Blätter* gradually changed. As George attracted "disciples" in Germany, it increasingly became the arena in which his followers exhibited their work.

As George's assurance grew that his ideas were gaining recognition within Germany, and more and more writers met his exacting standards, the international character of the *Blätter* was gradually altered, and the last seven volumes were almost exclusively devoted to works of the members of the *Kreis.* One element remained constant, however: the contributions by George himself, whether in the form of essays, translations, or poems. Many of the poems later published in individual volumes appeared for the first time in the *Blätter.* The changes which took place in the character of the journal were not the result of an intentional exclusion of non-German poets but came about because George felt that these models were no longer necessary for the development of his "new art."

When, in 1904, a prospectus for the *Blätter* was published, explaining the aims of the first six volumes, its contributors, the "Society [*Gesellschaft*] of the *Blätter für die Kunst,*" described themselves as follows:

The Society of the *Journal for the Arts*, which has been wrongly regarded as a secret league, is only a free assembly of artistic and esthetic men. It was founded by members of a new movement which contradicted Naturalism and which was aimed at a deeper spirituality [*Geistigkeit*], which in poetry is associated with the names Stefan George and Hugo von Hofmannsthal, in art with Ludwig von Hofmann, Reinhold Lepsius, and Melchior Lechter. Besides publishing the *Journal,* which appears at irregular intervals, it is responsible for artistic editions of ancient and modern poets and is attempting, through poetry recitals and performances, to let the new rhythmic forms be heard. It has nothing to do with conventional "belles-lettres." It has no statutes or laws, and its growth did not occur through publicity, but rather through vocation and natural affinities through the years.[25]

In order to emphasize the disparity between the aims of the *Blätter* and those of other writers, George also employed a new convention of orthography and punctuation in the journal, which to him was more rational and pleasing.

The reform of the German writing and printing systems had long been a hotly disputed question. The one side, which favored the *Fraktur* or Gothic typeface and the handwriting based on it, argued that it was somehow more German, as were the peculiarities of spelling, using such ligatures as "ß," "tz," and especially the quaint practice of capitalizing nouns. The other side favored the Latinate *Antiqua* typeface, generally used in writing English and the other western European languages, claiming that the *Fraktur* system, with its artificial peculiarities, formed an arbitrary barrier between the culture of Germany and those of its neighbors. This argument had gone on for almost a century, and in many fields, such as the natural sciences, the "moderns" had won the day. In literature, however, the question was still open, most writers being altogether indifferent to it or preferring *Fraktur.* With his Latinate temperament and desire for simple, rational, and uncluttered forms, George came out clearly for the *Antiqua* type style in all of his publications and for a reform in spelling, which stressed the elimination of unnecessary elements. Nouns were no longer to be capitalized, and capitals were to be used only at the beginning of a line in poetry or of a prose sentence, for proper names, and for the indication of a word to be stressed. George was quite well aware that this made the reading of a text more difficult—which was exactly what he wanted, claiming that this departure from conventional writing forced the reader to read more slowly and concentrate more intensely, emphasizing the difference between poetic and ordinary language. George was extremely interested in the details of the printing of his books, the paper, the type, the decoration, and the binding. For the collections of his poems, he chose a typeface closely resembling his own highly stylized handwriting, a "Stefan George type," adapted especially from the "Grotesque" typeface.

The friend who shared George's ideas on the graphic arts and inspired many of them was Melchior Lechter (1865-1937). An artist and craftsman in the tradition and style of William Morris, Lechter lived in Berlin, working as an illustrator and designer of stained-glass windows, which were an indispensable part of public and private architecture at the time. He was responsible for the elaborate first editions of George's books of poetry through *Der Siebente Ring* (1907). After 1907, however, George sought a new, more austere style in keeping with the tone of his later poems, for which the ornate serpentine borders in the manner of the William Morris Kelmscott Press would have been incongruous. Only Lechter's emblems for the *Blätter* were retained, among them the picture of a monstrance in the form of a Gothic spire, which was also used as the imprint for the edition of George's collected works.

The position of the Austrian poet Hugo von Hofmannsthal (1874-1929) as an exponent of the "new art" at the side of Stefan George, which was proudly proclaimed in the 1904 "Prospectus," was there declared at a time when the friendship of the two men had once again become so strained that communication even on matters concerning the journal was barely possible. The correspondence between them ceased abruptly in 1906 over a relatively minor quarrel concerning editorial rights. The relationship with Hofmannsthal, with its extreme episodes of attraction and repulsion, was based on mutual respect on the level of poetry and artistic integrity, but was marked, on the personal level, by a vain search for an empathy which perpetually eluded both men. George had first met Hofmannsthal in Vienna in 1891, where he spent several months after having completed *Algabal.* Six years younger than George, Hugo von Hofmannsthal was still attending the Gymnasium, but already was the author of incredibly mature poems published under the pen name "Loris." Such Viennese literary luminaries of the 1890's as Arthur Schnitzler were captivated by his work and personality. George believed, from reading these poems, that he had found the only other spirit kindred to his own in Germany at that time. Winning Hofmannsthal as a collaborator for the *Blätter* thus became his most urgent desire. After his experience in Paris, the encounter with Hofmannsthal was the next decisive moment in George's life—both in respect to the affirmation it brought him as a poet and to the personal disappointment which was to be inflicted upon him. In one of the most revealing letters George ever wrote, in which Hofmannsthal is addressed as "twin-brother," he describes his emotional crisis after *Algabal* as "the great desolation." Hoping that Hofmannsthal will be spared this experience for years to come, George sums up the events of his life that had culminated in his desire to meet the younger man:

For a long time in life I yearned for that person of a fastidious, penetrating, and highly subtle reason who forgives, comprehends, and respects everything and would soar with me over and above things and appearances—and, oddly enough, this being should nonetheless be somehow veiled in mist and be under the power of a certain romantic radiance of nobility and honor from which he cannot quite separate himself, like John in *Rosmersholm.* This person could have given me new impulses and hopes (for what I can write after *Algabal* is inconceivable to me) and stop me on the path which leads directly to the void.[26]

George goes on to describe his hope that he had found such a spiritual partner in Hofmannsthal, but, by the end of the letter, he gives voice to his resigned realization that such a friendship is possible only between much younger people. Hofmannsthal's answer to this letter was enigmatic and tortuous, reflecting the magnitude of what he felt George expected of him, that is, the answers to problems of being and creativity which only life itself could bring: "I believe that one human being can be much to another, light, a key, a seed, or poison . . . but where Destiny is enigmatically at work, there I see no [individual] guilt or merit or will which can help." He closes the letter with a remarkable insight concerning George: "You have shown me depths, but you delight in standing at the edge of dizzying cliffs, and proudly love the void, which only few can see."[27] In that intense desire for a creative partnership, Hofmannsthal obviously saw what many were to feel later; George's demand for exclusive and full commitment of the other's personality to himself, which George was fully prepared to reciprocate. This claim, which bore with it the implicit threat of icy contempt if rejected, obviously filled the young Hofmannsthal with apprehension. The intellectual liaison with George would have meant giving up too much else in life and art. He was just beginning to discover the world he was celebrating in his poems in all its melancholy richness. The foreboding with which George filled him is evident in the poem "Der Prophet" ("The Prophet"), which Hofmannsthal wrote at this time:

> He has received me in a spacious hall,
> Which strangely frightens me with all the power,
> Of sweet aromas sickeningly flowing,
> There birds so strange do perch and bright snakes hang.
>
> The door falls shut, the sounds of life fade out,
> And silent anguish muffles the soul's breath,
> A magic potion captivates each sense,
> And all else flees, helpless, ceaselessly.
>
> But he is not the one he always was;

> His eye compels, transformed are brow and hair.
> From his words, innocuous and soft,
>
> Dominion and persuasion emanate.
> He makes the empty air oppress and stifle,
> And death he can inflict without a touch.[28]

George was deeply hurt by Hofmannsthal's apprehensions and his retreat behind the manners of convention. For years he kept hoping for a change in Hofmannsthal's attitude, a realization that George was not, after all, as ominous a person as Hofmannsthal had implied in "The Prophet." Although he contributed poems to the *Blätter* until 1904, Hofmannsthal was ultimately to turn to the drama, which George abhorred in its modern form, and, through his collaborations with Richard Strauss, to the fusion of drama and music in operas, such as *Der Rosenkavalier.* Although all outward contact between the two ceased after 1906, the mutual inward preoccupation continued. As late as 1922, Hofmannsthal wrote of the impact which George had on German literary, intellectual, and cultural life in his time: "Almost alone, George, with the circle of his followers, opposed the general degradation and confusion. He was and is a glorious German and Western European phenomenon. Whatever was touched by his spirit has retained his imprint, and his disciples among the younger scholars, even more than among the poets, can be recognized by their uncommonly rigorous standards. To a shallow individualism he opposed the concept of spiritual and intellectual discipline, and thus instilled with new life the highest spiritual strivings of our youth, especially at the universities . . ."[29]

George's hectic desperation in relation to Hofmannsthal is difficult to reconcile with the austere and self-contained countenance he turned to the world in later years. During the period of the "great sadness" following the writing of *Algabal,* however, he tried to break out of the isolation to which he felt condemned. The harmonious meeting of the minds with his "twin-brother" Hofmannsthal had proven illusory, perhaps because of their very similarity.

His next quest for someone to pierce the veil of loneliness which seemed to envelop George also ended in failure. Several years later, George said to friends that there had once been a woman who was "my world." George had met Ida Coblenz in 1892 in Bingen. She admired his poems and showed a great understanding of them. Many of the poems in the *Preisgedichte* (*Eulogies*), *Das Jahr der Seele* (*The Soul's Year*), and even in *Der Siebente Ring* (*The Seventh Ring*) concern her. George saw Ida often, especially in the fall of 1894 and the summer of 1896. Her brief, unhappy marriage to a businessman in 1895 did not interrupt their friendship.

However, her relationship with the poet Richard Dehmel (1863-1920), which led to her marrying him in 1901, aroused a great resentment in George. With his enthusiastic championing of Naturalism and socialism, his sensual glorification of life as it is, Dehmel stood for everything George despised in the poetry of his time. In a letter to Ida, written shortly after he had met Dehmel before her house in Bingen, George wrote: "Our [friendship] arises from the fact that each of us is able to communicate what he thinks great and noble to the other—it rises and falls with this ability—and disappears entirely when something appears great and noble to one which is brutal and debased to the other."[30]

This encounter with Dehmel must have merely provided the outward occasion for an expression of disappointment which George had long repressed. The prose piece "Ein lezter Brief" ("A Final Letter"), published in 1903, is generally believed to be George's final inward reckoning with Ida Coblenz, although he never sent it to her. It contains indications that he desired from her a promise of exclusive loyalty and love, which she did not give of her own accord, but which he could not ask for:

> You are able to smile without loving, but I can only hate. Many may be contented with your light grace, I cannot take it as a substitute for the word you should have spoken and which would have been my salvation. For a whole summer you spoke of the well-formed clouds, of the mysterious sounds of the forests, and the sounds of the rustic flute, but there was one word you did not speak. What is all your beauty, all your enthusiasm if you are unaware of that? Not a word, less than a breeze, a touch. You saw that I waited for it day and night. I could not speak it, I could only sense it in dreams, I could not have said it, since you had to say it. So dream and act as you must—we have nothing in common any more: whenever you are close to me, I must hate you, and when you are far away, you are a stranger. (I, 488)

George had planned to dedicate *Das Jahr der Seele* (1897) to Ida Coblenz, but, instead, his sister's name appears where hers was to have stood.

All his life, George remained a wanderer, having no permanent residence; he was almost continually on the move, visiting his friends in Heidelberg, Munich, Berlin, and Switzerland at various times of the year. Some of the accounts of his friends compare him to a medieval emperor, who reigned in all parts of his "realm," rather than make his "capital" in any one province—a simile which accords nicely with George's imperious and yet gracious manner toward those close to him. Those relationships in which George's private emotions were too much involved invariably ended in pain and disappointment. The majority of his friendships, however, in which George acted as a poet, critic, and anthologist, and especially as a teacher, inspired in all those who knew him a fierce and reverent loyalty. The qualities which were remarked upon in his earliest days at Paris never left George: the aura of physical and intellectual distinction, of uncompromising integrity in matters of literature and ethics, and a mordant wit combined with a basically warm and generous spirit toward those to whom he chose to reveal it.

It was given only to a few of George's friends to understand and appreciate the totality of his personality, rather than one particular aspect. His two closest friends were Karl Wolfskehl and Friedrich Gundolf. Wolfskehl, one year younger than Stefan George, had also attended the Ludwig-Georgs-Gymnasium in Darmstadt. The son of a well-to-do family, he could afford to pursue his varied interests as an independent scholar without being encumbered by a profession. Wolfskehl's interests embraced poetic expressions of all nations and periods. He had received his doctorate of Philosophy in German literature from the University of Giessen, and soon had an outstanding reputation among German literary scholars. Wolfskehl read the first issue of the *Blätter* and *Hymnen* in 1892 and was struck by the tone of the earliest poems: "If there is one poet I could compare with you," he wrote to George, "–please forgive a literary historian the passion for parallels–it is Goethe in his most noble, most serious period of creation; in the years when the 'Trilogy of Passion' was written. Earnestly unique, introspective, and yet grasping, with wonderful subtlety, all sense and the external; thus your poetic individuality shows itself to me with the full magic of the most genuine talent on the one hand, and proudly in the full awareness of that talent on the other."[31] In this letter George recognized the readiness to serve the same ideal of art which impelled him, and invited Wolfskehl to visit him. This meeting has been described as Wolfskehl's "baptism," to which he came as a literary historian but went away as a poet. A close literary and personal association began between the two young men, which was to last until George's death. Wolfskehl's robustness and enthusiasm helped George through the acute personal crises of the early 1890's. From the second volume of the *Blätter* onward, he was a constant contributor to the journal, and he was among the first to interpret George's personal and poetic significance to the public outside the limited group reached by the *Blätter*. When Wolfskehl married in 1898, his home in Munich became George's domicile whenever he came to that city, where, in the so-called "*Kugelzimmer*" ("Globe-Room") poetry readings were held, the central events of gatherings of his friends.

Karl Wolfskehl was a major German poet in his own right. In his attempt to give a new voice and soul to poetry through a rejuvenation and redefinition of mankind's elemental myths, in his translations and transcriptions of old Germanic poetry and oriental lyric cycles, he exhibits a virtuosity of language, a discriminating taste and philosophy which place him in the mainstream of the quest for new directions and meanings in art in the twenty years around the turn of the century. Wolfskehl's own literary and critical stature make his profound, mystical devotion to George the most eloquent testimony to the poet's personality and its impact on his contemporaries. Like George, he believed that an improvement of poetic taste, a return to standards that had been lost through decades of poetry speciously imitative of Goethe and the Romantics, was necessary. One of Wolfskehl's contributions toward this goal was his collaboration with George in preparing the anthology *Deutsche Dichtung* (*German Poetry*), whose three volumes were devoted to *Jean Paul* (1900), *Goethe* (1901), and *The Age of Goethe* (1902). The editors claimed that, "In the case of our collection, any comparison with conventional anthologies, which collected patriotic German crudity or insipid sentimentalism is impossible. We selected those works which seemed to us to contain the noblest fire under the most felicitous artistic control."[32] George and Wolfskehl were trying to achieve no less than a reform of the modern image of the German literary tradition as part of their general concept of a "new art." They sought to emphasize the transcendental, poetic aspects of the works of German poets from Klopstock to Conrad Ferdinand Meyer, rather than those preferred by literary scholars of the time, who stressed, wherever possible, the nationalistic, pragmatic, and naturalistic aspects of these poets' works. In 1899, while the anthology was in preparation, Germany celebrated the 150th anniversary of Goethe's birth, an occasion on which George wrote a "poem for his time," which reflects this thought: "Yet you know not that he [Goethe] who's turned to dust/ Since then holds many a secret yet for you,/ And that of him, the radiant one, much now/ Has disappeared that you still call eternal" (I, 230).

It was through Karl Wolfskehl that George met Friedrich Gundolf, the son of a Darmstadt professor of mathematics, in 1899, when Gundolf was eighteen and George thirty. Gundolf was one of those very rare persons who, by character and inclination, were able to share George's outlook on life and to ease the painful awareness of loneliness—one of the main underlying currents in their letters to each other.[33] Gundolf became the first and most significant of George's younger friends.

For months at a time, particularly during Gundolf's student years, he was George's inseparable companion, helping to publish the books appearing between 1900 and 1910, sometimes acting as George's intermediary, but always his close friend and regarded by George as his equal. Their studies of the works of Shakespeare culminated in Gundolf's translations of most of the dramas and George's *Umdichtung* (recomposition into German) of the greater part of the sonnets. What Gundolf meant to George is most movingly set down in the first part of the group of poems "Gezeiten" ("Tides") in *Der Siebente Ring.* For Gundolf, brought up in the tradition of German classical idealism, George seemed to be the affirmation that the priestly poet, the Socratic teacher, the imperious judge of his age, did not belong only to the past, and was not merely an ideal to be sought in the works of Homer, Plutarch, and Shakespeare, but actually lived in his own time. George was a major inspiration for Gundolf in his vocation as a teacher.[34] His entire academic career is associated with Heidelberg, where he held his qualifying lecture (*Habilitation*) in 1911 and was a professor from 1916 until shortly before his death. Particularly his books, *Shakespeare und der deutsche Geist* (1911), *Goethe* (1916), and *George* (1920) show Gundolf's intuitive skill as an interpreter, his perception of the spiritual roots of art and scholarship. At Heidelberg, Gundolf, in his turn, widened the circle of young friends around George.

Goethe once said: "The most terrible fact for the disciple is that he must finally resume his own being in relation to his master. The stronger those things are which the master has given, so much greater is the sadness, even desperation of the receiver."[35] This statement proved to be all too true for the relationship between Gundolf and George. Contrary to many opinions,[36] George was not an autocratic "master," and Gundolf led a completely independent professional life, numbering George only as the most important among a large circle of friends. After World War I, George himself saw a "crisis of maturation" impending for Gundolf and feared that his friend would be diverted from developing to his full potential by the business of being a "Herr Professor." Gundolf, himself in failing health, desperately tried to bridge the chasm he saw opening inevitably between them and once more pledged his allegiance in the study *George*, which he wrote in 1920. Friction continued to increase until George implacably broke off all further contact between them. Both men felt a profound sense of loss, as though a tragic fate had forced them to go their separate ways after "a long journey" on which "strong ties had bound [them] insolubly in secret" (I, 271). Even if Gundolf felt that his friend had been too harsh in turning away from him, he never admitted it to George. His loyalty to the poet and the ideals for which they both stood remained unshaken until his untimely death in 1931, which, by a cruel irony, occurred on July 12, Stefan George's birthday. The last poem which Gundolf sent to George closes with the lines:

> See me as on a catafalque,
> With forgiving's downward glance,
> I am your child, . . . see what I was
> Even in conflict's cry by night.
> Let your first kiss glow once more
> Life-giving on my pale brow.
> I live because live I must
> Through you, for you, beneath your sign.[37]

The loyalty of both Wolfskehl and Gundolf toward Stefan George was shown in their unwavering adherence to him during the most decisive and critical experience of his life, the encounter with Maximin, from which George drew conclusions regarding life and art of so seemingly drastic a nature that some of his oldest friends maintained a dismayed distance from him. In June, 1904, George wrote a terse report of the past six months to his friends Reinhold and Sabine Lepsius in Berlin: "After the beginning winter in Berlin, much that was perplexing, much that was coming to its end, and the devastating conclusion: I am mourning an incomprehensible and early death, which threatened to bring me to the final abyss too."[38] Outwardly, the death which came so close to costing George his own life was that of a youth named Maximilian Kronberger, who died of meningitis one day after his sixteenth birthday. George's relationship to the boy, who greatly admired the poet, was that of a friend and teacher. The idealistic character evident in Maximilian's features had caught George's attention in 1902, and George encouraged and criticized the boy's poetic efforts. He introduced Maximilian to his friends, and the boy took part in the poetic pageants celebrated in Wolfskehl's home in the *Fasching* (Shrove Tuesday) seasons of 1903 and 1904. The importance which this youth, whom George called "Maximin," was to assume in his world is directly related to George's spiritual and intellectual concerns at the time.

Around the turn of the century, George had come into contact with the circle of the *Kosmiker* ("Cosmics") in Schwabing, the artists' quarter of Munich, where Wolfskehl lived. Wolfskehl belonged to this circle, as did the philosopher Ludwig Klages (1872-1956), and the scholar Alfred Schuler (1865-1923). As adherents of Nietzsche and the Romantic philosophers Carl Gustav Carus (1789-1869) and Johann Jakob Bachofen (1815-87), the *Kosmiker* proceeded from the idea of the total decay of the soul of mankind through rationalism and believed in salvation by reawakening the myths of those cultural strata which had become lost through the history of Judaeo-Christian Western civilization. Both Klages and Schuler believed that a re-establishment of man's mystical rapport with the ultimate forces of life could be brought about by an ecstatic embrace of paganism; in Klages' opinion that of the Germanic tribes before their conversion to Christianity, to Schuler that of the mystery religions practiced in Imperial Rome.

It is not surprising that Klages and Schuler, who were primarily interested in psychology and religious anthropology, respectively, should have committed themselves to such a system of belief. Since Nietzsche had proclaimed the functional "death" of the conception of God, around which western European culture had been centered for almost 2,000 years, men had been seeking a new approach to the divine outside the sanctioned channels of the established religions. Thus, simultaneously with the deliberations of the "Cosmics," such movements as theosophism, anthroposophism, and Christian Science drew wide followings at this time. This phenomenon can be seen as an attempt to oppose to the overwhelming weight of philosophical materialism a spiritual force as an alternative path for Western civilization to follow. It was almost inevitable that Stefan George should take an interest in this group. Klages and Schuler claimed to see in George's poems the communion with mythic forces which they themselves desired—qualities particularly apparent to them in *Algabal.* For the "Apollonian" George, however, the doctrines of the "Dionysian" Schuler were on the threshold of madness. He clearly felt the danger of "Schulerism" for his younger friends and opposed the mystical, irrational racism which the "Cosmics" ultimately proclaimed. On the day after an "orgy of talk" with Klages and Schuler, at which George had been present, Wolfskehl found on his desk a note from his friend: "Do not set the fakir in the place of the priest, the Magus [sorcerer] in the place of the Vates [seer], ghosts in the place of spirits."[39] A major clash with the "Cosmics" was unavoidable. Klages believed that Judaic doctrines were responsible for the decline of pagan Germanic strength in the German nation and of remnants of Roman paganism. In 1903, he demanded that George, whom he wanted to be the poetic voice for their group, sever all relationships with Jews in his circle, particularly with Wolfskehl. This George refused to do and promptly broke off all personal contact with Klages.

Perhaps one reason for the confidence with which George was able to make this decision was that he himself felt that he was approaching an answer to the question which concerned him increasingly: can the eternal, divine forces, which we *feel* to be present, which portend a promise of a higher, purer realm than this world of material phenomena and physical causes and effects, make themselves manifest in this day and age? It is apparent that George believed that he had found such a manifestation in Maximin. In his "Memorial Book for Maximin," George reports his recollection of their first meeting:

We had just passed the midpoint of our life and were fearful at the sight of our immediate future. We were approaching a Humanity distorted and grown cold, which was proud of its many-sided achievements and subtle sentiments, while the great deed and the great love were close to disappearing. Masses created laws and rules and, with the lies of their petty interpretation, suffocated those warners who were formerly more mercifully eliminated by murder. Impure hands rummaged in a heap of dross into which jewels had been arbitrarily flung, divisive arrogance masked desperate impotence, and impudent laughter prophesied the decline of all that was sacred. We were sufficiently mature not to rail any more against the fateful recurrence of the inevitable suffering; but now a plague seemed to rage for which there was no remedy and which would end with the death of the soul of this whole race. Already some of us took the path to the regions of darkness and called madness a state of glory—others closed themselves off in their huts full of sadness or hate; when the sudden arrival of one single person gave us back our trust amidst the general degeneration and filled us with the light of new promises.

When we first encountered Maximin in our city, he was still in his boyhood years. He walked toward us from the triumphal arch with the imperturbable firmness of a young gladiator and the expression of superior authority softened by that expressiveness and melancholy which had only come to the faces of the people through centuries of Christian culture. We recognized in him the representative of an all-powerful youth as we had dreamed of, with its untamed abundance and purity which even today moves mountains and can walk on the waters—a youth which could take our heritage and conquer new realms. . . . what we needed was one person who was moved by the elemental happenings and would show us things as the eyes of the gods see them. From the brilliance which suffused us, we knew that he had been found. . . . The better we came to know him, the more he reminded us of our ideal, [*denkbild*] and we revered the expanse of his spontaneous mind and the motions of his heroic soul as well as its manifestations in gesture, expression, and speech. (I, 522-23)

To George, Maximin represented the forces of life in an elemental concentration he had never before encountered in the world, the embodiment of a primeval force, an Eros universally present, but only exceptionally so purely manifested. When George compares and even equates Maximin with a god, then this must be taken in the Socratic sense, in which the god Eros temporarily possesses man. George saw in Maximin an affirmation and an explanation of the magnificent paradox of Greek antiquity, as he later expressed it in the *Blätter*:

If our leading spirits, especially Goethe, prostrated themselves before the Hellenic miracle and regarded Greek art, particularly statues, as the highest artistic goal, then there must be more behind this than the explanation that southern serenity and pleasing form had so captivated them that they even underestimated the powers and achievements of their own people. More to the point, they recognized that here, for all humanity, something incomparable, unique, and perfect lay hidden, which must be emulated at any cost and that the efforts of progress, so acclaimed by all, must first of all be turned to this end. Compared to the Greeks, the people of their own nation must have seemed like caricatures in spite of their powerful gifts. Indeed, these leading minds did not demand that purely external imitation which led to the undesirable "Classicism," but rather an interpenetration, fertilization, a Sacred Marriage. . . . Behind all of the explanations [for their love of Greece] of a historical, esthetic, or personal nature lies the belief that, of all the concepts of the millennia known to us, the Greek thought: the body—this symbol of transitoriness—The body is the God [DER LEIB SEI DER GOTT] is by far the most creative and inexhaustible idea, by far the greatest, most daring, and worthy of man,—to whose sublimity all other thoughts, even the Christian, must take second place.[40]

Maximin symbolizes this age-old idea. For George, the incapacity of modern culture to accept such a concept lay at the root of its ills. The view of the world as governed by merely physical cause and effect, of man's fate as determined merely by heredity and environment, was insufficient. In Maximin, the perfect fusion of body and mind seemed achieved in a self-awareness which, to George, was godlike. "The Maximin ideal needs to be understood humanistically. It asks something very simple of us: to serve the Apollonian spirit in childlike purity, to ennoble oneself and to open the eyes of our fellow men, so that they may once more see the Beautiful as beautiful, the great as great, harmonious order as the divinely ordained goal of life, and learn to hate nothing more than destruction and chaos."[41]

Stefan George's celebration of the life and death of Maximin must also be seen in the light of the poetic tradition of mourning a poet who has died too young. From this tradition come Milton's *Lycidas* and Shelley's *Adonais,* for example, in which the cosmic consequences of the poet's loss are no less striking than in the "Maximin" poems, the departed poet scarcely less endowed with godlike qualities. The Maximin "experience" and its impact on George is intimately associated with the poet's increasing quest for permanent values in the Hellenic tradition. Although the possibility for human perfection which Maximin represented to George never left him as a poetic and humanistic inspiration, he was far too intellectually honest and skeptical of his own feelings, too knowledgeable and reverent of the Greek and Christian traditions, to claim—as some critics interpret the "Maximin" poems— a new, universally valid incarnation of the Godhead in this youth or to place him at the center of an elitist cult.

Just as Stefan George's experience in Paris in the early 1890's had impelled him to return to Germany to give a new voice and form to German poetry, so the Maximin experience was a turning point in his life. Through his writing and the precepts of his own life he now wanted to shape the soul of a generation which would build a world in the spirit of that Hellas which was the ultimate goal of George's striving. His efforts in the early days of the *Blätter* had brought him distinction among a small circle of scholars and intellectuals who perfectly understood what George wanted, but had also attracted the attention of a far larger group which exaggerated George's intentions to one extreme or the other, such as the Cosmics, who praised him as the minstrel of a paganistic voluptuousness, or the literary critics, who stamped him as a mere esthetic dreamer in the sense of *Jugendstil.* So, too, the poems which George published in *Der Siebente Ring, Der Stern des Bundes* (*The Star of the Covenant*) (1914) and *Das Neue Reich* (*The New Realm*) (1928), attracted readers, especially among the younger student generations, who affirmed the purely spiritual and ethical essence of George's intentions. George's rising fame, however, also attracted men who saw in his poetry an affirmation of their own conservative and autocratic leanings, without understanding properly the archetypes to which George was referring.

Many of George's most striking utterances are indeed to be found in the didactic poems in which he describes conditions in his own time, which must be healed before a better day can dawn. These poems, such as the "Zeitgedichte"—whose literary forebears may be found in Roman satires, and in Germany among the poems of Goethe, Heine, and Nietzsche—were regarded by George's contemporaries as prophetic in character, forecasting the catastrophes which were soon to befall Germany. Thus, for better or worse, George's reputation as a seer and prophet was enhanced against his will. Toward the end of his life, what he had earlier envisioned in the realm of his spirit had apparently become hard political and military reality. Although he persistently attempted to judge his time and prescribe remedies for its ills from an Archimedean point outside the immediate historical context, developments in Germany, the social struggles of the Wilhelmine era, World War I, and the turmoil of polarization which the Weimar Republic engendered, made it unlikely that the words of so famous a poet could be read merely as a sibylline and purely spiritual interpretation of the world he experienced.

George saw contemporary history as being symptomatic of a cultural condition and weighed it in these terms, not judging the individuals involved or their immediate motives in his poems, although in private conversation he was a pungent critic. He did not feel that it was the task of a poet to be a political commentator. This refusal to become involved with immediate social and political questions was present in the first "manifesto" of the *Blätter* published in 1892, which laid George open to charges of being an esthete or a dandy, untroubled by moral concerns. He was, quite to the contrary, both in his attempts to give a new voice to German lyric poetry and to express a new humanism, moved by profoundly moral ends. The poet had to sacrifice too much, he felt, if he were to follow the vagaries of every political trend. He put it best in a brief poem to Albert Verwey, which he sent him during World War I: "If the poet tries to say/ Where truth and falsehood wander day by day/ He must with years of silent penance pay" (I, 449).

By 1920, at the age of fifty-two, George already seemed much older. "My years count double," he told a younger friend after a long illness.[42] The earlier years of almost uninterrupted work as a poet, translator, and editor had laid the pallor of exhaustion on George. The last volume of the *Blätter* had been published. Almost all of his later poems had been written. George was now to devote the remaining years of his life to encouraging the efforts of his many "grandchildren," as he called the youngest poets who had made their debut in the *Blätter*. At one of his last encounters with Karl Wolfskehl, George explained his silence, his refusal to write any more, with the words of Shakespeare's magician-king, Prospero, in *The Tempest*:

> But this rough magic
> I here abjure, and, when I have requir'd
> Some heavenly music, which even now I do,
> To work mine end upon their senses that
> This airy charm is for, I'll break my staff,
> Bury it certain fathoms in the earth,
> And deeper than did ever plummet sound
> I'll drown my book.[43]

As he grew older, George's fame increased, and his sixtieth birthday, coinciding with the appearance of his complete works in 1928, brought forth international critical tribute. Apparently withdrawn and solitary, he had become, to the public, a living monument to his art.

To a few, however, he remained the *Meister*, visiting those who remained loyal to him and what he stood for. In his old age, George was not a lonely man. As he himself had written to Hofmannsthal many years earlier: "In my youth, I was strong enough to triumph over the greatest adversity without help. Later, however, I would certainly have collapsed if I had not felt myself bound by the 'ring' [of my friends]. That is one of my final truths, that is one of the secrets."[44]

When Stefan George died in 1933, there was a grim dissonance between the eulogies from inside and outside Germany, the former claiming George as the prophet of the Third Reich, which had taken power that year, the latter often interpreting his silence as expressing his utter contempt of the new regime.

Before his death, attempts were made to use the poems of George, who was by this time Germany's greatest living lyric poet, to justify the dictatorship being imposed upon Germany and to inveigle the poet himself into accepting one honor or another from the hands of the regime, which would imply his active support. Stefan George steadfastly refused to do any such thing and finally even rejected the establishment of a Stefan George Prize for young poets. In August, 1933, he crossed the Lake of Constance into Switzerland, where he settled at Minusio. There his health rapidly deteriorated, and he died on December 4, 1933, surrounded by some of his closest friends. "A man should be buried where he dies," George had said. Despite the wishes of the German government to have an elaborate state funeral for the poet, he was interred in the village churchyard at Minusio. There a simple granite plaque marks the grave, which is flanked by laurel trees.

CHAPTER 2

The Quest

Je mehr einer Dichter ist, desto vollständiger ist er in seinem Werk zu finden.

Friedrich Gundolf

I Hymnen, Pilgerfahrten, Algabal

THE LYRIC poet is faced with a perpetual choice. He can become involved with the world around him, working in terms of the concrete occurrences and phenomena he encounters, aiming at empathy, even at reconciliation, with this world. The poet's other alternative is to achieve distance from this world by portraying it only in a veiled fashion and by symbolically representing his dreams for its betterment and that of his fellow men. Stefan George's entire poetic achievement can be understood as the construction of this second kind of symbolic "anti-world," hidden for him behind and within the natural world, the physical world of the senses, which the poets of his time celebrated. As Claude David observes: "The forty years which separate the last poems of Heine from the first poems of George are as poor in lyric poetry as was the first half of the eighteenth century."[1] It was against this imitative and hollow sentimental tradition that George was espousing the cause of a new "spiritual art." He was striving to be a poet of the kind Nietzsche had envisioned when he wrote: "Just as the poets of the past perpetually shaped the image of the gods poetically, the poet of the present should so shape the sublime image of Man and sense those instances in which, in the midst of our modern world and reality, the great and beautiful soul is still possible without separation or abstraction from this reality, in which it can even now be embodied in harmonious and proportioned circumstances... and [this soul] helps create the future through imitation and envy of its sublimity."[2] That George looked forward to such a future, beyond his time and the conventional measures of causality, is indicated already by the titles which he chose for some of his books, in which subjective time ("The Soul's Year") or a chiliastic future ("The New Realm") are evoked.

George was later to call his earliest poems the reminders "of the time of our purest enthusiasm and full desire to blossom" (II, 467). The *Hymnen,* published in 100 copies in 1890, are one step removed from this degree of spontaneity. They represent the very personal conclusions George had reached after his first contacts with the French Symbolists. The German title, which literally means "hymns," does not suggest liturgical poems but rather indicates the festively solemn and esoteric intention of the book.[3] In following the advice given by Verlaine in his poem, *Art poétique,* George was bringing to Germany the poetic values he had found in Paris, with a distinct intention of giving a new tone and form to German lyric poetry. This is evidenced by his pleasure at Carl August Klein's remark that *Hymnen* was a new "milestone" in German literature, comparable to Martin Opitz's *Buch von der deutschen Poeterey* (*Book of German Poetics,* 1624).[4] Accordingly, the book was dedicated to his own generation, the bearers of a new song, a "dream in blue and gold" (I, 8).

The *Hymnen* contains eighteen poems, divided into four parts. We are better informed about the times and places in which the *Hymnen* were written than about any of his later collections. George began to write them in Bingen around Easter, 1890, and completed the first seven poems during that summer in Berlin. The next four poems (I, 14-17) were written during his short journey to Copenhagen. "Hochsommer" ("Late Summer") (I, 18), in which George is clearly influenced by the tone of Verlaine's *Fêtes Galantes,* was written at Bad Kreuznach, and he wrote the last six poems of the cycle (I, 19-22) in Paris late in 1890.[5] *Das Jahr der Seele* is foreshadowed here in the sense that the poet is following a full year's experiences and feelings—the sequence of the writing of the poems determining the order in which they appear—rather than being subjected to the kind of artistic rearrangement so characteristic of the later George. There remains, then, in this first collection, this much of a link with the subjective, "confessional" tradition.

Despite this apparent adherence to the temporal sequence of the poems, *Hymnen* shows the cyclical unity which was later to become one of George's hallmarks. All of the poems exhibit a similarity of tone in the expression of closely congruous situations and atmospheres. As in so many of the later cycles, this tone is set by the opening poem, in which the poet, having fled into the natural world of the river bank, is confronted by his muse, *die herrin* ("the lady"), who descends to him after he has purged his mind of all earthly categories and reflections and has entered the realm of his imagination, where new laws prevail: "The flight of time loses its old names/And space and being exist only in images" (I, 9). This *herrin* is reminiscent of Baudelaire's Muse and Mallarmé's "fée au chapeau de clarté" ("fairy with the radiant headdress") in "Apparition"—to name only the Symbolist analogues—as well as the classical conception of the Muse of Poetry.[6] To her service the poet dedicates himself, and in return he is blessed.

While the first poem describes the greatest ecstasy imaginable to the poet—the exceptional instant of inspiration—the remaining poems reveal the conditions and moods which lead him to seek this solace. Without the kiss of the Muse, the poet is the loneliest of men. He knows of "destroying blazes" (I, 12) within himself, of a continuous "disturbance through thinking" (*denkerstörung*) (I, 9), and of his torment, anguish, and suffering. In describing the condition of the poet, George uses the words *dulder* (I, 16), *dulden*, and *duldung* (I, 20), all related to the concept of suffering and sufferance, with its strong associations, in German, with the martyrdom of saints, such as Sebastian. He is the "pilgrim with his hand on the staff" (I, 22), and his relationship to the world is one of distant remove. The poet is a mere observer and becomes painfully aware of the fact that, for other human beings, the barriers of estrangement which he feels everywhere are either nonexistent or only occasionally present. Only a momentary, transitory flash of communication can exist between the poet and those he loves. He feels he has nothing in common with ordinary men, who are able to find happiness and relaxation in evidently restricted circumstances, and in the feeble reflections of powerful nature, represented by carefully cultivated parks and public gardens. Half of the *Hymnen* touch upon this strained relationship between the poet and "society," for example: "Im Park" ("In the Park") (I, 10), "Von einer Begegnung" ("On an Encounter") (I, 12), and "Hochsommer" ("Late Summer") (I, 18). A mysterious curtain seems to float between him and the concrete reality which all other men are able to grasp and in which they find satisfaction and fulfillment. The light of day is harsh, dessicating, and blinding to the poet. He flees the definite forms of Apollonian "reality," preferring the cool, fog-shrouded contours of dusk or night—a world more like that of his imagination, the world of Diana, Apollo's nocturnal sister, and of dreams removed from the glaring sun, which, shining upon him, makes his isolation all the more conspicuous:

With silent gables and dead ramparts,
The long walls of the city stifling stand
Panting heat like sacrificial ovens.
In the courts surrounded by arcades
The play of dried-up fountains long has failed.
On beds where leaves of bushes dry and crumble,
The smell of flowers halfway withered lies.
(I, 12)

As a possible release from his isolation and estrangement from reality, the poet longs for love, but all he encounters is frivolity, well-meaning but falling short of the intensity of understanding he needs in his melancholy. The gracious self-contained world, in which love is reduced to a mutually understood social gesture, is captured with splendid irony in the poem "Hochsommer," which originally bore the title "Hohe Saison" ("High Season") and describes the languid, mindless atmosphere of a *fin de siècle* spa. These people, young and old alike, arouse not so much the poet's contempt as a kind of existential envy that they, devoid of higher ambition, can be so perfectly contented with their frivolous and vain pursuits:

Ton verklang auf den altanen·
Aus den gärten klänge tönen·
Unter prangenden platanen
Wiegen sich die stolzen Schönen·
Keck in eleganten zieren
Sie am arm den kavalieren
Milder lauschen und mit süssen
Winken grüssen.

Ja die reifen die sich rühmen
Feiner kinder flink im spiel
Huldigen dem leichten stil·
Auf den lippen eitle fragen·
Von verlockenden parfümen
Hingetragen.

Pauken schweigen· sachte geigen.
Ferner tritt· es nahen reiter·
Leises traben· langsam weiter . .
Zwanglos darf ein flüchtig raunen
Sie bestaunen.

Fröhliche galante leere
Feindlich trübem tatenmeere·
Weise schlaffheit· nur im bade
Wahre gnade.

Auf dem wasser ruderklirren·
Gondel die vorüberfuhr·
Sanfte takte sanftem kirren
Sich vereinen einer kleinen
Pompadur. (I, 18)

On the terrace echoes dwindle,
From the gardens chords are sounding,
'Neath luxuriant shade of plane trees
The proud beauties sway in languor,
Pert in elegant attire.
Arm in arm with courteous swains
They hearken gently and with gestures sweet
Each other greet.

Yes, the parents who can boast of
Such choice children, skilled at play,
Do homage to the sprightly style.
On their lips the vainest questions
Borne forth by alluring perfumes'
Sweet suggestions.

Drums are silent, soft the viols;
Distant hooves; approach of riders;
Gentle trotting, slowly onward.
Carefree comment in fleeting choirs
Them admires.

Merry courtly emptiness,
Foe of any urge to deeds,
Sophistic slackness: the watering place
Alone brings grace.

Stroke of oars upon the water;
Gondola which just passed by;
Gentle rhythm, gentle courting
Combined allure
A little Pompadour.

Just as the poet does not have any part in the affairs of society, so he is cruelly expelled by a Nature equally in harmony with itself, a harmony into which he cannot yet enter. All things in the natural world seen in *Hymnen* strive toward unity: the waves (I, 9), and the intertwining branches (I, 15). Here, even death is appropriate, leaves being blown to their resting place by the wind (I, 22) or shriveled by the sun (I, 12). In this teleologically ordered nature, as closed a system as the society of men, the poet has no place either. But its laws are more awesome than those of men and hold more of a promise of lending meaning to the poet's life, if only he can come into harmony with them. The way to the ecstasy of inspiration lies through nature, through a sense of its innermost pulse, the inhalation of its primal essence and its aroma, the *urduft* which intoxicates him prior to the apparition of the *herrin* in the first poem, "Weihe" ("Dedication"). Here, through communion with the Muse, another instance of which is depicted in the poem "Gespräch" ("Conversation") (I, 20), the poet finds the reward for his isolation from the world of men and his discord with the natural rhythm of life. This is affirmed in the poem "Im Park" ("In the Park") (I, 10), in which the poet is shown as an impassive onlooker in a luxuriant, sensuous garden, the very epitome of verdant life. He is unmoved because he is in communication with his spirits and must carry out his arduous craft, resistant and difficult though it be: "For he must wield the pen which balks his will."

A dim memory exists, however, of times when the split between reason and the mystery of life, between society and the poet, was not as wide as the poet now believes it to be. This happier condition existed in the early stages of mankind, as is indicated in "Nachthymne" ("Night Hymn") (I, 16), and in childhood, as in "Neuländische Liebesmahle II" ("Utopian Bacchanals II") (I, 14). In the latter poem, the solemn ritual he envisions reminds the poet of the time, now sunken in dreams, during his childhood, when he was a "king," his imagination dictating every aspect of his world—a supremacy which now has been lost to him. Thus, "Der Infant" ("The Infante") (I, 20), in which death in childhood is described as the ultimate blessing, because the realm of the imagination never has to be abandoned, is a significant part of the depiction of the world in which the poet lives. Only the playful interchange between the elf and the pale child was pure bliss. If he had grown up, he too would have fallen out of the state of grace and freedom and become just such a tormented man as the poet is. The Infante symbolizes the interchange between the supernatural and the human, a state of natural grace which the poet is able to reach only after long struggles. While childhood may know of this close communion, the totally devoted and self-assured artist may permanently achieve the state which the young poet reaches only sporadically. In "Ein Angelico" ("An Angelico") (I, 21), the painter Fra Angelico is portrayed as such an artist who transforms the world around him and its living substance into color and thus takes part in creation itself:

Er nahm das gold von heiligen pokalen·
Zu hellem haar das reife weizenstroh·
Das rosa kindern die mit schiefer malen·
Der wäscherin am bach den indigo. (I, 21)

The golden gleam he took from sacred goblets,
For radiant hair the straw of ripened wheat,
The pink from children scribbling with slate,
From the laundress at the stream the indigo.

So far the poet has experienced inspiration only as a fleeting moment. His desire that this moment might be prolonged, even unto eternity, is projected into the statues of "Apollos and Dianas" in "Die Gärten schliessen" ("The Gardens Close") (I, 22). George calls them "happy," thus indirectly expressing his own unhappiness. They are enveloped in veils of mist, protected and hidden by the shadows of the night. For the pilgrim, however, with whom George identifies himself and who is excluded from the garden and its static esthetic perfection, the quest for his place in the order of things must continue. It is no accident that in this closing poem of the *Hymnen,* Apollo and Diana are evoked as coexistent in a setting of order and art, even if their precise contours are shrouded. It is between the sunlit world of Apollo, of light and clarity of perception, and that of Diana, the world of night and moonlight, of dream and fantasy, that the pilgrim's path now lies. His goal is a realm of the spirit which transcends the immediate social context in which he lives and which implicitly rejects him, for the words of men cannot express what he feels. He proceeds onward, disdaining to expend time and effort in reproach:

Heisse monde flohen aus der pforte.
Ward dein hoffen deine habe?
Baust du immer noch auf ihre worte
Pilger mit der hand am stabe? (I, 22)

Hot moons fled swiftly through the gate of time.
Is your hope your sole possession?
Will you continue trusting in their words,
Pilgrim with your staff in hand?

In 1891, George published his second book of verses, *Pilgerfahrten* (*Pilgrimages*). The title indicates a new departure from the point at which the *Hymnen* closed, when the "sufferer" had given himself a new identity and purpose as the "pilgrim with his staff in hand." The *Pilgerfahrten* represent a spiritual journey, whose various stations are possibilities of being, which are examined, reflected upon, and usually rejected by the poet. At the outset, the goal of the pilgrimage appears to be that felicitous attitude toward himself and the world which escaped the poet in *Hymnen.* In the progress of the journey, however, it becomes apparent that the poet is to have no goal except yet another portal beyond which lies a new horizon of his art.

The initial poem, "Siedlergang" ("The Hermit's Excursion") (I, 27), depicts the tormenting conflict between the life of the spirit and the life of the flesh. Like "Weihe" in *Hymnen,* the poem sets forth the essential questions to be elucidated in the cycle. The hermit, a Faustlike figure, leaves his lonely retreat at spring's first beckoning, since his contemplations are now fruitless. Blinded by the sun's light, he finds himself before a group of dancing women who celebrate the coming of the new year. Formerly, the hermit had scorned women, mentally transforming their beauty into ugliness. Now he finds himself overpowered by desire: "Now my grief grasps for each pale countenance,/ I am blinded by a brow,/ My very mind's entwined about an eyelash/ About an arm bejeweled with tourmaline" (I, 27). The question is left open whether the hermit will surrender to his desire and join in the dance of the "red women" or return to his "loyal parchments" where sleep will overtake and dreams console him. The hermit is one to whom the readiness for commitment to human passion may have come too late, his love-hate having forced him to flee so far into the realm of the mind that he is unable to take part in the dance which had so long seemed a defilement to him. He is a figure to be pitied, and his fate is one to be avoided in favor of a better balance taken at the propitious moment.

The hermit's overly conscious and tortured preoccupation with the conflict between flesh and spirit is countered in the next poem, "Mühle lass die arme still" ("Let your arms be still, o mill") (I, 28), by the innocent and unconscious surrender of the children to their fates.

Little girls, dressed in bridal white, cross the ice on a day in early spring immediately following their First Communion, some of them still preoccupied with the "distant God of the Catechism," some with the gifts which await them at home. The children drown in the river when the ice gives way beneath them; but the poem suggests that perhaps supernatural powers, "dark lads from the depths" desiring their "brides," have drawn them down. At the end of the poem, the bells ring out signifying the disaster, a tragedy for the outside world but accepted without question or complaint by the children. Their "marriage" to the transcendent powers, signifying the end of their lives, seems to have come at precisely the spiritually appropriate moment, before they have lost the imaginative innocence of childhood.

In the four following poems, it becomes apparent that, for the poet, the problem of full commitment in love is a central one. He reveres and loves a woman but fears that, if he and she surrender to passion, the spiritual reverence, which is a primary force in his love for her, will be destroyed—all the while feeling that if he does not return her love on a sensual plane he will lose her. He wishes to revere her with the same complexly carnal and spiritual awe with which pious men regard the Virgin Mary:

> Frommen gleich die trotz ihrem grauen
> Wieder und wieder beim angelus schauen
> Zu einer madonna von ebenholz. (I, 29)

> As pious men despite their terror
> Look time and again while praying the angelus
> At a madonna of ebony wood.

He rejects the "warm bond" (I, 30) she offers him and is astonished at the passion he has inflamed in her. He suffers at rejecting her and tries to establish another kind of bond between them, one in which the perils of sensuality will not exist: "O Sister!/ You dislike this name?/ Let this riddle be/ When I depart/ . . . / A betrothal for us both" (I, 30). The poems "Lass deine tränen/ Um ein weib" ("Cease your weeping/ Over a woman") (I, 29) and "In alte lande laden bogenhallen" ("To old lands arcades call") (I, 30) explain this fastidious reticence. Both poems express a fear of surrendering to love too early, before a spiritual and emotional understanding of this most sublime and complex of human experiences has been attained. The poet must know the full truth before he can consider himself ready to love, and only in the ripening itself will the realization of this truth come—in Nature's own course, which it would be unseasonable to try to hurry through a hasty urging, despite the inner call of passion: "Before the June/ Concludes its feast/ Will you see her/ Without a veil?" (I, 29). In the second poem, this fear of an unseasonableness of the soul is most explicit. The poet has fled to the south, and an experience he has there symbolizes his dilemma:

> Am rand der gärten riss mich eine nadel·
> Teerose· gelbe rose!
> Mit sattem schmelz und ohne weissen tadel·
> Mächtige mildelose·
> Schon tropfen tau beklömmen ihren adel.

Zu früh noch . . . will ich mich am wohlgeruche
Erster veilchen beleben:
In heissen häusern ich sie spärlich suche·
IHR in die nähe zu schweben
Erlös ich freunden duft aus meinem tuche.
(I, 30-31)

At the garden's edge a thorn did wound me,
Tea rose, yellow rose!
Sated in smoothness and with no blot of white,
Mighty and merciless,
Even drops of dew would sully its perfection.

Too soon as yet . . . I must revive myself
With early violets' aroma:
I rarely find in hothouses these flowers,
To be close to HER I need
Only release the familiar aroma from my scarf.

Almost frightening in its sensual perfection, the yellow rose, which seems to reach out to grasp the poet is the emblem of the demands to which his passion and that of his beloved subject him. His spiritual state, however, requires the innocence of violets, which he must seek in hothouses, since they are out of season, while roses bloom in every garden. Thus, the poem is a portrayal of a state of mind out of season with nature; but to do the seasonable thing, to surrender to love without the spiritual ripeness, would be equally offensive to another aspect of the integrity of nature. The poet's scarf, redolent with the perfume of the beloved he has fled, is sufficient to arouse in him the full poignancy of his relationship to her. Physically remote from her, he can be as close to her as *he* wishes or can even tolerate. This impasse makes commitment to love impossible. Ernst Morwitz has suggested that these poems reflect Stefan George's friendship with Ida Coblenz, which began during the period in which *Pilgerfahrten* was written.[7]

The first two poems of the group "Gesichte" ("Visions") (I, 31-32) deal with the same problem of surrender to love but take the woman's standpoint into consideration. In the first of these poems, the woman, beautiful and fastidious, loses her dignity and integrity by giving her love in adultery to a man unworthy of her favors. It is not the adultery which is condemned, but the inappropriateness of the object of her love. The woman in the second of these poems is also intemperate in her passion. Although the man she loves pays her no heed, she is ready to surrender all that she is to her beloved, who does not realize the wealth of sweetness her love has to offer. Again, the man is not worthy of the devotion he inspires, and, paradoxically, the woman who offers it diminishes her worth in her own eyes and before the world. These admonitory ballads are intimately bound up with the question of the right human commitment and readiness for it, which is the central theme of *Pilgerfahrten*.

A very different possibility is explored in "Mahnung" ("Warning") (I, 32-33). In a manner prefiguring *Algabal*, the poet sees himself as a triumphant conqueror, a pagan emperor at the height of his victory through which his autonomous will is supreme; in other words, the highest possible realization of power over other men. The conquered people passes before him, completely at his mercy. A woman rends her dress in grief, the chaste priestess greets the emperor as his slave. But the poet, speaking to the conqueror, who is at the same time a projection of himself, says that in the moment he enjoyed the carnal power he had acquired, he would be lowering himself from his exalted heroic stature to the level of the beasts, and, lower yet, to the track in the earth which their passing claws leave. Thus, this dream ends in revulsion on the part of the poet. He will not use his suffering as a guide and will not take revenge upon the world because he cannot partake of it fully, since, once conquered, the "land" he longed for would be transformed into a place of suffering and pain:

> War so denn wirklich dein erstritten land?
> O überhöre jenen lockungschrei
> Und sag nicht dass dein leid dein führer sei
> Und wechsel nicht ein würdiges gewand. (I, 33)

> Was this the land you fought for long and hard?
> O do not hearken to that luring call,
> And do not say your suffering is your guide
> And do not change or lose a worthy garb.

The poet has therewith left behind him the world of harmony in love and greatness through deeds. The remaining poems of *Pilgerfahrten* are exclusively concerned with questions touching upon his vocation as a poet, which is to be his ultimate commitment, all other possibilities having been tried and found wanting. These questions concern the poet's place in the world, his quest for inspiration, his conquest of suffering, and his finding of the proper subject matter in a dialectic, almost narrative fashion. Despite their dissimilarity in form, the poems must be read consecutively if their total meaning is to become apparent. As a statement of George's quest for a poetic credo at the time, *Pilgerfahrten* is greater than the sum of its parts. At first, the poet seeks recourse from suffering in a dream realm within his mind (I, 33-34). This dream might become reality through his song and his words—a reflection of the Symbolist doctrine of the poet as creator: "In the pleasure in tones clear to the sense/ Which for moons rang in my mouth/ Does a seed lie for new images?/ Am I now coming home to true meadows?" (I, 34). In the ability to create a new world through his art the poet sees his salvation for the moment and determines to shape his life accordingly. His art shall no longer be a triumph over life, his song no more a "triumph over suffering" (I, 34), but pure art, completely divorced from his personal fate. Thus (I, 35), he buries his pilgrim's cloak and staff, the symbol of his earthly lot and suffering, and decides to undertake an indeterminate "gladder journey." But then his memories, from which he cannot separate himself and which he cannot bury, ascend to his consciousness, and he sobs that he had best smash his lyre against the selfsame tree under which he had buried his cloak and staff. The lyre, the Orphic instrument, here symbolizes "pure" art divorced from the poet's personal experience, through which he would become the medium for a world of objective meaning incomprehensible to the senses. But the poet's memory and his humanity come between him and the realization of this ideal of art. He cannot play this "lyre," for the attempt to do so would make all that he has experienced meaningless. This poem indicates the beginning of George's later parting of the ways with the full consequences of *poésie pure.*

Only in the fusion of experience and expression which achieves the intensification of the meaning of life through art can there be a felicitous solution for the poet, one which will justify his particular nature and fate. But this again raises the question of unseasonableness, of being in disharmony with the world: "But to struggle with my torment/ When men gladly seal betrothals/ Is it right? when fountains glisten/ Always with the moon to weep?" (I, 35). The consolation for present unseasonableness is hope for future ripeness: "Behold, many a rose will yet blossom,/ Still the grain awaits its ripeness" (I, 35). Until his season comes the poet must sing, and in this singing itself there is a solace. He must develop his art so that as an instrument it is ready at the time when his spirit is ready to make full use of it:

> Spenden nicht die kühlen finger
> Leise lust mit ihrem froste? . .
> Sei verjährter fahrten singer
> Dass der klangdraht uns nicht roste! (I, 36)

Don't your chilly fingers give
Subtle pleasure in their coldness? . . .
Be a singer of past journeys,
That our lyre string will not rust!

The poet's new-found equanimity, his readiness to follow his vocation, is expressed in "Neuer Ausfahrtsegen" ("The Blessing of New Journeys") (I, 36-37). Like "Lauschest du des feuers gesange," this poem has, at its center, the complex love of men for the Virgin Mary, a love that is both spiritual and sensual. The poet is in a cathedral, speaking to the image of Mary, whose eyes seem to regard him benevolently. When he was younger, Mary had seemed to him a premonition of his future beloved, his bride. Now, when his desire for this bride has cooled and he despairs of ever finding her, he asks himself the meaning of this new confrontation with the Virgin. His song rises in the cathedral, and he knows that his urge to sing, his need to live are being aroused in him and sanctified. Mary has now become for him, who was never able to accept her theological significance, another manifestation of the Muse, a seeming encouragement from another sphere of being:

Zur salbung fliess· mein eigen siedend blut!
Wo find ich wieder meinen pilgermantel?
Wo find ich wieder meinen pilgerhut? (I, 37)

Let my own hot blood flow now to anoint me!
Where can I find again my pilgrim's cloak?
Where can I find again my pilgrim's hood?

Newly fortified, then, the poet resumes his journey, first to become a "singer of past journeys," then toward the threshold of a new conception of art, using new expressive means, whose felicity is dubious to him from the very outset. Again and again, as in "Ihr alten bilder schlummert mit den toten" ("Slumber with the dead, images of old") (I, 36) and "Dass er auf fernem felsenpfade" ("Let him on paths of distant cliffs") (I, 37), the phantoms of autonomous images haunt him—images unrelated to his actual experiences, mere romantic fantasies, whose peril he senses. He would have his wanderer "bathe in the light" (I, 37) and avoid the swamps in which blooms a fascinatingly beautiful "white lily," which is at the same time a "wicked angel, seducing angel." Thus the "blue flower" of Romanticism, the symbol of longing for autonomous esthetic entities, is here transformed and depicted as the greatest possible peril for the pilgrim, both as man and as poet. Though the poet be forced by his fate, his peculiar way of viewing reality, to stand aside from more ordinary men, he must try to understand their world and not to escape from it into a surrogate, romantic world of subjective imagination. He must pay his tribute to the rhythm of nature and must consent to mature, ripen, and die, as do all living things. This links the "wanderer" (I, 37) to the woman depicted in the vignette "Die frühe sonne küsst noch ohne feuer" ("The early sun still kisses without warming") (I, 38). She is disconsolate at being past the prime of her youth. The flowers in her garden no longer seem to praise her as "the queen of this flower Eden" (I, 38). Thus, she is a disruptive presence here, her fluttering ribbons driving off the butterflies and her abrupt movements causing the potted palms to twitch and sway: "Sullenly she feels the pride of things/ Which have sprung up only to bloom" (I, 38). Her unhappiness lies in her inability to accept that she is subject to the same forces which govern the blooming of the flowers. Hers is a vain and self-defeating desire for esthetic permanence, a desire to be avoided in life and only conditionally to be achieved in art.

"Verjährte Fahrten" (Journeys Past"), I, II, III (I, 38-39), recollect some aspects of the poet's experience of the world: the piety of childhood, an island-garden at Aranjuez in Spain, so redolent with the melancholy of the dead past that the visitor almost expects an *Infante,* perhaps the one in *Hymnen,* to appear fleetingly. Especially in this second poem, the merging of a natural setting, in all its atmospheric density, with the subjective moment of imagination, in the sense which the poet's new conception of his art demands, seems to succeed fully. That no art can surpass the ingenuity of nature, however, and that no poetic imagination can create her wonders, is the truth expressed in the third of these poems. The poet describes a railroad trip across the Alps by night. As the sun rises, he sees the ice crystals on the pane of the train window:

> Wo farren gräser junge palmen
> Ganz aus kristall sich aufgestellt
> Mit ähren moosen schachtelhalmen·
> Wundersame pflanzenwelt! (I, 39)

> Where ferns and grasses and young palms
> Made of pure crystal did stand
> With wheat ears, mosses, slender reeds,
> Plants as in a wonderland!

As the final poem in *Pilgerfahrten*, "Die Spange" ("The Clasp") (I, 40), elucidates, the poet is here paying tribute to a spontaneity and appropriateness of art he himself cannot achieve and which it is humanly impossible to achieve. But his ideal is to come as close as possible to this degree of artistic felicity—a perfect imaginative intensification of the real world, not a flight away from it. With the "Verjährte Fahrten," the inner spiritual journey of *Pilgerfahrten* ends. After seeking new commitments and goals which would fill the void so apparent in *Hymnen*, the poet has achieved a new affirmation and dedication to a concept of art at once old and, for him, infused with new meaning—a poetry which will not attempt to escape from the verities of existence but which will seek to elucidate them and to encourage men to see beyond their own apparent limitations. Nature herself reveals all of these verities, but it is given to few besides poets to understand them; and this is to be the poet's mission in life. To communicate his own fantasies in his own cryptic language, in the manner of the most esoteric French Symbolists, was seen by the "pilgrim" to be arid and impossible. Yet he is still obsessed by this possibility and must explore it further, in an almost experimental situation, the world of *Algabal*, before he can turn away entirely from *l'art pour l'art* in the purely esthetic sense.

The poem appearing just before "Die Spange" seems to have a special place in the economy of *Pilgerfahrten*. It did not appear in the first edition of the volume, but was added in the edition of 1898, together with the motto: "So I went forth/ And became a stranger/ And sought one/ Who would mourn with me/ But there was no one"—a paraphrase from the Psalm 69.[8] This second edition bore a dedication to Hugo von Hofmannsthal. Evidently an element was lacking in the structure of *Pilgerfahrten* which was supplied by the addition of the poem "Beträufelt an baum und zaun" ("Does a balm sprinkle now...") (I, 40). The poem is reminiscent of "Im Park" in *Hymnen*. The poet, "the nameless one," appears here alone in an autumnal world of passionate color: "Red-yellow, speckled-brown/ Scarlet and uncanny green." But the poem has opened with a question: "Does a balm sprinkle now/ On fences' and trees' brittle wood?" which implies a new awakening that is almost miraculous in the face of the year's dying. But unlike the poet of "Im Park" who communes only with his "spirits," "the nameless one" is approached by a being who seems to understand his grief:

> Wer naht sich dem namenlosen
> Der fern von der menge sich härmt?

In mattblauen kleidern ein kind . .
So raschelt ein schüchterner wind
So duften sterbende rosen
Von scheidenden strahlen erwärmt. (I, 40)

Who comes to the nameless one
Grieving far from the crowd?
In garments of pale blue a child . . .
Thus rustles a hesitant wind
Thus dying roses perfume
Warmed by departing rays.

The "nameless one" and the "child" walk hand in hand through the garden "like siblings in fairy tales," ecstatic and with faltering gait. Most readers of this poem, especially Morwitz and Goldsmith,[9] interpret the line "In mattblauen kleidern ein kind . ." as referring to a young boy. Claude David[10] goes so far as to see a reflection of Hugo von Hofmannsthal in this *kind.* For the noun *kind* to be valid in denoting a boy in German, he could be no more than twelve years old; and it is hard to imagine a youngster, no matter how ethereal his disposition, walking with "slow and hesitant" steps, as the poet and his companion do at the close of the poem. This kind of inconsistency is alien to George, whose figures achieve their vividness through the credibility of their actions and motions.

Hugo von Hofmannsthal was sixteen when George first met him, and, as George's letter to him, quoted on p. 28 indicates, George was hardly seeking the companionship of a childlike mind in approaching him. These inconsistencies disappear, however, if one recalls that in German the term *kind* may also be applied to describe a young girl of any age up to the threshold of puberty, perhaps up to fourteen or fifteen years of age. George uses *kind* in this sense in several other poems.[11] The simile "Wie märchenhafte geschwister" ("Like siblings in fairy tales") in the last stanza would seem to support the likelihood that George meant just such a girl, since, in fairy tales, "siblings" are invariably sister and brother, two brothers being, if anything, hostile to each other. Such a girl would be far more likely to walk with her companion in the manner specified and to wear "garments of pale blue." The reiterated causal "So . . . / So . . ." in the fourth and fifth lines of the stanza indicate that this child is imaginary, a creation of the wishes of "the nameless one," the poet, evoked by the aroma of the dying roses and by the rustling of the wind.

What, then, is the place of this poem in *Pilgerfahrten?* The problem of love between a man and a woman, and the question of why the poet felt unable to give himself fully in love, were subsumed in the general problem of the triumph of art over individual suffering after having been intensively treated in the first several poems of the cycle. The problem was never resolved, and no counterimage was ever opposed to the poet's sense of being out of season with his own physical nature and that of the beloved. This poem presents such a counterimage, the poet's dream of a love in which he could find felicity and inner repose: the voluntary approach of a girl with the beauty and innocence of childhood, who would not demand passion or gratification (*ein heisses band*) (I, 30) from him but would be content to be as he, silent, dreaming, joining in an ecstatic, purely spiritual companionship, uncomplicated and undefiled by physical love. Thus, as the "Verjährte Fahrten" gave examples of the poet's striving for expression in art congruous to his nature, "Beträufelt an baum und zaun" closes, for the moment, the circle by opposing a dream of ideality to the painful reality depicted in the first several poems of *Pilgerfahrten*.

"Die Spange" ("The Clasp") (I, 40), with which *Pilgerfahrten* concludes, compresses the poetic problem with which George had been struggling throughout the cycle in a final striking image and points ahead to a new manifestation of these same problems, but by no means to their solution. The author likens himself to a craftsman who makes clasps in the same way in which the poet makes poems. The making of a clasp is identical to the making of a poem, and a poem is a clasp. A clasp is a device for holding things together. A poem for George has very much the same function, as became clear in *Pilgerfahrten*. Ideally, it holds together the poet's intimation of the world in the form of arbitrary symbolic language in which these intimations must find expression. The poem links the subjective mind with objective reality. Just as the pilgrim (I, 34-35) cannot play his lyre without longing for his buried mantle and staff and must come to terms with life in his poetry and give it some relation to nature, so the poet in "Die Spange" wishes to use the ordinary materials of life to form his "clasp":

Ich wollte sie aus kühlem eisen
Und wie ein glatter fester streif·
Doch war im schacht auf allen gleisen
So kein metall zum gusse reif. (I, 40)

I wanted it of coolest iron
And like a smooth and solid band

Yet in all shafts throughout the mine.
No such ore was ready for the mold.

The use of the word *reif* ("ripe, mature") to denote the ore's unsuitability is striking. It evokes echoes of the poet's own sense of immaturity, his preference for the violets over the yellow rose (I, 30-31), his sense of unseasonableness in relation to nature and the world in his function. Thus, he has not yet found the proper material and the maturity within himself to give his "link" the ultimate form he desires, simple, natural, and functional, made of a material all men revere for its utility. But, in order that "the lyre string will not rust" (I, 36), he must continue to sing, must fashion his "link" of the material which comes most readily to hand:

Nun aber soll sie also sein:
Wie eine grosse fremde dolde
Geformt aus feuerrotem golde
Und reichem blitzendem gestein. (I, 40)

But now it shall be like this:
Like a large exotic bloom
Shaped of gold red as fire
And rich sparkling gems.

Large and exotic blooms, whose form his art is now to take—as we have seen in the case of the "yellow tea rose" (I, 30) and the "white lily" (I, 37)—always indicate a dangerous temptation for the poet, from which he knows he must ultimately recoil if he is to retain his wholeness. "Iron" is the metal of the everyday world of experience. It cannot become "ripe" in the poet except through the passing of time, and the poet has, as he seems to acknowledge himself, not passed through enough time to become "ripe," in this as in so many other ways. He has not experienced enough of the world to make his "link" out of its materials. Thus, almost in resignation and desperation, he turns to "gold," which symbolizes the world of fantasy. Gold has a much smaller material function than does iron. Its preciousness lies only in the minds and imagination of men. The same is largely true of the stones which men call precious. Turning to the world of autonomous imagination implies the attempt to create a pure poetry in the sense of the Symbolists, that is, completely divorced from the reality of life, from the world of "iron." The decision to commit himself temporarily to a poetic doctrine whose dangers the poet recognizes and has stated, is made reluctantly. The poet intends, in time, to fulfill his original dream of the form he will give his poems, but because the time is not yet ripe, he creates the world of *Algabal,* in which the same problems as in *Hymnen* and *Pilgerfahrten* are treated, out of the richness of his imagination and the matter of history.

In 1892, shortly after the appearance of George's third book of poems, *Algabal,* Carl August Klein wrote in the *Blätter für die Kunst*: "The three books *Hymnen, Pilgerfahrten, Algabal* seem to be conceived as a trilogy... Everywhere the protagonist is the soul of the modern artist. In *Hymnen* we see [this soul] hovering over gardens and shorelines with still apparent pleasure in the world. In *Pilgerfahrten,* we see it symbolized as a wanderer, with longing, but suppressed cries of suffering. In *Algabal* symbolized as the Byzantine *Imperator* who mourns himself to death amidst the rustling of metals and sumptuous garments. In the first book, drums and trumpets predominate, in the second the lyre and the flute, in the third, long vibrating, violin tones, which sound of despair and confuse the senses."[12] In 1898, these three books were published together in one volume, thereby underscoring Klein's appraisal and establishing the unity which they have represented in all subsequent editions.

Victor A. Oswald[13] has presented evidence that, in creating *Algabal,* Stefan George studied at least some of the historical sources available to him and that many historical episodes are reflected in the events of this cycle. Algabal is the name George uses for the Roman emperor known variously as Heliogabalus, Elagabalus, or Algabal, who ruled from A.D. 218 to 222. His reign was marked by hedonism and lasciviousness, self-deification and cruelty, in a degree remarkable even for that period of Rome's decay. Algabal (Varius Avitus) was rumored to be an illegitimate son of Emperor Caracalla, who had been killed in A.D. 217. He had taken the name of the sun-god, Heliogabalus, in whose cult he had been a priest in his native province of Syria. Like his father Septimius Severus (A.D. 146-211), Caracalla had been popular among the soldiers, and Algabal's reputed ancestry, together with his exceptional physical beauty and his priesthood, gained the soldiers' favor for him. Through the connivance of his grandmother, the soldiers elected him Emperor, withdrawing their allegiance from his predecessor, Macrinus. During a riot of the soldiers in Rome, Algabal was killed and his body thrown into the Tiber. He had lived eighteen years.

As Friedrich Gundolf has pointed out, the poem "Mahnung" in *Pilgerfahrten* foreshadows Stefan George's interest in this enigmatic figure, who combined the outward dignities of a priest and emperor with esthetic and sensual appetites of equal and unmatched depravity.[14] In speaking to the *du* of the conqueror in "Mahnung" (I, 32-33), the poet already weighed and found wanting the delusion that any man's will could reign untrammeled without his having to pay an excessive price in terms of his own humanity. In the book of *Algabal,* George examines the artistic and existential consequences of total subjectivity in all of their aspects, beginning in the realm of art and proceeding through the essential sectors of life.

The autonomy of will and imagination in art were embodied for George in the most extreme attitudes of the French Symbolist poets—the later Mallarmé and especially Rimbaud—whose involvement in their personal symbolic universe was tantamount to philosophic solipsism, the rejection at will by the artist of the claims of anything outside his personality to meaning or binding reality. George's mistrust of such a subjective unhinging of the self from some moral relationship to reality and to the poet's own empiric past was clearly expressed in *Pilgerfahrten.* Yet he felt within himself a power and compulsion of the imagination which all too easily could have led him to find refuge from his alienation from men in a splendidly structured artificial world of image and symbol. Through the creation of *his* Algabal, "a unitary metaphor of omnipotence, sacral dedication, beauty, and the autonomy of the dream,"[15] George established a surrogate *persona,* an intensification of the possibilities latent within himself, to express, in his stead, the totally amoral artist and man.

In *Algabal,* George may be said to purge himself of the potentially destructive urge to live and create an art unbounded by the moral categories of man in his highest natural expression. In portraying the aridity and cruelty arising from Algabal's spectacularly unnatural attitude toward reality, George affirms, by opposition, nature and the sane interchange between the subjective mind and objective reality. As a closer examination of the poems will show, *Algabal* plays much the same role in George's creative biography as *The Sorrows of Young Werther* plays in Goethe's, although critics like Claude David are at pains to deny such an idea.[16] Both books can be seen as expressing intensifications of dark urgings which, once objectivized, lose their compulsive, almost magical lure for the poet. In this connection, it is interesting to note that George, on the very rare occasions he spoke about this cycle, always avoided any formulation which would have implied identity between himself and Algabal. Thus, in the dedication of *Algabal* to King Ludwig II of Bavaria (I, 44), who had died under mysterious circumstances in 1886, George indicates his own youthful admiration for Ludwig, but he lets Ludwig's "younger brother" Algabal, greet him beyond the grave, thus tacitly dissociating himself from identity with his creation. In 1920, talking about Nietzsche, George said that it had not been Nietzsche but *Algabal*[17] who was beyond good and evil. The opposition of a poetic *persona* to a real person, the avoidance of the opportunity to say that he, George, had been beyond good and evil, seems to make sharp and intentional the disjuncture between him and Algabal, thereby denying the identity which is usually claimed.[18] Algabal was to venture "beyond good and evil," into a realm of artistic and human amorality which at once tempted and repelled George.

The twenty-two poems of *Algabal* are divided into three sections, "Im Unterreich" ("In the Subterranean Realm"); "Tage" ("Days"); "Die Andenken" ("Remembrances"); and a closing poem, "Vogelschau" ("Augury"). The first part depicts the world of Algabal's creation and, by implication, the emperor himself. Algabal's domain underground, below the city's buildings and the bed of the river, is born of his "radiant intoxication" (I, 45). Here we find gelid springs and grottos formed of rare metals, jewel-studded and illumined by eternal candles. On subterranean lakes, boats without oars are carried by the waves to lands where dragons wait. The creator and "master" of this imaginative opulence, the emperor himself, is only "sometimes" gladdened by its sublime novelty, where "no will rules beside his own/ And where he the light and the climate commands" (I, 45). Among other wonders, the nether realm has chambers of the "yellow glow and the sun," of "pale radiance," where the myriad possibilities of white reveal themselves to the eye, and a coal-black garden, "which has never seen a Spring." Like the house of des Esseintes in *A Rebours* by Huysmans, Algabal's "underworld" is an imitation of nature assembled from the rarest and most precious substances. But the illusion which these creations are meant to evoke is not a fulfillment. There is an oppressive tension between the surrender to the illusion and understanding of the reality constituting it, of the discrepancy between the objective and subjective levels of truth:

> Daneben war der raum der blassen helle
> Der weisses licht und weissen glanz vereint·
> Das dach ist glas· die streu gebleichter felle
> Am boden schnee und oben wolke scheint. (I, 46)

Close by there was the room of pallid radiance
Uniting white reflected and in rays,
The roof is glass, the carpet of bleached furs,
The floor of glowing snow with clouds above.

Surely these chambers achieve the desired effect of externalizing the artist-emperor's fantasy, the isolation and concentration in the work of art of qualities only arbitrarily present in the natural world: the quintessence of gold and of the sun; of silver, snow, and cloud; of total blackness captured in an artfully sculpted garden of coal.

But this triumph of art over nature is rendered pathetic by the constant disruption of art's illusion. The minds of the reader, of the poet, and of the emperor himself are not long permitted to linger undisturbed in the fullness of the artistic effect achieved, for the artist's imagination is never entirely released from the bondage to its material and to craftsmanship. The evanescent and abstract totality of "pallid radiance" is immediately juxtaposed to the reality of "glass" and "bleached furs." Other elements call this universe of autonomous artifice into question. Even here, the emperor cannot flee memory and moral responsibility. The sight of a stone sphere with which he played as a boy moves him to tears, and on that day he refrains from his accustomed vices. In the fastnesses of a world created to the measure of the artist's imagination, an existential universe beyond the esthetic one manifests itself and cannot be denied. An earnestly moral irony underlies these poems which, at first, appear to be showpieces of *fin de siècle* decadence with heavy leanings toward *art nouveau.* In the closing poem of "Im Unterreich" (I, 47), the emperor describes the garden he has built, which requires neither sun nor air, being made entirely of carven coal and lava. The birds are lifeless, and the fruits never ripen and fall. The garden is entirely black, its light a dull gray shimmer denying the times of the day. This garden is the consummate artificial paradise, perfect but lifeless. Algabal ponders how he can bring true life into it through the creation of a "dark, large, black flower":

Wie zeug ich dich aber im heiligtume
—So fragt ich wenn ich es sinnend durchmass
In kühnen gespinsten der sorge vergass—
Dunkle grosse schwarze blume? (I, 47)

But how create you in the sanctuary
—So I asked when in thoughts I paced through its paths
In bold speculation forgetting my cares—
Dark, majestic flower of black.

H. Stefan Schultz has suggested that, in the act of speaking the words "Dunkle grosse schwarze blume," Algabal has answered his own question, has created the impossible, according to the Symbolist belief that whatever is expressed in words exists.[19] This purely conceptual act of creation, however, differs sharply from Algabal's other artistic acts, which require an utmost degree of material artifice for their realization. As it evolves out of the question whether or not it can be created, the black flower, a mocking of the Romantic dream of the blue flower, gains an ominous reality, which the other elements of Algabal's nether realm never achieve. It is only in total withdrawal from confrontation with the pragmatic world into the subjective dream that truly autonomous creation is possible. There, the awareness of necessity underlying even the most effective artifice is suspended. In creating the "black flower," Algabal has momentarily retreated into an even more inaccessible "underworld" of art, the realm of total solipsism, where, for a time, he can ignore his cares, but whose imaginative reality he cannot transpose into objective form, try as he might, because of the exigencies of the eternal dialectic between matter and spirit.

The futile barbarism of the attempt to transform dreams into reality, expressed in the *Unterreich,* has its counterpart in the world in which Algabal must live, act, and confront the reality embodied in other men. Outwardly, his power is supreme, and his esthetic perfection is so complete that a Lydian slave who startles the emperor while he is feeding the pigeons gladly commits suicide for having disrupted the harmonious beauty of a moment, both for the emperor and for himself (I, 48). But the emperor's scorn is aroused by the Lydian's readiness to lose his life for so apparently trivial a cause, out of an awe which the emperor cannot feel for himself. As a tribute to this act, he has the slave's name engraved upon his drinking cup, which he can never again use without recollecting a sacrifice he knows he did not deserve—aware of the discrepancy between the role he must play and his human frailty. He feels that an arbitrary fate has cast him into this role, but "To hesitate in sorrow is not seemly/ For us born by Chance for the purple robe" (I, 53).

Algabal's sense of his own limitation is apparent in his warning to his "mother's mother" (I, 49), who has plotted against him because he did not share her political aims, preferring to create a world far from her concerns, in which his will has supreme power: "O let me only, neither praised nor hated/ Freely follow my restricted path." If he is provoked and forced to exceed his limits, terrible visions, arising in his troubled mind, will be transformed into murderous reality. At other times, Algabal gives free rein to his despotic fancy, literally suffocating his guests in a shower of roses at an orgiastic banquet (I, 50-51). He is fatalistic in regard to his approaching death and plans suicide before the mob can murder him: "Yet know/ Your ruler has departed from you/ Ere the town even dares to grumble its plaint" (I, 53). As he is completely skeptical about the genuineness of human passion, estheticizes warfare, and doubts even the mourning of the bereaved (I, 52-53), Algabal can find no existential possibility in the glory of military leadership. His days are emptily voluptuous, his nights sleepless. He is lulled only by the music of Egyptian flute players, which "kills" him in respect to reality, closing his eyelids with the weight of dreams (I, 51). The music of Syrian musicians, reproducing, in abstract compression, the totality of life in its pain and beauty, draws Algabal back from the chasm of suicide, which would be the supreme gesture of the autonomy of his will (I, 54).

Through his pessimistic self-awareness, his understanding of his own sensual humanity, Algabal lacks the Neronian contempt for the rabble which would enable him to rule with vigor, to impose his esthetic amoralism upon Rome, turning it possibly into his ultimate artifice:

> So sprach ich nur in meinen schwersten tagen:
> Ich will dass man im volke stirbt und stöhnt
> Und jeder lacher sei ans kreuz geschlagen.
> Es ist ein groll der für mich selber dröhnt.
>
> ICH bin als einer so wie SIE als viele·
> Ich tue was das leben mit mir tut
> Und träf ich sie mit ruten bis aufs blut:
> Sie haben korn und haben fechterspiele.
>
> Wenn ich in ihrer tracht und mich vergessend
> Geheim in ihren leeren lärm gepasst
> —Ich fürchte—hab ich nie sie tief gehasst·
> Der eignen artung härte recht ermessend.
>
> Dann schloss ich hinter aller schar die riegel·
> Ich ruhte ohne wunsch und mild und licht
> Und beinah einer schwester angesicht
> Erwiderte dem schauenden ein spiegel. (I, 52)
>
> I said this only in my darkest days:
> My will is that the mob must groan and die

That he who laughs be nailed upon the cross.
This is an anger droning for myself.

I am as one as they as many are,
I do whatever life has done to me,
And could I draw their blood with supple whips,
Still they have grain and gladiatorial bouts.

When dressed like them, forgetful of myself,
I secretly have shared their empty noise,
—I fear—I never deeply hated them,
Appraising right the hardness of my kind.

To flee the throng I bolted fast my door,
I rested gentle, light, without desire,
And almost a sister's countenance
In mirror's surface came before my gaze.

Algabal is unable to affect the people of Rome deeply in any way. Within himself, he feels the totality of their desires and diversions, the flight from the tyrannic reality of existence into an orgy of "bread and circuses." In their midst, though their brutish lusts are the very opposite of his abstract estheticism, he cannot bring himself to hate them, although his fastidiousness will not let him be like them. It is only in his confrontation with his own image in the mirror that Algabal can find "a sister's countenance," the complementary image of his own unique nature, which neither the world of art nor that of action can offer him. Algabal cannot wrest the fulfillment of his artistic dream from the brittle material reality with which the artist must work, and he must sadly acknowledge that his "underworld" is only an approximation of the inner reality of his fantasy. Through words alone, in the solipsistic interchange between spirit and language, the most pliable of artistic media, he can "create" the sensual manifestation of his dream, the black flower. In this poem the mirror symbolizes an analogous solipsism, the tragic constitution of a man fated by the "hardness of his kind" never to find the correspondence in the empiric universe to the overpowering images of his subjective imagination.

In the existential consequences he draws from this fate, Algabal is the extreme expression of this problem, which we have seen as the major constituent theme in George's preceding books, *Hymnen* and *Pilgerfahrten.* Algabal is not the heroic exponent of an *art nouveau* esthetic carried to its artistic and amoral extreme, but the victim of an arbitrary fate which has made him what he is and cast him into a role he cannot really play. The barbaric retreat into total preoccupation with his own dreams, "beyond good and evil" and safe from any moral acknowledgment of the reality of the empiric existence "outside his door," must end tragically. Reality, depicted in the form of the mutinous mob which murders Algabal, avenges itself on those who most spectacularly defy its imperatives. It was precisely from such an absolute defiance on his own part that George constantly withdrew, never permitting himself to surrender to the temptation of a personal world of poetic symbol, constantly attempting to establish a functional continuity between subjective and objective perception of the universe. In *Algabal,* the tragic consequences of just such a surrender are patently apparent, presenting a negative possibility which George overcame within himself. The problem in itself persists, however, and is a significant factor in all of the later works.

The closing section of *Algabal,* "Die Andenken" ("Remembrances"), evidently depicts Algabal on the threshold between life and death. His youth, a time when he dwelt only in the realm of the ideal, is a world irrevocably lost to him: "Days of greatness when in spirit only I was called the ruler of the world,/ Cursèd day when in my homeland I departed from the temple./ There I conversed with gods about their highest plan/ Their children came down for my delight and service" (I, 55). In his final hours, he admonishes himself to confront his fate in the fullness of his beauty (I, 56). In accord with the elegiac mood of the "Andenken," ruefully tender memories engulf Algabal. He had married a priestess of Vesta (I, 56), hoping to find in her the counterpart to his own sublime dignity and contemplative aloofness from the fate of mankind, the esthetic remove permitted only to the gods. But he banished the priestess back to her temple when he discovered that she, too, had, "like the others a flaw." This "flaw" consists not, as many interpreters believe, in her femininity, but rather in her humanity, her capacity for feeling, which Algabal senses in himself, and which stands between him and his dream of totally transforming the world in terms of his imaginative ideal.[20]

The theme of the singular mercy of an early death appears already in "Der Infant" in *Hymnen* (I, 20-21). Algabal tells how he had poisoned a youth and a lass he found sleeping after their lovemaking. Wishing to spare them punishment by their fathers—the destruction of their joy—he endows them with the gift he had been saving for himself, the poison from his ring:

> Begnadete! da ich euch gütig nahte
> Und kein erwachen euch ein glück ermattet

Das nur der traum so herrlich euch gestattet
Als ich es jezt aus euren zügen rate. (I, 57)

Blesséd ones! since I benevolently came,
And no awakening dulled your happiness,
Which only dreams can grant you with such glory,
As I now guess it from your countenances.

As he had often done in the deepest despair of his youth, Algabal is now waiting for his death, the "saddest solace, son of night" (I, 58). His life seems to him like the bud of a flower he sees in the temple, denied its natural blossoming by a fate which has placed it before the altar, drenching it in rare essences, but, at the same time, killing it (I, 58).

Algabal summarizes the stages of his life in "Vogelschau," the closing poem of the book. He affirms his desire to return to the ideality of his earliest dreams, possible now only through the intermediation of his death, for which he is supremely ready:

Weisse schwalben sah ich fliegen·
Schwalben schnee- und silberweiss·
Sah sie sich im winde wiegen·
In dem winde hell und heiss.

Bunte häher sah ich hüpfen·
Papagei und kolibri
Durch die wunder-bäume schlüpfen
In dem wald der Tusferi.

Grosse raben sah ich flattern·
Dohlen schwarz und dunkelgrau
Nah am grunde über nattern
Im verzauberten gehau.

Schwalben seh ich wieder fliegen·
Schnee- und silberweisse schar·
Wie sie sich im winde wiegen
In dem winde kalt und klar! (I, 59)

Once I saw white swallows flying,
Swallows snow- and silver-white,
Rocking in the wind and flying,
In the wind so hot and bright.

Gay-feathered quails I saw hopping,
Parakeet and colibri
By the wonder-tree trunks slipping,
In the wood of Tusferi.

Then I saw large ravens flutter,
Jackdaws black and darkest gray,
Flying low o'er nests of vipers,
In the enchanted forest's vale.

Again I see white swallows flying,
Band of snow- and silver white,
How they rock in wind and flying,
In the wind so cold and clear.

The first three stanzas of the poem are in the past tense; the final strophe is in the present. The motif of the white swallows occurs in the first and last stanzas, symbolizing the purity of the ideal realm in which Algabal had dwelt in his youthful dreams and which he now hopes to re-enter. But in his youth, the air through which the birds flew was "hot and bright," warmed by his faith in the gods, with whom Algabal had communed then. Now the wind is cold and clear with the chill of his lost hope that his ideals might find a congenial realization. The understanding that these hopes have been in vain seals Algabal's readiness for death, which will be an enlightenment, a release for him, and is anticipated without terror or despair. The two middle stanzas of the poem, presenting first colorful, exotic birds, and then black ravens and daws, symbolize Algabal's life: first his attempt to manifest his fantasies in art, as in the underworld, then his despair over his inability to do so, and the existential consequences this implied. The new augury of the last stanza is Algabal's triumph over this despair. In his return to the disembodied ideals and dreams of his youth, he is free of a necessity with which he cannot come to terms.

II Die Bücher der Hirten- und Preisgedichte, der Sagen und Sänge und der Hängenden Gärten

The title of *The Books of Eclogues and Eulogies, of Legends and Lays, and the Hanging Gardens* is emblematic of Stefan George's quest for appropriate forms to reflect the many facets of his imagination and world view. In this collection, published in 1895, three different historic realms are evoked: pastoral antiquity, medieval Europe, and the Persian Orient. George cautiously specified his intentions for choosing these settings: "Nowhere is there the intention of depicting an historical or cultural period; [these works] contain the reflections of a soul which has temporarily fled into other times and places and found comfort there. . . . Every age and every spirit, in forming that which is historic and exotic, moves on the plane of the personal and present, and of our three great cultural spheres [*Bildungswelten*], no more is contained here than still lives on in some of us" (I, 63).

George wanted these poems to reflect his present and real situation through the poetic and human attitudes of archetypal cultural eras. In his essay "Poems by Stefan George" (1896), Hugo von Hofmannsthal saw no negative reason for the apparent denial of present reality in these poems.[21] Admitting that they require close analysis, he regarded them as "signs of the exalted soul of a genuine poet," in contrast with works which "greedily swallow up life and spew it out again in lumps of sensation."[22] Hofmannsthal noticed certain significant attitudes: a victory of life through nobility of the soul and purity of vision and a feeling of triumphant youthfulness. "The inborn kingliness of a self-possessed spirit is the subject of the three books. . . . The concise style reveals the artist's intention, certain images are taken from the leaping fire, from the starry heaven, the most elemental tools, so to speak. The manifold, isolated, and splintered condition of our relationship to the world has been cast into the monstrous abyss of silence."[23] Against the background of this silence of the present, elemental human situations can unfold. Removed from the "splintered" context of the present, the persons involved are projected into a sphere of experience beyond immediate time and space and postulated as continually valid by the poet. Archetypal values of past times and distant cultures, still latent in all men, are thus made operative for the poet's present as alternatives to the overly intellectual attitudes of the immediate historical context. Outside the realm of poetry, the modern age is too conscious of the historical "pastness" of these cultural spheres to find their values binding any longer.

The first fourteen poems, constituting the "Book of Eclogues," directly invoke a pastoral culture in which nature deities dominate man, who feels himself to be part of nature. The forces of nature are personified in satyrs and sylphs who inhabit trees and river banks. The plasticity and mythic atmosphere of the landscape description is reminiscent of the paintings of Arnold Böcklin, which also depict nature in this way. Although the names and reminiscences evoked are Greek, this is not solely the world of Greek pastoral antiquity, many of the elements having been taken, as George said, "from our own still undesecrated valleys and forests" (I, 63). There is an element here of literary "Arcadianism," in that universal types are presented in a setting free of the inhibitions and rationalizations of a more complex society.

The first three poems depict two women, first in their common loss—their bridegrooms having died on the same day seven years before—then in their common hope that the gods might have a happier fate in store for them:

> Schwester! von damals an hiessest du mir Serena
> Und wir gestanden uns unser tiefstes geheimnis:
> Dass wir noch von den flimmernden fluren droben·
> Schwan oder Leier· das schöne wunder erhofften. (I, 65)
>
> Sister! from that day on I called you Serena,
> And we confessed as one our deepest common secret:
> That we from the flickering fields above,
> If Swan or Lyre, still hoped for the wonder so fair.

In this historically indefinite pastoral world, the despair of the sisters over their loss is made bearable by a "secret," the hope brought about by their natural faith in the gods, whose will is revealed in the stars, "the flickering fields above." The "wonder so fair," a fulfillment of their hope in love, might come in the form of a swan—a constellation they see—as Zeus came to Leda, or bearing a lyre, as Orpheus, the most faithful of lovers, sought out Eurydike after her death, even in the underworld. The conception of love as a divine wonder, the identity of the lover with the gods, at any rate his function as a bearer of their will, is possible only on this naïve level of culture, where men still live ritually, as a function of the will of divine forces manifested in nature. In "Loostag" ("Day of Decision"), the woman speaking in all of these poems notices that her companion turns away from her toward "a vineyard lattice in the West." The poem closes: "O, what if a secret looms/ From these vines, taking you from our midst!" (I, 66). The divinely ordained love for which both had hoped—here in its elemental form, the Dionysian abandon symbolized by the vines—threatens their bond. Thus, the first three poems sum up significant qualities of George's vision of the pastoral world: the conquest of suffering through remembrance and ritual; the complete submission in faith to the will of benevolent gods; and, finally, the recognition of the elemental and irresistible force of a godly, Dionysian nature.

In the *Hirtengedichte,* men, demigods, and legendary creatures represent mythic aspects of existence. The joys and travails of the bard are the concern of a number of these eclogues. Thus, in "Der Tag des Hirten" ("The Shepherd's Day"), a young herdsman leaves his flock and the cultivated fields of civilization to wander in a dark forest, where "exposed the beeches' black roots intertwine"

(I, 66). He falls into a deep sleep, awakens at the end of the day and climbs a peak, where he crowns himself "with sacred foliage" and intones his song to the darkening clouds. In this world, it is a natural and proper act of sacred reverence to follow the mysterious voice, the urge to sing, far from the paths of men. Far more often, however, these figures are the victims of an ineluctable fatality, which they endure with resignation, often culminating in gestures of martyrdom. The figures in the *Book of Eclogues* are, for the most part, essentially tragic, un-Arcadian, no matter how idyllic their world may seem. Thus, the satyr in "Flurgottes Trauer" ("The Satyr's Sorrow"), despairs because the girls he lures with his music are frightened by his ugliness: "Among gray mists/ I will speak my plaint to the Lord of Harvests because/ With life eternal he did not endow beauty" (I, 67). The discrepancy between the artist's song and his empiric being here becomes an essential aspect of the world of myth. Like the *herrin* in "Gespräch" (I, 20), the *Flurgott* is fated not to find solace in union with mortals, love them as he may.

"Der Herr der Insel" ("The Lord of the Island"), possibly influenced by Baudelaire's "Albatros," which George had translated (II, 238), develops the theme of the poet's isolation. The poem is a legend, similar to that from the *Arabian Nights* in which Sinbad encounters the gigantic bird, Roc, on an island. The "Lord of the Island" was a magnificent bird, so tall that, standing on the ground, it could reach the tops of the tallest trees. In flight, borne by its purple wings, it resembled a gigantic black cloud. At sunset, it came to the shore and raised its "sweet voice" while the dolphins, "the friends of song," swam closer:

> So habe er seit urbeginn gelebt·
> Gescheiterte nur hätten ihn erblickt.
> Denn als zum erstenmal die weissen segel
> Der menschen sich mit günstigem geleit
> Dem eiland zugedreht sei er zum hügel
> Die ganze teure stätte zu beschaun gestiegen·
> Verbreitet habe er die grossen schwingen
> Verscheidend in gedämpften schmerzeslauten. (I, 69-70)

> In this way he had lived since time began,
> Only the shipwrecked had ever seen him.
> For when, for the first time, the white sails
> Of men, borne on by favorable winds,
> Came steering toward the island, to the hill
> He climbed, once more the precious realm to see.
> And then, 'tis told, he spread his giant wings,
> Expiring with soft, gentle cries of pain.

The fate of the bird is analogous to that of the poet. For both, life is the fulfillment of seemingly ritual acts to which they are compelled by their very nature, which has set them apart from other beings. With the magical causality of legend, the "lord of the island" is destroyed by a principle which threatens his sovereignty. So too, the poet's very being is endangered by confrontation with a culture whose values are irreconcilable with the sense of fatalism and self-sacrifice in which he finds his fulfillment.

Not only for the artist is the human society an incompatible element. Almost all of the figures in the *Book of Eclogues,* for one reason or another, stand outside the circle of their fellow men. The children in "Der Auszug der Erstlinge" ("The Departure of the First born") must leave the city because of a promise made by their fathers to the gods in order to drive off misfortune.[24] They have been sacrificed by their society for a cause they do not understand, but they do not complain, for that is their lot:

> Wir schieden leicht· nicht eines hat von uns geweint·
> Denn was wir tun gereicht den unsrigen zum heil.
> . . .
> Wir ziehen gern: ein schönes ziel ist uns gewiss
> Wir ziehen froh: die götter ebnen uns die bahn. (I, 70)

> We left with ease, not one of us did weep,
> For what we do will save the ones we love.
> . . .
> We gladly go: sure of a goodly goal,
> We go with joy: the gods will smoothe our path.

The chorus of children affirms their faith in the gods and that what their society has required of them is right, even if it ends in their destruction. This readiness for sacrifice in the name of faith or art is characteristic of the figures in the second half of the *Eclogues,* such as the young men in the poem "Geheimopfer" ("Secret Sacrifice") (I, 70-71). The two "Favorites of the Populace" (I, 72), the wrestler and the lute player, are shown entirely in their outward aspects, the impression they make on the admiring throng. They have become sacrifices to their arts and to the adoration of the crowd, completely losing their individuality. This is the ultimate identity of the artist with his society, possible only in a cultural context in which the whole society constitutes the artist's public, a circumstance which the present state of the poet's own culture does not permit.

The poetess presented in "Erinna" and likewise universally

adored, is preoccupied with her love for a young man, which makes her unfeeling for her public role. The discrepancy between her "role" and her actual feelings is stated as a natural part of life, her dreams as a fate to be endured. More problematic is the future of the two young men in "Abend des Festes" ("The Eve of the Feast"). The feast is an initiation ceremony for the chosen servants of the temple. Of all of their companions they have not been chosen, because they were not fair enough. Rejected by the god, they no longer can return to their lives as common men:

> Wir können mit den schäfern nicht mehr weiden gehn
> Und mit den pflügern nicht mehr an der furche hin
> Die wir das werk der himmlischen zu tun gelernt.
> Gib deinen kranz! ich schleudr' ihn mit dem meinen weg·
> Ergreifen wir auf diesem leeren pfad die flucht·
> Verirren wir uns in des schwarzen schicksals wald. (I, 73)
>
> We can no longer go and with the shepherds graze,
> And no more with the plowman by the furrow walk,
> We who have learned to do the service of the gods.
> Give me your wreath! I'll throw it far away with mine,
> On this abandoned path let us take flight,
> Let us then lose our way in the forest of black fate.

The identity, in the mind of the speaker, between the choice of the priests and fate, the realization that a higher life, once seen and now lost, allows him no return to the society of other men, brings about a tragic insight and the resignation to his fate. There is no struggle with circumstances, at most a statement, hardly a complaint, that things are as they are. This is a realm of existential resignation to the higher will of the gods who still live and affect men because men's faith in them is still alive. Just so, the legendary hero in "Das Ende des Siegers" ("The End of the Victor") (I, 74) withdraws in resignation from the sight of men, when, after many conquests, "his strength leaves him" in a struggle with a serpent, the gods withdraw their protection, and he suffers a wound which can never heal. He lives his remaining days "carefully hidden/ . . . From growing heroes, favored friends of the gods." George, whose previous work has been the mirror of his struggle to understand and come to grips with his peculiar fate as a man and poet, has here created a poetically historic realm in which such an understanding, such an accommodation to his existence, would have been more easily possible, regardless of what fate would have willed for him.

The eleven "Preisgedichte auf einige junge Männer und Frauen dieser Zeit" ("Eulogies on Several Young Men and Women of This Time") initiate a tradition which remains unbroken in the remainder of Stefan George's works. From now on, each of his books will contain a group of poems dedicated to the poet's friends, such as the "Widmungen und Überschriften" in *Das Jahr der Seele*, "Lieder von Traum und Tod" in *Der Teppich des Lebens*, "Tafeln" in *Der Siebente Ring*, the second book of *Der Stern des Bundes* and, finally, the "Sprüche an die Lebenden" and "Sprüche an die Toten" in *Das Neue Reich*. The years in which the "three books" were written, 1892 and 1893, mark the end of George's period of greatest isolation. Many significant relationships were formed, such as the friendships with Ida Coblenz, Ludwig Klages, and Alfred Schuler, as well as less momentous friendships, which, for the moment, meant much to George, such as that with Paul Gérardy and Edmond Rassenfosse. As Gundolf remarks: "For the first time he finds friends who understand him, sympathetic companions who aid him, living poets whom he honors as men and from whom he can learn for his art, a spiritual and intellectual atmosphere in which he can breathe."[25] At this time, because of the encouragement received from his friends, George finally realized his long-cherished plan of publishing the *Blätter für die Kunst*.

The "Eulogies" present portraits of the poet's friends, who are given Greek names in keeping with the pastoral tone of this book.[26] They are not depicted as individuals; but rather, one or two characteristics are singled out, so that they tend to emerge as types. The poet's tone is affectionate, now gently mocking, now admonitory. Present-day situations are stylized in such a way that they are suggestive of the Greek world without becoming explicitly anachronistic. Thus, in "An Damon" (Albert Saint-Paul), the Louvre is transformed into "our house on the northern hill, the scene/ Of new and lonely joy./ Marble images decorated it, godly nakedness/ Which we admired and honored" (I, 75). So, too, Bingen becomes "Phlius" (I, 79).

But such incidental mannerisms should not detract from George's insight about these friends. They represented to him types of human integrity and genuineness he found only too rarely in his time. He placed them into another historical context precisely because he felt that their historical being was purely accidental and their human significance universal, so that they, like he, would have deserved the setting of an age and clime better suited to their qualities. He valued their souls, not their place in this world, whose criteria he explicitly rejects: "Mocking and scourging I spoke of those who always with forethought/ Can consider the useful, their goals midst this turbulent life" (I, 77). It is precisely the immediacy with which his friends experience the turbulence of life itself and their own souls that George regarded most highly.

Pastoral antiquity served George as a setting in which credibly to present figures who accepted their destinies with an innocence born of unquestioning knowledge of the gods' existence and of the powers of the natural universe these gods inhabit. The *Book of Legends and Lays,* set in the chivalric Middle Ages, illumines another aspect of human existence. The knights and ladies, poets, hermits, and monks of whom the "Legends" tell, are almost all involved in a conflict within themselves, the struggle between flesh and spirit, between desire and duty. They see their fates not as preordained, but as chosen—the resolution of a conflict. The existential choice once made, however, becomes fate, absolute and unquestioned, whatever images the tormented soul may present. These situations are indeed modern, and the conflicts universal, but George is presenting them here in elemental circumstances of love and warfare, in which the choices are more absolute and not prone, as in more complex "modern" times, to be relativized. George does not create a Romantic or historic medieval world, but a transparent universe of existential values, adding only enough medieval detail to evoke, through the estate or activity of the person, the latent remembrance of a time when these existential attitudes had arisen. The form of the poems is definitely modern, rarely betraying any imitation of medieval forms.

Whereas in the *Eclogues* the will was depicted as powerless against Fate, it is the determining factor in the *Legends.* Faith and devotion to duty are not immediate and spontaneous but an act of will and moral judgment. Thus in "Sporenwache" ("The Knight's Vigil") (I, 82-83), the young knight, praying on the night before his consecration to God's service, makes the sign of the cross to dispel an "earthly image" of a lovely young girl, which disturbs his reverence. He prays to the infant Jesus:

"Ich werde diener sein in deinem heere
Es sei kein andres streben in mir wach·
Mein leben folge fortab deiner lehre·
Vergieb wenn ich zum lezten male schwach" (I, 83)

"I will be a servant in your legion,
No other striving shall awake in me,
May my life follow henceforth your decree,
Forgive me that I was one last time weak."

This first poem of the *Book of Legends* states an essential theme of conflict in the book. The will of the young knight must choose between desire and duty. Since faith is a viable alternative and the Savior seemingly manifest, the decision for duty and service is clear, almost easy, the vision of the girl paling to unreality before the massive, seemingly breathing existence of the church in which he prays.

Often enough, the extremity of will is depicted darkly, particularly in relation to poets. "Frauenlob" (1250-1318) was a *Minnesänger* whose tomb is in the cathedral of Mainz. The wall tablet covering his niche depicts richly dressed ladies surrounding the bier of the poet. In the poem, Frauenlob tells how he had celebrated the beauties of the city and its women through "A life of stubborn burdens/ A whole life of dark suffering" (I, 85). But even in reproaching the women for their coldness, their total lack of response or recognition of his suffering, he paints an animated and lovely picture of them:

> Weisse kinder der bittgepränge
> Mit euren kerzen fahnen bändern·
> Führerinnen der heitren klänge
> In farbigen lockeren gewändern·
> Bleiche freundinnen der abendmahle·
> Patriziertöchter stolze hochgenannte
> Die unter heiligem portale
> Die schweren kleider falten der levante—(I, 85)

> White children of the shrove procession,
> With your candles, pennants, ribbons,
> Singers of the merry songs,
> In colorful, languorous garments,
> Pale devotees of the sacrament,
> Patrician daughters proud, of noble name,
> Who 'neath the sacred portal,
> Stand in folds of heavy silk from the Levant.

When they mourn at his bier, he tells them, they will, "in common widowhood," weep for him whom they had spurned. Similarly, the knight-poet in "Im unglücklichen tone dessen von..." ("In the Unhappy Tone of...") (I, 87) undertakes heroic deeds at the whim of his beloved, who continues to reject him; but despite his wounds and his poverty, his will and his love continue steadfast to the point of absurdity:

> Ihr saht wie ich mein glück und meinen leib
> In eurem dienst verdarb·

Euch grämte nicht in fährden mein verbleib·
Ihr danktet kaum wenn ich in sturm und staub
Euch ruhm erwarb
Und bliebet meinem flehen taub.

Nun leid ich an einer tiefen wunde·
Doch dringt euer lob bis zur lezten stunde·
Schöne dame· aus meinem munde. (I, 87)

You saw how I my fortune and my life
In serving you did ruin,
You cared not where in dangers I did lie,
You barely thanked me when in combat's dust
I earned your fame,
And deaf to my pleadings you stayed.

Now I suffer from a deadly wound,
But to the last hour your praise shall sound,
Lovely lady, from my lips.

The surrender to an existential decision once made is displayed here more in terms of its humanly painful aspects than in those of a higher glory. In the "Tagelied" ("At Daybreak") (I, 86), the only one of the "Legends" reminiscent of a medieval poetic form, that of the *tageliet,* the lover, about to depart for the wars after a nocturnal tryst with his beloved, reassures her of his worshipful devotion and of the deeds he will do in her name. For her, however, his fortune in arms can only bring pain and tears, for she can comprehend only the fact of parting. The "Knights Errant" (I, 88), precursors of the "Templer" (I, 255-56) in *Der Siebente Ring,* perform heroic deeds for the glory of an unnamed "pale, proud lady," perhaps a beloved noblewoman, or even Mary. They suffer for the safety and well-being of men, who praise, but then forget them. The knights sacrifice all human consolation, living outside the pale of society, which weaves strange legends about them, all for the sake of an ultimate reward in a chivalric Valhalla much like Amfortas' castle in *Parzival.* Yet, like "The Knight Who Lost Himself to Love" (I, 90), he who surrenders to earthly temptations will be forever tormented by hallucinatory sounds of knightly life in which he cannot participate. "The Hermit" (I, 91) tells of his farewell from his son, a young warrior, who desires the honor of great deeds. His father has found peace in contemplation but cannot pass on his experience of the world and the vanity of action to his son:

Ich hätte ihm so gerne meinen leichten
Und sichern frieden hier bei mir verliehn.

Doch anders fügten es der himmel sorgen—
Sie nahmen nicht mein reiches lösegeld . .
Er ging an einem jungen ruhmes-morgen·
Ich sah nur fern noch seinen schild im feld. (I, 91)

So gladly would I have given him my gentle
And certain peace here in my house.

But otherwise ordained the thoughts of heaven,
They deigned not to accept my ransom rich . . .
He went at dawn of day that promised fame,
I only saw in far-off mead his shield.

The closing poem of *Legends,* "Das Bild" ("The Image") (I, 91-92), resumes a theme stated in *Pilgerfahrten,* particularly in "Neuer Ausfahrtsegen" (I, 36-37), the intermingling of spiritual adoration with sensual love. The complex Marianism of the Middle Ages is captured in the figure of a monk who retreats to his cell at sundown to adore, in a spiritual and sensual ecstasy, the image of Mary, to beg her for a visible sign that his love for her is in some form requited. Legends of miracles tell him that such things can happen, that the lady to whom he offers his *minne* can appear, but his hopes are eternally in vain. Now, even if a sign were to come, even if she herself were to appear, "I fear my arm is now too weak for an embrace,/ Upon my lips the burning love expired" (I, 92). The intensity of the monk's will that his heavenly love be realized in earthly terms has exhausted his capacity to live, and has brought him to the outermost limits of his mortal existence. "Sporenwache" stated the conflict of flesh and spirit and its resolution through the power of the human will in optimistic terms. In contrast, the closing poem depicts the pessimistic possibility, the crumbling of the will under the weight of an insoluble riddle, the impossibility of defining the limits between spiritual and earthly love, which are only explicable and open to experience, the one in terms of the other.

Lays of a Wandering Minstrel are the lyrical counterpart to the more epic *Legends.* The minstrel himself is much like one of the figures of the *Legends,* however, for the love songs he sings are addressed to a beloved who will not respond to his pleas, whom he may have only seen in his dreams and whose image he carries always with him (I, 93). The songs are simple and direct, lyrically understated, for "Words deceive, words flee,/ Only song can touch the soul" (I, 93). The *Lays* tell more of loss and resignation than of wooing. So great are his love and his sorrow that he prefers to leave rather than burden his beloved (I, 95). An ironic inner voice tells the minstrel that he shall survive his renunciation of love and that another fate, whether joyful or sorrowful, is in store for him. As the final personal statement of the *Legends and Lays,* this attitude bears striking similarity with that adopted at the close of the *Pilgerfahrten.* The six closing poems of the second "book" recapitulate the romantic and magical qualities of this medieval world. In a ballad (I, 96), a young noblewoman is made to forget her pledge to her lover by the enchanting songs of a minstrel. In "Erwachen der Braut" ("The Bride's Awakening") (I, 98), a maiden has a premonition of the victorious return of her lover. Between these reminiscences of a balladesque, chivalric world appear the three "Songs of the Dwarf" (I, 97), the magically powerful prince of the dwarves, the fairies' child. He appears to men unexpectedly, perhaps in the midst of children dancing and lambs gamboling, to communicate to men what fate has intended for them. The dwarf is the analogue to the longed-for "herrin" of the *Hymnen,* here a part of a universe in which the natural and supernatural effortlessly coexist. In his third song, the dwarf prophesies the riches of nobility to one, the victories of knighthood to another, and to the minstrel a special destiny, a more definite affirmation than George was able to perceive in his own time, from which magic had fled:

> Dir kein ruhm· dir kein sold–
> Dir allein im liede liebe und gold. (I, 97)
>
> For you no fame or fortune's foretold,
> You will find in songs alone love and gold.

Just as the *Book of Legends and Lays* had opened, it closes with a tribute to the religious spirit of the medieval period, this time in a prayer to Mary, the "Lily of the Meadows" (I, 98).

In his essay, "Poems of Stefan George," Hugo von Hofmannsthal wrote: "The poems of the third book have a freer, more indefinite background. Sometimes beyond the world, sometimes drilled into the silent core of the earth, always far from the ways of men. Designating this dreamlike condition, it is called *The Book of the Hanging Gardens.* ... But also in these profound stupors of the imagination, we find once more the spirit which revealed itself to us in the *Eclogues* and the *Legends and Lays.* If [the spirit] was tender there, desirous of life, admiring and worshipful, then the poems of the *Hanging Gardens* are sumptuous, even proud and passionate, full of the idea of a highly personal kingship, and of gloomy and fearful experiences. But a highly cultivated inner purity and a feeling of true vocation are not lost; the gestures, in all moods of tension and relaxation, show no coarsening weightiness."[27] In *The Book of the Hanging Gardens,* Stefan George continued the tradition of Oriental motifs in German poetry that had begun with Goethe's *West-östlicher Divan.* There, Goethe's experience and the poetic art of Persia had merged to artistic perfection. During the nineteenth century, such poets as Platen, Rückert, and Bodenstedt ("Mirza Schaffy") had made a convention of oriental imitation, reducing it to a manner for the conveyance of a drily moralizing, Epicurean attitude toward life. George took up some of the motifs and metrical peculiarities of poems in the *Divan. The Book of the Hanging Gardens,* however, represents the transposition of personal experience into the oriental realm and not, as is the case with Goethe's successors, the importation of a pseudo-Persian philosophy and poetry into the German poetic idiom.

In the *Book of the Hanging Gardens,* many of the problems of the earlier books are once more concentrated: the relative validity of the active and the reflective life, the tendency of each to diminish the claim to real value of the other, the overpowering nature of love, and the solace of an early self-willed death. As in *Algabal,* the central figure of the book is a poet-king, but he is of quite a different nature than Algabal. In his ironic attitude toward his actions, even toward his power and greatness, he is more human. His passion is intense and immediate, free of the barbaric estheticism of the Roman emperor. Instead of attempting to impose his inner reality upon the world, this king seeks, like the young poet of the *Hymnen,* a confirmation of the purpose of his existence in the world he sees and celebrates.

The thirty-one poems of the book are divided into three sections of ten, fifteen, and six poems. In the first part, the king's various moods in relation to his role in the world and his inner life are set forth. Though born to rule (I, 101) and thus set apart from the fates of other men, he is as much drawn to moods of contemplative repose as to his career as a ruler and conqueror. In the midst of warlike and worldly pursuits, other voices call him to devote himself to the life of the soul (I, 99-100), and when he has subdued a city, his first act is to raise his sword in tribute to the god who has made his victory possible (I, 100-101). In repose, his mind denies the claims of the empiric necessity by which he must live:

> Zierat des spitzigen turms der die büsche erhellt·
> Verschlungnes gefüge
> Geschnörkelte züge
> Verbieten die lüge
> Von wesen und welt. (I, 102)

> Decor of sharp minaret which illumines the hedge,
> Convolute structure,
> Whimsical flourishes,
> Forbid the illusion
> Of being and world.

The lie of "being and world" which these capricious decorations seem to refute is the idea that matter and spirit are necessarily disparate, that they cannot be fused in formal perfection. But such perfection, such a union is only possible in the static realm of art and architecture. For the king, who is obliged to act, the realization of his desires is doomed to fall short of ideality, as in the poem "Vorbereitungen" ("Preparations"), in which the contradiction is foreshadowed between the ideality of his priestlike kingship and his knowledge of his own limitations:

> Und du selber?—liebst dich lang zu läutern·
> Mit den reinen zauberkräutern
> Deinen geist in einsamkeit zu schonen·
> Ihn mit der erharrung schauer lohnen
> Bis der vorhang birst
> Vor dem ausbund aller zonen—
> Den vielleicht du nie berühren wirst. (I, 103)

> And you yourself?—love to refine yourself at length,
> With the magic herbs so pure,
> To spare your soul in solitude,
> Reward it with anticipation's tremor
> Until the curtain tears
> With the splendor of all climes,
> Which you perhaps will never touch.

The second section depicts the confrontation of this meditative, skeptical ruler and conqueror with love. It is an illicit love for a woman who is perhaps married, perhaps promised to another, as various hints (I, 106, 108) indicate. The passionate, all-consuming nature of this love calls to mind the exquisite containment of the Hatem-Suleika poems of the *Divan*:

Wenn ich heut nicht deinen leib berühre
Wird der faden meiner seele reissen
Wie zu sehr gespannte sehne.
Liebe zeichen seien trauerflöre
Mir der leidet seit ich dir gehöre.
Richte ob mir solche qual gebühre·
Kühlung sprenge mir dem fieberheissen
Der ich wankend draussen lehne. (I, 107)

If today I do not touch your body
Then my soul's sustaining thread will tear
Like a bowstring stretched too tautly.
Signs of love must be weeds of mourning
To me who suffer being yours alone.
Judge whether to me such torment is just,
Coolness sprinkle for me, hot with fever,
For me leaning weakly at your door.

These poems represent one of the rare occasions in the poetry of Stefan George in which love is depicted as rapturous and joyful, in a fulfillment which magically transforms the lover's view of the natural world, as shown in the poem "Das schöne beet betracht ich mir im harren" ("Waiting I regard the lovely flower bed") (I, 108). But, for reasons left unexplained, the lovers must part, and the cycle ends on a note of desolation:

The hissing throng of brittle leaves
Unseen hands thrust harshly on
Outside the pale walls of my Eden.
Sultry and o'erclouded is the night. (I, 110)

The third section is narrative in nature, centering about the further fortunes and the end of the ruler. The experience of love depicted in the second cycle was the most profound of his life, overshadowing even his kingship in its significance (I, 111). The king's vigilance is diminished by his commitment to love and by his dwelling in dreams. The will to heroic action has left him. Enemies have entered his land and conquered half of it, and he is powerless to resist them. Only in song, in giving form to the movements of his spirit, can he find meaning. In failure, the king becomes a poet. Unlike Algabal, who tried to make the world the medium of his artistic will, the king's medium is music. Poetry becomes the only solace for a will all of whose purposes have failed:

Ich muss mein schönes land gebeugt betrauern·
Dieses sei allein mein trost:

Der sänger-vogel den zertretne fluren· mauern
Und dächer· züngelnd wie ein feuerrost·
Nicht kümmern singt im frischen myrtenhage
Unablässig seine süsse klage. (I, 111-12)

With bowed head I my lovely land must mourn,
This be alone my consolation:
The singer bird, whom trampled fields, walls
And roofs, flaming like a fiery grid,
Do not alarm sings in the balmy myrtle grove
Unendingly his sweet lament.

Like the minarets of the first section, this static image of formal esthetic perfection is a solace to the king amidst catastrophe; it is more real to him than all he has lost. The king now abdicates his throne and leaves his kingdom (I, 112). As a poet, he enters the service of a pasha:

I gladdened him through long weeks loyally
With songs of jubilation which I sang,
With wreaths of triumph which I wove for him,
Full of awe before him I bowed down,
To him who had subdued all mutineers,
And subjugated many alien foes. (I, 112)

This pasha is the unreflecting man of action which the former king could not be, a good ruler beloved by his people. In serving such a lord, the former king has a dignity of his own, for George saw an intimate connection between ruling and serving and felt that the servant has as much dignity and value in his station as the ruler. In this connection, Goethe had said: "What Western man, however, will never be able to understand, is the spiritual and physical submission to one's lord and superior, which stems from those ancient times, when kings first stepped into God's place."[28] Just as the king should not have lost himself to love, should have remained a ruler rather than becoming a poet, he now should serve in the capacity for which his fate has designated him. But of this, too, he is incapable. He plots to kill the pasha, but, seeing him "great and proud" on the day of his triumph, he cannot bring himself to do so and departs. All nature seems to whisper to him now of his former grandeur (I, 113-14). He returns to his homeland, there to mourn beside a stream, which seems to lure him to his death in a way comparable to the closing poem of Wilhelm Müller's *Die schöne Müllerin*:

Liebende klagende zagende wesen
Nehmt eure zuflucht in unser bereich·

Werdet geniessen und werdet genesen·
Arme und worte umwinden euch weich. (I, 115)

Loving, lamenting, timorous beings,
Come take your refuge here in our realm,
You will be happy and you will be healed,
Softly arms and words will entwine you.

Stefan George's second volume of poems has given as little in the way of final answers to the problem of life as did the first. Archetypal remembrances of past epochs of human history have proven more felicitous to the quality of George's imagination than his own time as reflected in *Hymnen.* Yet the tragic possibilities latent in the quality of feeling prevailing in those times proved perhaps even greater. Behind all the varieties of historical experience George tries to recapture, and behind all of the masks through which he tries to speak in a more certain voice, is his mind carrying the knowledge that it is fated to see too much. George can find the repose of unreflecting certainty in none of the ages or *personae* he has inhabited in the "three books." Amidst the "hanging gardens" of the imagination, his "oriental" king is prey to the same fatal necessity of penetrating the illusion which his own being represents as was Algabal.

CHAPTER 3

The Artist and the Angel

Kein freund war nahe mehr· sie alle gingen
Nur ER der niemals wankte blieb und wachte. (I, 187)

I Das Jahr der Seele

THE appearance of the "public" edition of *Das Jahr der Seele* (*The Soul's Year*)in 1898 extended the knowledge and appreciation of Stefan George's poetry beyond his immediate circle of friends. Presently, critical articles on his works began to appear, and by the end of the decade his name was mentioned in literary histories and essays summing up the last quarter of the nineteenth century. Poems by George, particularly from *Das Jahr der Seele*, were printed in anthologies. They were even parodied in a popular journal—a significant, if backhanded tribute to wider awareness of his style. *Das Jahr der Seele* was George's most readily accessible work to date, eschewing the apparently esoteric and historical attitudes of the earlier books in favor of a more immediate "confessional" poetry. A variety of subtle lyric moods is presented through the medium of vivid images from nature, strikingly stylized and set in extraordinarily mannered patterns of rhythm and rhyme. For Friedrich Gundolf, the book was liked for the wrong reasons, since people seemed to see in it "that charming twilight of feeling, in which the German reader felt most at home."[1] In terms of the book trade, too, *Das Jahr der Seele* was one of the best-received of George's books, going through eleven printings in twenty-four years.

In his foreword to the edition of 1898, George was at pains to diminish the biographical aspect of *Das Jahr der Seele* for which friends had evidently desired explanation:

> We should not unwisely concern ourselves . . . with the human models of a lyrical work or the landscapes which inspired it: through art they have undergone such a transformation that they have become insignificant for the poet himself, and for others any knowledge of these facts is confusing rather than illuminating. . . . In very few books are 'I' and 'thou' as much the same soul as in this one (I, 119).

The confidence that he can transform the people and places of his actual experience into artistic entities represents a new departure for George, whose central problem had been the enforced juxtaposition of the subjective world of his imagination with the objective perception and insights he could not bring himself to ignore. Thus, *Das Jahr der Seele* represents a significant change in George's poetic attitude.

The book contains ninety-eight poems symmetrically divided into three sections. The first part, to which the title of the volume most directly applies, consists of three sections: "Nach der Lese" ("After the Vintage"), "Waller im Schnee" ("Pilgrims in the Snow"), and "Sieg des Sommers" ("Summer's Triumph"). The second part, "Überschriften und Widmungen" ("Inscriptions and Dedications"), contains the "Sprüche für die Geladenen in T." ("Aphorisms for the Guests in T.") and the brief tributes to George's friends, who are now, as will be the case in future collections, identified by their initials. The closing section of thirty-two poems is entitled "Traurige Tänze" ("Mournful Dances").

In all of these cycles, as George himself conceded in his foreword, not imaginary or abstract, but immediate human experience is depicted, even if knowledge of the precise details is not required. The most important relationship thus reflected was George's friendship with Ida Coblenz, which had ended in 1896. Originally, *Das Jahr der Seele* was to have been dedicated to her, and not to George's sister. "Nach der Lese," "Waller im Schnee," several of the "Traurige Tänze," and the "Erinnerungen an einige Abende innerer Geselligkeit" ("Memories of Some Evenings of Inner Harmony") in the second part testify to the emotional tensions of the friendship experienced by George and Ida Coblenz. In 1894, the first three poems of this section had appeared in the *Blätter für die Kunst* with a dedication to "I. C." For the poet and his work of art, however, the experience itself, with all of its pain and disappointment, was now irrelevant and was no longer connected with the poems it had engendered, which were to be autonomous entities.

In *Das Jahr der Seele,* George is close to achieving the task which had oppressed him in *Pilgerfahrten* (see the poem "Die Spange"), namely the integration of experience in a consummate work of art. The poems of this volume represent a synthesis of the immediacy of the German "confessional" tradition with the color, music, and esthetic fastidiousness of the French Symbolists. George has learned to express actual experience and his responses to the states of being of others with the same affinity and empathy once reserved for the world of his subjective imagination. It is significant that Stéphane Mallarmé, who received *Das Jahr der Seele* in 1898, the year of his death, praised it warmly by saying: "In [this book], you make the seasons dependent upon your soul. This is excellent, because all intimate poetry is enacted within the pageant of some ideal year." Mallarmé found in the book the "nobility and ingenuity of the dream" and "supreme imaginative music."[2]

The first four poems of the "Widmungen und Überschriften" speak directly of the poet's relationship to the world in terms of his art. They are the most useful guides to the changes in George's art and attitude which are to be found in *Das Jahr der Seele.* Many of the problems raised previously are restated. The first poem echoes the feeling expressed at the end of the *Pilgerfahrten* six years earlier:

Lieder wie ich gern sie sänge
Darf ich freunde! noch nicht singen·
Nur dies flüchtige gedränge
Scheuer reime will gelingen. (I, 136)

Songs as I would like to sing them,
I may still not sing, my friends!
As yet but this hasty flurry
Of timid rhymes can come from me.

The poet still has the feeling that he is presenting only what he is able to "rescue over into life" from the "hard struggles" of his youth. George regards his way as a poet retrospectively, characterizing each of his works as a phase of his life, ending with the figurative "martyr's death" of his soul, first through *Algabal* and subsequently in *Das Buch der Hängenden Gärten.*[3]

The question of the justification for his art arises, and his answer is a new one:

Und heut geschieht es nur aus Einem grunde
Wenn ich zum sang das lange schweigen breche:
Dass wir uns freuen auf die zwielichtstunde
Und meine düstre schwester also spreche:

Soll ich noch leben darf ich nicht vermissen
Den trank aus deinen klingenden pokalen
Und führer sind in meinen finsternissen
Die lichter die aus deinen wunden strahlen. (I, 137)

Today it happens for one reason only
If I my lengthy silence break to sing:
That we look forward to the twilight hour
And my dark sister says these words to me:

If I am meant to live I must not lack
The draught your ringing goblets offer me,
And guides through all my darkness are to me
The radiant lights that shine out of your wounds.

According to Goldsmith,[4] this was the dedicatory poem George originally intended to use for *Das Jahr der Seele* and first sent to Ida Coblenz. Morwitz[5] asserts that the "dark sister" of the poem is George's own soul. The circumstances cited by Goldsmith, however, seem to indicate that the "dark sister" is some person other than the poet himself, very likely Ida Coblenz. In this case, the implications of the poem are momentous for George's self-awareness in his vocation. The poet appears here as a Christlike martyr, who suffers that his "dark sister"—that is, by extension, all souls akin to his—might live. This alone gives meaning to his life and art. Particularly the "sister's" assertion that she is guided by the "light" which radiates from the poet's "wounds" bears an unmistakable resemblance to pictorial representations of Christ crucified with rays of light emanating from the nail wounds. The poet's "wounds" are here surely those inflicted upon him by his experience of the world, an often-used metaphor, quite frequent in the case of George. Through the "light" from these wounds, the artistic transformation of that experience, he helps the "dark sister" continue to live, just as George aided and consoled Ida Coblenz—partly through his presence and partly through his art—through a difficult period of her life. Quite aside from the question of the propriety or decorousness of evoking so powerful a religious analogy, there can be no doubt that George saw a new *raison d'être* for his "singing" in the fact that it can help others by redeeming them from their own darkness.

In the third of these poems, the aspect of redemptive martyrdom is supplemented by another, which is presently to assume central importance in Stefan George's concept of the poet, namely, the idea of the poet as seer, judge, and magical namer of things:

Des sehers wort ist wenigen gemeinsam:
Schon als die ersten kühnen wünsche kamen
In einem seltnen reiche ernst und einsam
Erfand er für die dinge eigne namen—

DIE hier erdonnerten von ungeheuern
Befehlen oder lispelten wie bitten·
DIE wie Paktolen in rubinenfeuern
Und bald wie linde frühlingsbäche glitten·

An deren kraft und klang er sich ergezte·
Sie waren wenn er sich im höchsten schwunge

Der welt entfliehend unter träume sezte
Des tempels saitenspiel und heilge zunge.

Nur sie—und nicht der sanften lehre lallen·
Das mütterliche—hat er sich erlesen
Als er im rausch von mai und nachtigallen
Sann über erster sehnsucht fabelwesen·

Als er zum lenker seiner lebensfrühe
Im beten rief ob die verheissung löge . .
Erflehend dass aus zagen busens mühe
Das denkbild sich zur sonne heben möge. (I, 137)

The seer's word is shared by very few:
Already when the first bold wishes came,
In an exotic realm austere and lonely,
For all things he invented his own names.

Some of them thundered like colossal calls,
Commands, or whispered, lisping, soft as pleas,
Some flowed, now like Paktolus' ruby fire
And then like gentle, murmuring brooks in Spring.

He oft delighted in their ringing strength,
They were for him when he in ecstasy
Immersed himself in dreams far from this world
The temple's sacred music, holy voice.

He chose but them alone and not the stammer
Of gentle lore of motherhood when he
With nightingales and May intoxicated,
Of fabled creatures early longed-for dreamt.

When asking of the guide of his life's dawn
In prayers if the promise was a lie,
Imploring that from fearful bosom's travail,
The image of the dream rise to the sun.

Words, that is, the names the poet gives to what he imagines and experiences, have magical power, in that they give tangible form to that which is abstract. Through them, he can hope to make real—let "rise to the sun"—the image of his dream, the *denkbild*. Although, as the preceding poem shows, the poet can comfort those who turn to him of their own accord, his vision of the world, his "word" will be inaccessible to most men. This is now seen as immutable circumstance, no longer subject to doubt or giving rise to lament. In this context, the word *seher* must be understood less in the sense of "prophet" than as meaning simply "one who sees," that is, one who has a peculiar way of experiencing the world and expressing what he sees. After the "pilgrimage" of the first two volumes, Stefan George has come closer to knowing what his place in the world as a poet must be, and he assumes it with assurance, but also with a sense of resignation that what is commonly understood as "happiness" can never be his, that his "names" have a higher claim in his life than the "stammer/ Of gentle lore of motherhood," which ordains the continuity of physical existence to the detriment of the spirit.

In *Das Jahr der Seele,* the sense that the poet is a being set apart by fate and must live accordingly, renouncing many aspects of life, is stated as a condition. In the earlier books, only the symptoms of this condition were described, without a distinct cause of the poet's malaise being yet stated. In the "Sprüche für die Geladenen in T . ." (I, 138-39), the theme is further developed. Although each stanza of the first of these poems was written for a different one of the "guests" at Tilff in Belgium, where George stayed together with Paul Gérardy, Léon Paschal, and Edmond Rassenfosse in May, 1892, the complete poem is a single entity expressing George's insights regarding the nature of the poetic vocation. In it, the poet's childhood is described. Even at his mother's breast, a "malevolent fairy" sings to the infant of "shadows" and "death" and gives him eyes "dark and strange" in which "the muses submerge." "Great and stern" thoughts will preserve him and keep him from committing demeaning acts. Stoically, he can tell of his suffering only to the wind at night, while his "brothers" may freely complain. Finally and unrelentingly, his fate decrees that he must make a heavy sacrifice:

> Vergiss es nicht: du musst
> Deine frische jugend töten·
> Auf ihrem grab allein
> Wenn viele tränen es begiessen–spriessen
> Unter dem einzig wunderbaren grün
> Die einzigen schönen rosen. (I, 139)

> Do not forget: you must
> Kill your youth in all its freshness,
> Upon its grave alone
> When watered by many a tear–appear
> Surrounded by miraculous green
> The only truly beautiful roses.

The work of art can only be born through the death of the spontaneity and passion of the artist's youth. From the lament over this sacrifice, seemingly, the formal beauty of the "roses" can arise. It is significant that the poem, first written in French (II, 598) and published in the *Blätter für die Kunst* (Vol. I, Pt. 4) in 1893, should be included in *Das Jahr der Seele.* George had reached these conclusions at least five years earlier, at the time of *Algabal.* He chose, however, to express them differently, through *personae,* rather than speaking in his own right as a poetic subject. It is only in *Das Jahr der Seele* that he achieves the necessary assurance to do this.

The crucial poems of the "Widmungen und Überschriften" are an explanatory coda to the cycles which constitute the "year of the soul": "Nach der Lese," "Waller im Schnee," and "Sieg des Sommers." The loneliness of the poet, the lack of comprehension he must feel even in those he loves and who love him, is the central theme of these three cycles. In the glowing autumn landscape of "Nach der Lese" and the wintry world of "Waller im Schnee," the poet and a woman he loves find moments of silent communion with each other and harmony with nature. Ultimately, however, they must part, each unable to comprehend what the other desires and needs, perhaps because neither really knows his own needs. The relationship begins on a note of cautious hope on the part of the poet, who finds colors and textures of surprising and tender beauty in an apparently desolate world:

> Komm in den totgesagten park und schau:
> Der schimmer ferner lächelnder gestade·
> Der reinen wolken unverhofftes blau
> Erhellt die weiher und die bunten pfade.
>
> Dort nimm das tiefe gelb· das weiche grau
> Von birken und von buchs· der wind ist lau·
> Die späten rosen welkten noch nicht ganz·
> Erlese küsse sie und flicht den kranz·
>
> Vergiss auch diese lezten astern nicht·
> Den purpur um die ranken wilder reben·
> Und auch was übrig blieb von grünem leben
> Verwinde leicht im herbstlichen gesicht. (I, 121)

> Come and behold the park they say is dead:
> The shimmer of the distant smiling shores,
> The unexpected blue 'twixt pristine clouds,
> Illuminate the ponds and dappled paths.
>
> There take the deep yellow, the gentle gray,
> Of birches and of box, the wind is mild,

> The roses last to bloom are not yet sere,
> Select and kiss them and a garland bind,
>
> These last few asters you should not forget,
> The purple round the tendrils of wild grape,
> And also what remained of verdant life,
> In the autumnal image deftly weave.

The neologism *totgesagt* lends to the autumn landscape a quality of something rare and fleeting, to be cherished before it is too late. By virtue of their very existence, the clouds, the sky, the leaves, and the flowers are a triumph over death. And who has said the park is "dead"? Implicitly, those who do not understand the austere beauty of autumn. The unspoken understanding that *-gesagt* questions the truth of *tot-*, establishes a rapport between the poet and his companion, setting them and, by implication, the reader, apart from those who cannot see what they cherish. The familiar imperative verb forms, *Komm, schau, nimm,* etc., reinforce the sense of an intimate *Ich-Du* relationship between the speaker and the listener. In the description of the autumn colors, there is an apparently systematic avoidance of modifying a specific noun with a color adjective. Rather, the relationship between adjective and noun is mediated by a preposition, so that the color is mentioned at an appreciable interval preceding the noun, which only seems to explain the presence of the color. The substantive-attribute relationship is thus effectively reversed, creating an ambience in which colors rather than objects dominate. The autonomy of the color impressions in the poem emphasizes their symbolic qualities, and the progression of colors within the poem is significant. To the white of the clouds is added the "unhoped-for" blue of the sky, illuminating ever richer tones, the soft gray of the trees, yellow, the red of the roses, a tone reinforced by the deeper red of the asters, finally culminating in the purple of the vines. All of these yellow and red tones symbolize passionate life, still present in this park "they say is dead," which now has become a symbolic landscape too, identical perhaps with the poet's own soul, in which there is still to be found something "of green life," the vigor and hope of his youth.

Yet, for all the beauty which the park still holds, these are the "weeks of dying filled with radiance" (I, 122) both of the year and of the poet's love for the woman he addresses. They enjoy moments in which their disparate beings are subsumed by the rhythm of nature:

> Wir fühlen dankbar wie zu leisem brausen
> Von wipfeln strahlenspuren auf uns tropfen

Und blicken nur und horchen wenn in pausen
Die reifen früchte an den boden klopfen. (I, 122)

We feel the faintly humming specks of light
Drop down on us from branches, gratefully,
And start and listen only when at times
The ripe fruits falling thump upon the earth.

When they speak, however, there is a sense of insufficiency, of the inability of one to reach the other. The woman can understand the poet's esthetic appreciation of their surroundings but apparently does not choose to see his suffering:

With clever words you echo what I say,
Of what delights me in the vivid book,

But do you know too of the deeper joy,
And can the silent tear win your esteem?
Shading your eye upon the bridge,
You watch the passing of the swans. (I, 123)

An increasingly elegiac tone permeates the vivid autumnal images, portending the final admission of disillusionment:

Die wespen mit den goldengrünen schuppen
Sind von verschlossnen kelchen fortgeflogen·
Wir fahren mit dem kahn in weitem bogen
Um bronzebraunen laubes inselgruppen. (I, 124)

The wasps that have the scales of golden green
Have flown away from blossoms that have closed,
With our boat we move in a spacious arc
Round groups of islets decked in bronze-brown leaves.

and:

Vom tore dessen eisen-lilien rosten
Entfliegen vögel zum verdeckten rasen
Und andre trinken frierend auf den pfosten
Vom regen aus den hohlen blumen-vasen. (I, 124)

From garden gate whose iron lilies rust,
The birds take flight to the leaf-covered lawn,
And others on the pillars shivering drink,
The rain out of the hollow flower vases.

In a letter in which he concludes: "Too great a span still parts us from our joy" (I, 125), the poet tells her all he has not said, she has not felt. Her dropping the letter from her hands signifies the end of hopes cherished by both of them, different as they might have been, which have never really been stated. It is almost as if the white page fluttering to the ground were the first snowflake of the impending winter, "the boldest color on that faded scene" (I, 125).[6] Their relationship has a brief sequel before the scenery of a winter landscape, beginning with a sense of rediscovery and of a common fate, but ending in the same inadequacy of communication. The impenetrable, placid melancholy the poet feels in his companion pervades these poems:

> Ich lehre dich den sanften reiz des zimmers
> Empfinden und der trauten winkel raunen·
> Des feuers und des stummen lampen-flimmers·
> Du hast dafür das gleiche müde staunen.
>
> Aus deiner blässe fach ich keinen funken·
> Ich ziehe mich zurück zum beigemache
> Und sinne schweigsam in das knie gesunken:
> Ob jemals du erwachen wirst? erwache!
>
> So oft ich zagend mich zum vorhang kehre:
> Du sitzest noch wie anfangs in gedanken·
> Dein auge hängt noch immer an der leere·
> Dein schatten kreuzt des teppichs selbe ranken.
>
> Was hindert dann noch dass das ungeübte
> Vertrauenslose flehen mir entfliesse:
> O gib dass—grosse mutter und betrübte!
> In dieser seele wieder trost entspriesse. (I, 128)
>
> I teach you to perceive the gentle charm,
> And hear the inner voices of this room,
> The fire and the silent, flickering lamp,
> By all of this you are fatigued, bemused.
>
> Out of your pallor I can strike no spark,
> I rise and go into the neighboring room,
> And silently in kneeling I reflect,
> On whether ever you'll awake? Awake!
>
> As often as I turn and look at you,
> You sit in thought exactly as before,
> Your eye is still fixed upon emptiness,
> Your shadow falls upon the selfsame place.
>
> What hinders then the unrehearséd prayer,
> In which I place no hope, from pouring forth:
> O grant that—Mother great in your own grief—
> In this soul solace may spring forth again.

Almost in desperation, the poet prays to Mary to lift the burden of sadness from the woman's soul. Although its objective causes are never stated, this melancholy is the emotional ambience in which their relationship lives. He feels he must himself strive to be sad, in order the better to share her sorrow (I, 129). The poet states how carefully he had tended a plant, now dying, whose present sad state makes him sorrowfully recall the days of its blooming (I, 128). He destroys the "pale flower with the sick heart," rather than being uselessly embittered by it, only to realize, in the next instant, that something precious has been lost: "Now once again I raise my empty eyes/ And into empty night my empty hands." He cannot break the spell in which the fruitless relationship with this woman holds him in the same way, for in destroying it, he would divest his own life of its meaning, although he feels incapable of helping her.

It is only the coming of spring which makes the poet feel free to leave her, which he does abruptly, declaring: "I must not take you with me into Spring" (I, 130). Symbolically, he erects a "funeral pyre" (I, 130) for his memory of her. On the opposite shore of the river, to which he will now row, a young man, perhaps the companion of "Sieg des Sommers," awaits him waving a welcoming banner. The two young men are bound together by a common striving for an ideal realm of art in which the past, especially the immediate past, will and must be forgotten. Under the benevolent reign of summer, theirs is to be a "realm of the sun," where only joy prevails:

> Du singst das lied der summenden gemarken·
> Das sanfte lied vor einer tür am abend
> Und lehrest dulden wie die einfach starken·
> In lächeln jede träne scheu begrabend:
>
> Die vögel fliehen vor den herben schlehen·
> Die falter bergen sich in sturmes-toben
> Sie funkeln wieder auf so er verstoben—
> Und wer hat jemals blumen weinen sehen? (I, 132)

> You sing the song of the melodic lands,
> The gentle song before the door at evening,
> And how the simply strong endure you teach,
> Shyly they bury every tear in smiles:
>
> The birds fly from the sloes that yet are bitter,
> The butterflies seek shelter from the storm,
> They glitter once again when it is past—
> And who has ever seen a flower weep?

After the strained, melancholy tone of the two preceding cycles, we have here a sense of exuberant release, of surrender to the forgetfulness of nature, which always looks forward unburdened by memory. According to Morwitz, these poems describe George's brief friendship with the young Belgian Edmond Rassenfosse: "what bound them together was the ability and willingness of the younger man to place Art at the center of life, as the poet was doing."[7] The inability to find lasting human companionship in love between man and woman, shown in "Nach der Lese" and "Waller im Schnee," is here overcome. On the plane of art and the spirit, beyond the torment of memory and human conflict, the poet's soul can for a time commune effortlessly with others. The barriers which differing personal experiences and problems create are transcended by existential values that are universal in art. The poet's special view of the world and his difficulty in reconciling ideality with reality become his salvation from loneliness, whereas they had once been the primary causes of his isolation. Momentarily at least, he has found a companion who understands him. The primacy of ideality over reality for the poet is now stated unequivocally:

> Und törig nennt als übel zu befahren
> Dass ihr in euch schon ferne bilder küsstet
> Und dass ihr niemals zu versöhnen wüsstet
> Den kuss im traum empfangen und den wahren. (I, 134)

> And rightly call it folly to condemn
> That distant inner images you've kissed,
> And that you cannot ever reconcile
> The kiss that's true with that received in dreams.

But the friendship is of short duration, and the "triumph of summer," too, must end. The friendships memorialized in *Das Jahr der Seele* are only fleeting approximations of the fulfillment of the poet's inner ideal, which he is to seek first in the sublime form of the "angel" in *Der Teppich des Lebens* and which he finds, for a time, in the incarnation of Maximin.

"Traurige Tänze," the cycle which concludes *Das Jahr der Seele,* recapitulates, often in a more decisive form, the thematic concerns of the collection. Some of the poems are purely lyrical, capturing with surpassing musicality and intensity of feeling the mood of a moment, such as "Es lacht in dem steigenden jahr dir" ("The scent of the garden still quickens") (I, 153), "Keins wie dein feines ohr" ("None but your subtle ear") (I, 159), or "Es winkte der abendhauch" ("The evening breezes beckoned") (I, 167). Others are brief ballads like those encountered in *Hymnen.*

But the greater part of the "Traurige Tänze" is concerned with the destiny of the poet, the impossibility of finding a soul attuned to his, and the triumph of his art over his suffering. As in "Nach der Lese," love is no answer, for the beloved, try as she may, cannot understand his special grief, the poet's fear that his creative powers have left him and that he no longer has anything to live for (I, 152). Tacitly, he admits that he cannot help her find a way out of her despair either. She implores him to "sing" as he had once done, but suffering has made this impossible:

Gib ein lied mir wieder
Im klaren tone deiner freudentage–
Du weisst es ja: mir wich der friede
Und meine hand ist zag.

Wo dunkle seelen sinnen
Erscheinen bilder seltne hohe·
Doch fehlt das leuchtende erinnern·
Die farbe hell und froh.

Wo sieche seelen reden
Da lindern schmeichelhafte töne·
Da ist die stimme tief und edel
Doch nicht zum sang so schön. (I, 153)

Sing me one more song
In your clear tone of days of happiness–
You know why not: my peace has fled
And my hand hesitates.

Where dark souls contemplate
Appear images, rare, sublime,
But glowing memory is missing,
The color bright and glad.

Where ailing souls do speak,
Pleasant tones can soothe the pain,
There the voice is deep and noble,
But not for singing fair.

In the uneven metric pattern of each stanza, the grating off-rhymes (*wieder*/ *friede*, *freudentage*/ *zag*, etc.,), the absence of the musical, lyrical impulse, and the will to bend content to form, are made palpable, especially since the will and the ability to do so are abundantly present elsewhere. This poem offers a premonition of a later stage in Stefan George's development, when the musical element of his works will recede in favor of the tone of "dark souls'" contemplation. This will be a harsher, driving tone, which dispenses with rhyme and quite often also with strict observation of the niceties of scansion. George's "philosophic age" is prefigured here, the style of the later works, in which direct statement takes precedence over grace and musicality of form. For the moment, however, this new voice, "not for singing fair," conveys only the possibility of solace in despair. The woman in whose love he had placed his hopes does not return his love, does not understand his longing. Her words are as "unfeeling as the shrill song of children" (I, 154).

For the first time, the poet's grief is expressed directly in "Traurige Tänze," no longer solely through the mediation of a symbolic landscape or *persona.* The following poem is remarkable for its immediacy and expressiveness despite the evident artistic skill and the mannerism of its style. Abstract movements of the soul are no longer projected through phenomena of the empirical world but are expressed as though they themselves were physical entities oppressing the poet. Here again the tone of the "Maximin" poems in *Der Siebente Ring* is distinctly anticipated:

Dies leid und diese last: zu bannen
Was nah erst war und mein.
Vergebliches die arme spannen
Nach dem was nur mehr schein·

Dies heilungslose sich betäuben
Mit eitlem nein und kein·
Dies unbegründete sich sträuben·
Dies unabwendbar-sein.

Beklemmendes gefühl der schwere
Auf müd gewordner pein·
Dann dieses dumpfe weh der leere·
O dies: mit mir allein! (I, 158)

This pain and burden: to forget
What just was near and mine.
This futile opening of my arms
To what is now a dream.

This useless numbing of myself
With empty "no" and "none,"
This reasonless still struggling on,
Against a certain fate.

This suffocating heaviness
Of anguish now grown old,

Then this dull pain of emptiness,
O this: with me alone!

Out of the despair arising from the emptiness of his empirical existence the poet wrests a commitment to his art, to the transforming magic of language. Only in his poetic craft can he hope to find a plane on which his subjective idealism and his empirical being can be reconciled. Experience, whether of love or friendship, in and of itself, is chaotic, meaningless, and transitory, unless it can be given tangible meaning and permanence in an esthetic structure, which crystallizes its significance and places it in the universal, humane context of art. On the other hand, just as has been realized in the earlier collections of George's poems, a poetry arising merely from the poet's autonomous imagination, reflecting nothing of objective experience, is sterile. There must be a continual interrelationship between world and work, and it is the poet's, often agonizing, task to be the medium of this interchange:

Da vieles wankt und blasst und sinkt und splittert
Erstirbt das lied von dunst und schlaf umflutet
Bis jäher stoss das mürbe laub zerknittert·
Von ehmals wilde wunde wieder blutet– (I, 164)

When things do totter, pale, and sink, and splinter,
The song must die engulfed in mist and sleep
Till sudden blast the crumbling leaves will banish,
The ever painful wound will bleed anew.

Once more the wound is the stigma imposed by life upon the poet, painful, but necessary. There is no longer the alternative possibility that experience, hence also "wounds," can be shunned in favor of a retreat into an imaginative world of esthetic ideality and pretended harmony. The closing poem of *Das Jahr der Seele* definitively states the interrelationship of life and art for Stefan George:

Willst du noch länger auf den kahlen böden
Nach frühern vollen farben spähn·
Auf früchte warten in den fahlen öden
Und ähren von verdrängten sommern mähn?

Bescheide dich wenn nur im schattenschleier
Mild schimmernd du genossene fülle schaust
Und durch die müden lüfte ein befreier
Der wind der weiten zärtlich um uns braust.

Und sieh! die tage die wie wunden brannten
In unsrer vorgeschichte schwinden schnell . .
Doch alle dinge die wir blumen nannten
Versammeln sich am toten quell. (I, 167)

Will you yet longer on the ground swept bare
Yesterday's richer colors seek,
And fruits await among the ashen wastes,
And harvest ears of long-gone summers' grain?

Contented be if veiled in shimmering shadow,
Fulfillment known you once more may behold,
If through the torpid air a liberator,
The wind from far away blows tenderly.

Behold! the days which once did burn like wounds
In our life's story quickly pass away,
But all the things we saw and once named flowers
About the dry, dead fountain cluster now.

The opening poem of *Das Jahr der Seele* was concerned with the possibility of finding experiential, sensual beauty in an apparently dead world, transitory as this beauty may be. Fixed in the framework of the poem, it attains permanence and provides solace. The closing poem reaffirms this statement, asserting that only those things of beauty that are gifted with permanence by the magical act of being *named* remain to cluster about the "dry, dead fountain" of the poet's soul and revive his artistic inspiration. In the "shimmering veil" of his art, he can perceive a happiness once known and realize it in retrospect perhaps more consciously, more fully than at the actual moment of experience. For the moment, however, seeking felicity in immediate experience is futile.

Friedrich Gundolf aptly called *Das Jahr der Seele* "the last great poetic work of the European *Weltschmerz*, which is not a 'suffering because of the world,' but the 'suffering of the world itself.' Since the disappearance of the gods, every higher human being has known it, especially lovers and artists, those with reverence for nature and life."[8] It is significant that it is the *last* such work in Gundolf's estimation, for *Das Jahr der Seele* terminates the early period of Stefan George's maturation as a poet. Henceforth, the mythopoetic, constructive aspects of his work, the subordination of the chaos of experience to the organizing expression of art, will take precedence over the reflective, existential fatalism of the earlier works.

II Der Teppich des Lebens und die Lieder von Traum und Tod mit einem Vorspiel

In his sixth collection of poems, published in 1899, Stefan George draws the full consequences from the conclusions of *Das Jahr der Seele. The Tapestry of Life and the Songs of Dream and Death with a Prelude* proclaims the mastery of the artist over his fate and the world he perceives. He achieves this through his art. The very title asserts the ordering of the variety and rhythm of life within the borders of a tapestry, in which every pattern has its place in the total design, which is fixed by the artisan-artist. Dream and death are contemplated through the mediation of song, of controlled language, and no longer with the spontaneous expressiveness of the soul. Accordingly, there is an architectonic order evident in the book, which once again contains three parts. Each part contains twenty-four poems, most of which are rhymed, each of them consisting of four stanzas four lines in length. Only rarely is a metrical exception made to the iambic pentameter. As Claude David points out: "Here, for the first time, the well-known definition applies, which Gundolf gave for George's lyrical poetry: well-proportioned, assured writing, which does not subordinate itself to the flux of feeling; a uniform rhythm, which absorbs the melody; a permanent poetic 'state' in contrast to the inspiration of the 'occasion.'"[9] In *Der Teppich des Lebens,* Stefan George creates a universe of humane serenity in which the suffering of transitory experience is made bearable by intimations of a higher plane of existence accessible through esthetic and moral insight, *das schöne leben,* "life in all its beauty."

How the artist himself, after the disillusionment conveyed in *Das Jahr der Seele,* gained the strength, through a spiritual rebirth, to create this poetic universe is set forth in the *Vorspiel.* The initial situation is one of desperation and the exhaustion of poetic power, as at the end of the previous book, where only the recollection of beauty once known and captured in words could console him:

Ich forschte bleichen eifers nach dem horte
Nach strofen drinnen tiefste kümmernis
Und dinge rollten dumpf und ungewiss—
Da trat ein nackter engel durch die pforte:

Entgegen trug er dem versenkten sinn
Der reichsten blumen last und nicht geringer
Als mandelblüten waren seine finger
Und rosen· rosen waren um sein kinn.

Auf seinem haupte keine krone ragte
Und seine stimme fast der meinen glich:
Das schöne leben sendet mich an dich
Als boten: während er dies lächelnd sagte

Entfielen ihm die lilien und mimosen–
Und als ich sie zu heben mich gebückt
Da kniet auch ER· ich badete beglückt
Mein ganzes antlitz in den frischen rosen. (I, 172)

I sought the trove with fervor pale and mortal
For strophes in which sorrow without cure
And nameless things rolled muffled and obscure–
A naked angel then stepped through the portal:

Toward my heart and mind with thought turned in
A burden bore he, flowers that richly teemed,
No less than almond blooms his fingers seemed,
And roses, roses clustered round his chin.

Upon his head and brow no crown did weigh
And almost like my own his voice I knew:
In all its beauty life sends me to you
A herald: while he smiling this did say

There fell from him the lilies and mimosas–
And when to gather them I bent me down
Then HE knelt too, I bathed enthralled with joy
All my countenance in the dew-fresh roses.

There is no implication that the angel is a messenger from a transcendent realm, as in Klopstock's "Stunden der Weihe" or like the angels which are presently to dwell in Rilke's verses. The angel's voice is almost like the poet's and when the poet kneels to gather the blossoms, the angel does so, too. He seems to be, in fact, a mirror image of the poet, the higher analogue to his empiric being, his ethereal counterpart, and his *denkbild* of himself. Two motifs we have encountered in earlier works come to a confluence in this angel: the "Herrin" of the *Hymnen* and the mirror image, almost of a sister's face, which Algabal, alone in his chamber, contemplates (I, 52). *Die herrin* had appeared to the poet as a consoling visitor from another, higher sphere of being, affirming the essential rightness of his yearning. In his own countenance, Algabal sees the only being he can truly love, with whom he is in perfect communion, a postulated ideal which is, for Algabal, "I" and "Thou" at once.

Claude David has observed that the "angel does not exist; he is only a symbol, possessing no tangible presence. He is drawn in such a way that no one could possibly imagine that he is real. He represents that part of the soul in which reside volition, plans, and self-assurance, that image of the self which reflection posits as a model and the soul strives to equal."[10] The angel is not identical with the poet but rather manifests his ideal potential, almost in the sense of the notion of *Genius* as Goethe uses it in "Wanderers Sturmlied." But there is an important difference between this "good spirit" and the solipsism of the emperor in *Algabal*. The poet acknowledges the higher imperatives of the angel, and that he himself is only an imperfect embodiment of "life in all its beauty." Algabal, on the other hand, sees himself as the highest instance of perfection. Through the alienation of his empirical being from other men, the poet attempts a synthesis of two possibilities that are ever latent within him: the "muse," the voice of a higher volition, formerly externalized; and the autonomous, self-reflecting will, whose extremity is modified by the sense of an order higher than the individual will. Like the *Herrin*, the angel must indeed be seen less as a mystical being than as the symbolization of a force which the poet feels within himself.

"Life in all its beauty," *das schöne leben*, whose herald the angel is, seems to play the role of the Platonic realm of ideal forms, of which our empirical existence is only a distorted reflection. As we shall see, it is the poet's "service" to the angel to show men this eternal perfection and order which transcends temporal forms. Only insofar as the poet recognizes the ideality of these forms and the forces that create and control them is there a sense of a religiosity in the *Vorspiel*. The poet does not claim to know these forces, however, and gives his allegiance to no religious doctrine. Rather, the significant directions of men's present relationship to the gods are surveyed from a sovereign height to which the angel leads him. He identifies himself with none of them, thereby implying that the forces guiding man's destiny are not accessible to knowledge or even worship:

> Ich bin freund und führer dir und ferge.
> Nicht mehr mitzustreiten ziemt dir nun
> Auch nicht mit den Weisen· hoch vom berge
> Sollst du schaun wie sie im tale tun.
>
> Weite menge siehst du rüstig traben
> Laut ist ihr sich mühendes gewimmel:
> Forscht die dinge nützet ihre gaben
> Und ihr habt die welt als freudenhimmel.

Drüben schwärme folgen ernst im qualme
Einem bleichen mann auf weissem pferde
Mit verhaltnen gluten in dem psalme:
Kreuz du bleibst noch lang das licht der erde.

Eine kleine schar zieht stille bahnen
Stolz entfernt vom wirkenden getriebe
Und als losung steht auf ihren fahnen:
Hellas ewig unsre liebe. (I, 176)

I am your friend, your leader, and your guide,
You must in others' causes no more fight,
Though they the wisest be: from mountain's height
Regard what men do in the vale below.

A large and staunchly pacing crowd you see,
Loud is their strident and laborious throng:
Delve in all things and rightly use their gifts,
And you will have the earth as paradise.

Earnest swarms in smoky mists do follow
A pale man yonder upon a white horse,
Their psalm they sing in discipline and fervor:
Cross, you long shall be the light of earth.

A little troop more quiet paths pursues,
In proud remove from action's turbulence,
And as a motto on their banners stands:
Hellas our love forever.

The poet's inner intimation of ideality, the angel, is to determine his actions in the world as the final criterion. No existing philosophies or creeds are to have a higher claim than his insight and will. Raised by the angel, the poet stands above them all: the rationalistic believers in man's progress and perfectibility on earth, the followers of Christ, who believe that the cross, the symbol of suffering, guides man to a better life after death, and even above those whose ideal is Hellas, the world of classic temporal harmony between men and the gods. The vitality and beauty of life itself is the object of the poet's reverence. The question of what gods have created or control it is left open. The use of the angel as a symbol, as well as the frequent occurrence of biblical motifs in the *Vorspiel,* is intended to convey the intensity of his spiritual awakening for the poet by analogy to what the religious experience had once meant to men.

In the *Vorspiel,* the relationship of the poet to the angel is described, his new energy and creativity under the angel's influence, and the state of his soul, especially in relation to other men. It seems that the angel was always with the poet, who served him, but was often impatient in his role as the angel's bard. He was momentarily drawn from the influence of his "Lord" by love (I, 174), but the angel brings him back under his redeeming spell. Thus, the painful, melancholy encounters of *Das Jahr der Seele* are reduced to mere episodes, guilty betrayals of the poet's soul and mission. The higher love has displaced all thought of surrender to earthly instinct. With this almost priestly foreswearing of the "baser" aspects of his humanity, the poet has attained a new harmony with his soul, a new perspective from which to view life:

> In meinem leben rannen schlimme tage
> Und manche töne hallten rauh und schrill.
> Nun hält ein guter geist die rechte waage
> Nun tu ich alles was der engel will. (I, 173)
>
> Unhappy, evil days ran through my life,
> And many tones resounded harsh and shrill.
> Now a good spirit strikes the truer balance,
> Now I need follow but the angel's will.

The poet acquires new confidence in his art and the ability to accept the insight that his life must be one of toil and renunciation. While man's physical being lures to the fulfillment of desire, the angel summons him to deeds. If the profusion of life and its forms cause the poet to hesitate, if the magnitude of the world causes him to despair, the ideality represented by the angel is the ultimate criterion: "Though thousandfold may be the forms of things/ For you there is but one—Mine—to proclaim" (I, 178). The poet has always been the angel's "ward" through his love of classic beauty, of elemental and pristine form, which he is to continue to cultivate: "Your early love for light endured, for noble/ Vistas of gentle mountains, slender pine/ For color pure and strong and the clear line,/ And for the whispering of the garden's blossoms" (I, 180). Though artists, "selecting and rejecting like princes," can seem to change the world through the force of their imaginative and expressive power, the poet complains, they are condemned to eternal longing which, when fulfilled, is revealed as futile and illusory. The angel reminds him that only *through* their art are the images they revere so majestic and so compelling (I, 179) not only to themselves but to all men.

This power of transfiguration gives the poet a momentous role and moves him close to the pinnacle of the seer, an idea only faintly hinted at in earlier works:

Er darf nun reden wie herab vom äther
Der neue lichter zündete im nachten
Erlösung fand aus dumpfen lebens schmachten
Der lang verborgen als ein sichrer täter

Die welken erden hob durch neue glänze
Und seinen brüdern durch sein amt bedeutet
Wo sie vor allen wahren ruhm erbeutet
Und das geheimnis lehrte neuer tänze.

Ihm wird die ehre drum wie keinen thronen
Dem sich in froher huldigung ergaben
Die seherfrauen und die edlen knaben
—Die herrscher denen künftig völker fronen.

So steigt allein den göttern opferbrodem
Wie ihm der heiligen jugend lobesstimme
Die über seine stufen höher klimme
In ihrem odem viel von seinem odem. (I, 182-83)

He now may speak as though from airy spheres,
He who has lit new torches in the night,
Redemption found from life's dark languishing,
Who though long hidden has with certain deed

Glorified anew the tired earth,
And shown his brothers in his calling sure,
Where they in all men's eyes have earned true fame,
And taught the secret step of dances new.

For this he'll sit on Honor's highest throne,
He who ecstatic tribute does receive,
From sibyls and from noble-hearted boys,
—The kings whose will o'er nations hold sway.

So rises to the gods the altar's scent,
As comes to him the praise of sacred youth,
Who must upon his steps climb higher still,
Much of his breath commingled with their breath.

No longer do his words redeem him alone from suffering. His "brothers," too, are judged by him, and their actions praised or condemned. The poet is no longer a pilgrim or minstrel, but a bard, whose prophecies cause even *seherfrauen*—sibyls who delve into the will of the gods—to pay him tribute. For the first time, he has a place in the lives of his fellow men, a role in their society, which is once more conceived in archetypal, heroic terms. Through his words, the poet has shown men hope, the beauty of life, and the path of right action. This gives him the right, indeed the duty, to speak with the authority of a medium of the gods, "as though from airy spheres." His most important office, however, is to serve as teacher and example for the youth, the future rulers, who shall strive ever higher toward perfection on "his steps," his visions and judgments. Through this power, he now believes that he can play a decisive role in the destinies of men.

The concept of discipleship is developed, using explicitly religious terminology. The poet's friends and followers are called *Jünger*, "disciples" (I, 186), the word most commonly associated in German with the first followers of Jesus. The poet must choose these followers carefully, and their relationship is based on a "common suffering" (*schmerzgemeinschaft*) (I, 181) and a certainty that the same "noble fire" burns in them which inspires him. More warlike reminiscences of the medieval relationship of the serf and soldier to his lord are also evoked. The "disciples" are, in their own hearts at least, unswervingly loyal to their "lord" and put their lives entirely into his hands:[11]

> Was uns entzückt verherrlicht und befreit
> Empfangen wir aus seiner hand zum lehn
> Und winkt er: sind wir stark und stolz bereit
> Für seinen ruhm in nacht und tod zu gehn. (I, 187)

> Whate'er delights, exalts us, makes us free,
> From his hands we receive it as a fief,
> At his command we're ready, proud and strong,
> For his fame's sake to face the night and death.

He is the arbiter of their ethics. If they live in such a way—centering their lives on the search for beauty—that the "people's delusion" condemns, indeed boasting of their deeds, the poet smiles benevolently. He recognizes the inmost kinship which these actions reveal (I, 176-77). By his authority, he is a higher judge of the good than the opinion of ordinary men. He is not "beyond good and evil" by virtue of his "office." Rather, he is a judge of the innate quality of a man, especially of his "disciples," and the good man cannot do other than good, questionable as this "good" may seem in the eyes of the society.

Despite the devotion of his followers, however, the poet knows that, ultimately, he is alone with his "angel." In a poem which bears strong overtones of the theme of Christ in the Garden of Gethsemane (I, 186), he learns from the angel that he must endure his suffering, for he "thrives in worthy combat." Although the "sun is still rising," the first half of his life is not yet over and the poet sees a torturous journey before him. The angel, the ideal self, can do little to comfort him, promising only "a balm to soothe . . . the bloody stripes" of the whiplashes of adversity which his empirical being receives. The poet's friends and "disciples," in whom he places his hopes, are dismissed by the angel: "The disciples love, but are weak and cowardly." "Only you and I remain," the angel tells the poet, trembling with pity at the thought that the poet, as a man, must struggle on alone, without hope of further human solace.

The *Vorspiel* yields yet another important new element in the artistic consciousness of the poet: a reawakened interest in his native land and the life around him. "The earth from which you came is calling you" (I, 181), says the angel. His subject matter is, henceforth, not to be sought in the past or in perilous journeys to exotic lands, in the beauty of Venice or the glory of Rome. The "life-green Stream," the Rhine, whose waves guard its people's treasure, now lures him more strongly (I, 175). The poet is to celebrate and glorify the life and heritage of the seemingly ordinary people:

> The market and the harbor you must see,
> The moving sinews of the strong and slim,
> The people's joy and anger, songs and wisdom,
> The graceful, naked limbs glide in the waves.
>
> Then in new form and color will emerge
> The strife of man with man and beast and earth . . . (I, 182)

True poetic revelation, however, comes only in the seclusion of night:

> The mighty word will rise—a grace sublime—
> A star that glimmers on mysterious paths,
> The word of new delight and pain: a dart
> That breaks into the soul to flash and glow. (I, 182)

The hints given in the poems of the *Vorspiel* indicate that the poet's "struggle," which it is his "office" to carry on, is not merely one for solace to his mind through his expressive power. Nor is it to be construed any longer as a striving for pure estheticism, for an understanding of "art for art's sake." The mission of the poet, with its prophetic implications, is aimed at his own time and land, at his contemporaries. In *Der Teppich des Lebens*, the urgency of the poet's message is still subdued and limited to veiled suggestions that the greatness of the German cultural tradition is to be sought in examples other than those favored by his contemporaries. No note of condemnation is as yet sounded. Most importantly, the concerns are cultural—largely artistic—without any suggestion of the national or political destiny of Germany yet being called into question. These concerns will become strikingly more apparent in *Der Siebente Ring*.

Stefan George's belief in the poet's "mission" to the world in which he lived had begun to evolve even before the publication of *Das Jahr der Seele*. The first poem of the *Vorspiel* was published in the *Blätter für die Kunst* in 1895 under the title "Der Besuch" ("The Visitation"), and the following four poems, developing the theme of the poet's relationship to the angel, were published in 1897 in the fourth volume of the *Blätter*. Stefan George published his poems only when the state of mind they reflected had been transcended. This accounts for the comprehensive way in which the central questions of each book are developed and orchestrated, and in which the close of each of the collections seems to point ahead to the concerns of the next, so that there is a continuous thematic progression. The only exception is the transition from *Der Teppich des Lebens* to *Der Siebente Ring*, since, in 1899, George had not yet encountered Maximin, around whom *Der Siebente Ring* centers.

Several of the poems in the second section of the book, the "tapestry of life" itself, and of the final section, *The Songs of Dream and Death*, were also published in the *Blätter* before their appearance in the completed book; they were evidently written while George was still assembling the poems which were to appear in *Das Jahr der Seele*. In these poems, however, the new poetic attitude is strikingly evident. The poet has achieved a new distance from the subjects he describes, and only rarely are the poems couched in the first person. Instead of "fleeing into congenial times and landscapes," as he had done in the *Bücher*, George transposes empirical perceptions and experiences to a plane which is ultimately mythic. Although they are to some extent individualized, the figures presented in *Der Teppich des Lebens* are, in the final analysis, allegorical, representing universal aspects of human action and feeling. Like the "Gestalten" ("Pageant") of *Der Siebente Ring*, which they anticipate, each of these types represents, positively or negatively, a response to destiny which is typical and, in many cases, necessary for the culturally productive social existence of mankind. This cultural significance transcends the interest in the individual figure, adding a new dimension beyond the lyric moment caught in the poem. In a new degree of concentration, these persons are shown in interaction with others—either in cooperation or conflict, but no longer alone. Several of the poems are concerned, as the *Vorspiel* suggests, with figures whom George considered representative of German culture. Claude David has pointed out that Stefan George was, at the turn of the century, in the broadest sense, concerned with the German cultural and artistic tradition from which he had emerged.[12] Through his friendship with Karl Wolfskehl and their collaboration on the three-volume anthology *Deutsche Dichtung*, George became more acutely aware of the affinity of earlier German poets, particularly Goethe and Jean Paul, to his own poetic striving, and began to see himself more as a specifically German poet, strong as his interest in other European literatures was to remain. This led, however, to a concern with contemporary German culture, which by and large rejected or ignored precisely the poetic qualities of austere, compressed form and symbolic imagery which George prized.

In "Der Teppich" ("The Tapestry"), the introductory poem to the second book of the collection, a tapestry is described in which figures of men, beasts, plants, the moon, and stars are woven together in fixed, but apparently confused and contradictory relationships, in a "frozen dance" (I, 190). One evening, the tapestry springs to life, the figures step forth in their proper relationships and resolve the apparent mystery. This higher understanding of the secret of men's common existence in the context of civilization and culture is intuitive and inspired: "It cannot be forced by the will: is not for every/ Ordinary hour: is not the treasure of a guild./ To the many it will never come, and never through talk/ As an image it comes seldom to the rare" (I, 190). Life in all of its complexity is not to be rationally understood; its secret cannot be the possession of a "guild" of scholars. The people at large, the masses, can never understand it; and rational concepts expressed in words cannot grasp it. Only the "rare" person, who "sees" in visionary images and can express these images—the poet—can, at times, understand life's secret. Thus, the poet's claim to a special wisdom pertaining to the mythic powers of humanity, set forth in the *Vorspiel*, is asserted even more forcefully.

The poems of *Der Teppich des Lebens* set forth George's ideas on the origins and attributes of a vigorous culture in images which, in their totality, take on the force of theses. Culture is the common heritage of the economic and political history, the crafts and arts of a nation. Its origins in man's mastery over nature and his careful cultivation of all that is useful and wholesome to him are indicated in "Urlandschaft" ("Primal Landscape") (I, 190) and in "Der Freund der Fluren" ("The Friend of the Fields") (I, 191).

"Gewitter" ("The Storm") and "Die Fremde" ("The Stranger") (I, 192) emphasize the role which nature myths and magic play in enriching the tradition and imagination of the people. The people themselves, with sovereign ambivalence, are characterized as "lambs" ("Lämmer") (I, 193), which move through the meadows in wavelike herds, their feelings immediate and determined by the caprice of the light—happy in the sun and melancholy by moonlight. Incapable of deeper feelings or desires, they are empty and vain of heart, but they are proud of the golden bells of their "leaders." The "lambs" are old and yet forever young; their steps are heavy and steady, but their leaps are light. At times they are cautious, at times fearless of any cliffs. In their instinct for physical comfort and security, they are "lambs of the well-kept cisterns"; in their unfailing, apparently naïve faith, they are the "lambs of the fearless horizons." The great movements of the peoples, their sense of the collective destiny which they must follow, is now hardly understood and was celebrated only in the half-forgotten beauty of the heroic epics, whose remembrance has paled in the minds of men. For all the apparently ignoble qualities which the poet here attributes to the "herd," the mass of the people, their faith and their surging collective movement is their strength, the elements without which no culture, no matter how gifted its leaders, can exist.

Six pairs of poems stand at the center of *Der Teppich des Lebens*. The figures presented in these antithetically or complementarily arranged poems embody qualities essential to the intensity and grandeur of "life in all its beauty." The concern of the first two poems, which are complementary, is the individual whose innate feeling is in disharmony with the prevailing mood of the culture. Thus, the "Herzensdame" ("Lady of Hearts") (I, 194) sees a deeper, redemptive meaning in a miraculous sign from a statue of Mary than do her medieval contemporaries, who only fear punishment for their sins. In "Die Maske" ("The Mask") (I, 194), a figure departs from a rococo Mardi Gras ball and commits suicide, overwhelmed with melancholy and religious dread, which the "silken puppets" of that "jesting century" cannot feel or comprehend. The motif of murder for revenge—the most extreme instance of fundamental justice and a cornerstone of human relationships—is depicted in "Die Verrufung" ("The Curse") (I, 195) and "Der Täter" ("The Assassin") (I, 196). The injured man can find no honorable repose until the offender is dead and justice has been done. On the eve of his deed, the future murderer feels a sense of peace, of contempt for those who do not feel his passion, even though he knows that tomorrow he, in turn, will be pursued by avengers.

The "Schmerzbrüder" ("Brothers in Suffering") (I, 196) are opposed in their limitless longing, which lets them see nothing of immediate hope and possible fulfillment, to the unquestioning, loving devotion of "Der Jünger" ("The Disciple") (I, 197). "Der Erkorene" ("The Chosen") (I, 198) has been crowned by the "masters of song" for his purity and willingness to revere and serve. "Der Verworfene" ("The Rejected") (I, 198) is denied the wreath, for he has sold himself and his art for easy praise, for popularity, and can come before the truly "pure" only with shame. It is generally assumed that George meant this poem as a reproach to Hofmannsthal.[13]

The final two pairs of poems are specifically concerned with phenomena of German cultural history. "Rom-Fahrer" (Pilgrims To Rome") (I, 199) celebrates the enrichment brought to the German tradition by the lure which Italy exerted on the medieval German emperors, which has widened the scope of the people's imagination ever since. This outward movement is contrasted with the life of the soul exemplified by "Das Kloster" ("The Cloister") (I, 200), which celebrates the great German monastic tradition. "Wahrzeichen" ("Landmarks") (I, 200) and "Jean Paul" (I, 201) exemplify the elements which George found most essential and fruitful in German art and literature: the austere dignity and beauty of late medieval representations of the madonna, especially those of Hans Holbein the Younger, and the novels of Jean Paul Richter, which made a "miraculous forest" of his native landscape. In their intention, if not in their form, these poems, but particularly "Landmarks," bear a strong resemblance to Baudelaire's "Les Phares," which Stefan George also translated (II, 241-43), celebrating the essential qualities of specific artists.

The seven poems entitled "Standbilder" ("Monuments") describe allegorical figures of women. They represent significant influences and forces in the poet's life: the spirits of Greek paganism and of Christianity, disillusioned hope, duty, love, and passion in the work of art.[14] The last of these figures, shown in the poem "Der Schleier" ("The Veil") (I, 205), represents the art of poetry and exemplifies Stefan George's artistic ideal at this time. It is represented as a magical veil which, wafted over the world, transforms the prosaic and everyday into mythic entities. George's closeness to the Romantic poetic tradition is rarely as evident as it is in this poem. Poetry claims the major role in determining man's imagination, his higher impulses and thus his fate: "As my veil waves so will your longing be" (I, 205).

Die Lieder von Traum und Tod contains twelve poems addressed to the poet's friends and twelve of a more lyrical, personal nature. Of the first group, the poem "Den Brüdern" ("To My Brothers"), dedicated to the Austrian poet Leopold von Andrian, is of particular interest, for it demonstrates Stefan George's new conception of himself as a German poet. In 1891, he had sought the cooperation of Hugo von Hofmannsthal in bringing about a renascence of poetry in the German language, which would make a contribution to what he felt to be a European poetic phenomenon. Now, toward the end of the same decade, he sees the German tradition as more viable and flourishing than the Austrian, which he characterizes here as possessing the "tremulous beauty of those near death, a richly colorful decline" (I, 214).

The lyrical, intimate mood of the last twelve poems of *Die Lieder von Traum und Tod,* written in the same tone which had predominated in Stefan George's early works, now seems to be in sharp contrast with the drama and monumentality of *Der Teppich des Lebens,* the ascetic pathos of the *Vorspiel.* These poems capture the initial situation of the poet before his commitment to the angel. They state, once more, the despair he had attempted to overcome by viewing life as a "tapestry," all of whose apparently arbitrary parts are interrelated, meaningful, and ultimately beneficent. To find and express such meaning in life made bearable the torment of existence, the loneliness of the personal vision. In the orders of civilization and culture, in the perspective of history and kindred artistic striving, he had found a meaning in life beyond his own existence, and thereby, a higher purpose for his own life. All of this, however, has not changed the personal situation of the poet. Although he has found friends and admirers who understand him up to a certain point, he is still alone with his private despair, as at the outset, which the poem "Lachende Herzen" ("Laughing Hearts") (I, 218), with its ironically waltz-like dactylic meter, conveys:

> O laughing hearts who have seen Joy embodied
> As a maid floating down from airy clouds,
> With gifts to give, highest goals of your striving,
> You whose hopes grow from one feast to the next:
>
> You who unite all delight of the sunlight
> In the pink blossoms of your radiant cheeks,
> Dark days enduring as a brief atonement,
> Sad thoughts you banish with your graceful pleas:
>
> O dancing hearts I admire and seek you,
> I stoop not to hinder the bright balls you throw,

You light ones who move me—for moments fulfill me,
You whom I honor, to your surprise:

You who entwine me in your round dances,
'Tis but my costume that makes me like you,
O playful hearts, though close you embrace me:
How distant you are from my beating heart!

After the "tapestry of life," it is significant that the poems which deal with real persons, the relationship of the poet to his friends, should be "songs of dream and death." Contrasted with the eternal flowing pattern of human life and culture, the individual existence subsumed in this pattern is a visionary dream of meaningfulness in the face of the unalterable fact of death. Only through the dream, the willful imaginative postulation of one's individual existence as a purposeful element in the grand design of the tapestry, can the despair of existence be overcome. Hence, the concluding poem, "Traum und Tod" ("Dream and Death") (I, 223), shows the individual not in despair or loneliness but governed by ineluctable mythic structures of fatality, whose omens are written in the stars:

Pride and fame! so we wake to the world,
Hero-like we subdue crag and sea,
Young and great the mind looks without rein,
At the field, at the flood surging free.

On the path a light breaks, visions fly,
And the bliss with its pain shakes the soul,
He who ruled now must weep, know and bow,
"Thou my grace, thou my fame, thou my star"

Then the dream, pride's high flight, rises up,
To its will God who sent it to bend...
Till a call strikes us down from on high,
Us, so naked and small before death!

All this storms, tears and beats, flashes, burns,
Ere for us late in night's firmament,
There appears, shimm'ring, still, jewel of light:
Pride and fame, bliss and pain, dream and death.

CHAPTER 4

Maximin

Du kamst am lezten tag
Da ich von harren siech
Da ich des betens müd
Mich in die nacht verlor. (I, 279)

Der Siebente Ring

DURING the first decade of the twentieth century, the poetic voice of Stefan George took on a distinctly new tone. In the place of the solitary singer who summons up moods of exquisite existential melancholy, there emerged gradually the critic of his times, proclaiming a new idealism which would redeem men from impending catastrophe if they would only understand and live by it. Concern for the fate of the nation and the culture was previously latent in George, but, beginning with the fifth volume of the *Blätter,* or, for a wider audience, the appearance of the first "public" edition of *Der Siebente Ring* in 1907, it becomes a dominant theme of his work. Although a strong continuity with his practice of the past is evident, many of his later poems exceeding the earlier degree of lyric concentration, George had clearly reached a turning point in his life and art around 1900.

This change was precipitated by a complex of three roughly simultaneous experiences, each of which heightened the personal significance of the others. Aspects and themes of George's later work can be traced to each of them. The earliest of these experiences is the confrontation with the circle of the "Cosmics" in Munich. George had known Ludwig Klages and Alfred Schuler since 1893, but more intensive contact began only when Karl Wolfskehl settled in Munich in 1898. The Nietzschean contempt of the "Cosmics" for modern civilization and their belief that the magic and myths which motivated great cultures of the past must be revived, surely struck a sympathetic chord in George, even if he studiously avoided the occultism and mystical racism which Klages and Schuler expounded at the time. The following outburst by Klages in a letter to Gundolf is fairly typical for his outlook: "Humanity besmirches itself more from day to day. What can one do, considering these vermin which stink to high Heaven! Rather, one must attempt intensely to forget that human beings exist at all; this coat of mildew on the putrefying crust of our globe. But the decay can be scrubbed off and the idols made to totter, for everything is rotten to the core."[1] In the poems which George wrote before *Der Siebente Ring*, "humanity" in general or such pejorative variants as "the crowd" and "the herd," rarely appear as motifs and are treated neutrally, at worst with irony and as a part of life to be shunned. Beginning with the "Zeitgedichte," however, *die Menge* becomes more prominent as the object of George's contempt and cold fury for its ignorance of its innate higher humanity, its destruction and misunderstanding of all of those who try to realize man's divine capability. George did not surrender to the tragic despair which such a view could engender, nor did he hope for a cataclysmic resolution. Rather, just as he and his associates were doing in the narrower area of the arts in the *Blätter*, he chose, by precept and example, to proclaim his vision that the possible heights embodied in the totality of the culture of ancient Greece might be scaled once more.

George's friendship with his first younger "disciple," Friedrich Gundolf, also had its beginnings in Munich around the turn of the century. Shortly thereafter, the poems collected in the section of *Der Siebente Ring* entitled "Gezeiten" ("Tides"), which memorialize the early phase of this relationship, were written. George delighted in Gundolf as a friend, as a poet, and as a kindred intellect, possessed of great intuitive gifts. He clearly hoped that the younger man would, in turn, educate disciples of the new ethos in the same way as George was doing with him. The new role into which George was cast—the role of Socratic pedagogue—lent to his tone a new urgency, an apodictic terseness, the voice of unshakable certainty evident already in the later poems of the cycle "Gestalten" ("Pageant"). Through the friendship with Gundolf, who was to be followed by growing numbers of young men, George saw that his mission in life, at least in part, was among the young, and that if they were made aware of how life has a higher goal than pragmatic ends, Western humanity might ultimately be saved from its own ever increasing depravity. It was the encounter with the youth he called Maximin, however, which brought both his tragic vision of humanity and his vocation as a teacher into a meaningful interrelationship. Maximin provided the example of what George meant by the divine fusion of body and spirit. The central part of *Der Siebente Ring*, entitled "Maximin," celebrates the human significance and ideality of this experience, which was to strengthen and impel George for the rest of his life.

The number seven, revered since antiquity for its mystical and magical power, is the unifying architectonic emblem of *Der Siebente Ring,* which appeared in a private edition in 1907, as the seventh collection of George's poems (after *Hymnen, Pilgerfahrten, Algabal, Die Bücher der Hirten- und Preisgedichte, Das Jahr der Seele,* and *Der Teppich des Lebens*), seven years after the appearance of the last of these. The collection contains seven cycles of poems, the number of poems in each of which is divisible by seven and ranges from fourteen to seventy. Each cycle displays an inner unity of theme and a similarity of form in its poems. A definite progression is evident in the arrangement of the cycles within the book. At the center stands the cycle "Maximin," preceded by the groups "Zeitgedichte," "Gestalten," and "Gezeiten," and followed by the last three cycles "Traumdunkel," "Lieder," and "Tafeln." There is a movement from the external, the objective, the earthly, through ever more personal and subjective realms of experience and vision to the ultimate fulfillment of Maximin. The last three cycles bring the reader gradually back to the "world" in the "Tablets," which correspond in many respects to the "Zeitgedichte." The unity imposed by this carefully planned structure belies the fact that the poems were written in the course of nearly a decade, there being little or no relationship between the order in which they are arranged and that in which they were written. As in all of his collections, George took pains that the poems should appear as an esthetic whole rather than as sequential revelations of his inner state.

Like the whole of *Der Siebente Ring,* the first cycle, "Zeitgedichte" ("Poems for My Time"), constitutes an intellectual and emotional process. The sequence "Dante und das Zeitgedicht," "Goethe-Tag," "Nietzsche," and "Böcklin" represents a descent into cultural pessimism whose end is only reached with "Porta Nigra." The two poems at the heart of the cycle, "Franken" and "Leo XIII," represent the point at which an ascent toward new hope begins. Although the figures celebrated in "Die Gräber in Speier," "Pente Pigadia," "Die Schwestern," "Carl August," and "Die tote Stadt" seem to hold out slender hope indeed, they embody the strength and perception of a higher reality necessary to counterbalance the brutishness of mankind shown in the first part of the cycle. In the first and last poems, both entitled "Das Zeitgedicht" (I, 227 and I, 244),[2] George speaks of his own relationship to his contemporaries, as he does in "Franken" which, significantly enough, is the seventh poem of the cycle.

The German literary tradition of writing poems commenting critically on the poet's own times goes back to the Middle Ages, the *Sprüche* of Walther von der Vogelweide being a prime example. Juvenalian satire, too, was a favored medium through the ages in western European literature. The term *Zeitgedicht* itself seems to have originated in the eighteenth century.[3] It is not unlikely that George encountered it in the poetry of Heine, who wrote twenty-four sharply satirical *Zeitgedichte* in 1844.[4] Although George's poems differ considerably from most of Heine's "Zeitgedichte," the intent is similar: to arouse the contemporaries to an awareness of their situation and their own spiritual blindness. Right perception is the dominant concern. The poet ceaselessly condemns the failure of the many to share the redemptive vision of the few, to see the great forces still present in the world. Throughout the first six "Zeitgedichte," intellectual tension is engendered by the difference between the view of the *Menge, Ihr,* and that of the poet.

George's condemnation of the failure of cognition is stated as a challenge in the first lines of "Zeitgedicht I":

> Ihr meiner zeit genossen kanntet schon
> Bemaasset schon und schaltet mich–ihr fehltet. (I, 227)
>
> Companions of my time, you've known me long,
> Have measured and reproached me–but you erred.

The poet's contemporaries err because the criteria with which they measure are insufficient. The verbs *kennen* and *bemessen* imply merely superficial, quantitative estimation on their part. They had judged him to be a "scent-intoxicated prince, who, gently cradled, scanned his poems," taking at face value the image George had apparently presented to the world. In reality, the poet's past had been a time of agonizing struggle for him, "an entire youth full of harsh deeds," a seeking of allies in a hostile society, "the enemy's house." Of all of this, they had guessed nothing:

> Ihr kundige las't kein schauern· las't kein lächeln·
> Wart blind für was in dünnem schleier schlief. (I, 227)
>
> You knowing ones read terror not, nor smile,
> Were blind for that which slept beneath the veil.

The irony of the poet's calling his contemporaries "knowing ones" is heightened by the inadequacy of *raten* ("guessing") or *lesen* ("reading") with regard to full cognition. Now that he, like the Piper of Hamelin, has led them on his path and has shown them beauties through his poems that have made the "real" world distasteful to them; now that others are imitating his tone, "murmuring in the Arcadian mode," the poet will ride into battle in earnest, visible to all. His mission is the spiritual renewal of his fellowmen, and his spurs will "wound the rotten flesh." George asserts that the will to bring about such renewal has been constant in him from the beginning; and if his contemporaries believe that he has changed essentially, it is because of their imperfect conceptions about him and their blindness to his true nature: "Ihr sehet wechsel· doch ich tat das gleiche" ("You perceive change, but I remained constant") (I, 228). This militant stance, the contemptuous ferocity, are necessary in this moment of cultural crisis, but they are not permanent. A better time is foreseen:

> Und der heut eifernde posaune bläst
> Und flüssig feuer schleudert weiss dass morgen
> Leicht alle schönheit kraft und grösse steigt
> Aus eines knaben stillem flötenlied. (I, 228)

> And he who sounds the martial trumpet now,
> And launches sheets of flame knows that tomorrow
> All beauty, strength, and greatness well may come
> From gentle flute songs piped by a young boy.

If these more harmonious times are to come, however, they will result from an ever constant attitude and intention.

The succeeding poems amplify and vary the theme of "Zeitgedicht I": the tragic disparity between the artist and his age and a posterity which values the wrong aspects of his achievement. In the celebration of Dante, Goethe, and the Swiss painter Arnold Böcklin (1827-1901), George emphasizes the isolation of each man through the inability of his contemporaries to perceive his striving and judge and reward it rightly.

For many years, George had been working on translations from the *Divine Comedy*, of which excerpts appeared in almost every issue of the *Blätter* from 1901 (Volume V) onward. The partial translation of the *Comedy* constitutes a volume of George's collected works (X/XI). It is generally regarded as one of the best translations of Dante into German. The *Divine Comedy* is the "poem of his time" as indicated in the title of "Dante und das Zeitgedicht," in which George pays tribute to the poet with whom he felt such a strong affinity. It is the spirit of Dante which speaks. He reports how he was ridiculed in his youth when he was faint with his adoration of Beatrice, and how, as a man, was exiled from his native Florence as a "reward" for his advocacy of what he knew to be right. Dante's anguish over mankind's self-inflicted pain, his rage at the lax, the low, and the debased, crystallized into the hard, bronzelike form of the *Inferno*. Then many listened, and Dante's fame spread, but men did not feel the "fire and the claw" in their own hearts. When he described Paradise, Dante was scorned for his "softer tone," that of a "boy or an old man." What seemed weak and gentle was the "full fire" which Dante needed to illumine the love of the highest and for the "exaltation of the sun and all the stars." Compared to this pure fire, whose warmth no one felt, the flames of the *Inferno* were merely like sparks from a glowing log Dante had blown upon:

> . . . o toren!
> Ich nahm aus meinem herd ein scheit und blies–
> So ward die hölle· doch des vollen feuers
> Bedurft ich zur bestrahlung höchster liebe
> Und zur verkündigung von sonn und stern. (I, 229)

> . . . o fools!
> I took a log out of my hearth and blew–
> Thus Hell was made, the full fire I required
> To illumine rightly supreme love,
> And for the meaning of the sun and stars.

The end of the poem echoes the conclusion of the *Paradiso,* which also celebrates the "love which moves the sun and stars."[5] The parallel structures of "Zeitgedicht I" and "Dante und das Zeitgedicht" indicates the intimate kinship which George felt between himself and Dante. The serene note of resolution on which both poems end suggests the ultimate inward triumph of the poet in his private knowledge over the ignorance and adversity which confront him.

In the following three poems, George's criticism of the Victorian-Wilhelmine culture of Germany of his day reaches its highest pitch of anger. "Goethe-Tag" ("Goethe's Birthday") describes the poet's feelings on the 150th anniversary of Goethe's birth, August 28, 1899, a time when elaborate public tributes to his memory were given, at which the serene, humane "Olympian" Goethe was to be praised, the *Klassiker,* and not the tormented, daimon-driven man known only to the few, the aspect George was soon to show in the second volume of *Deutsche Dichtung.* The poet comes to Goethe's house in Frankfurt early in the day, stands reverently before it, and then leaves. He grimly anticipates the course of the day, the vanity of the celebration, of "those who must touch to believe," who see in Goethe's humanity and mortal frailty the justification for their own grossness, and who, in praising him, are really praising themselves. They do indeed possess his instincts, but in the lower sense, like animals. They do not know "that he who's turned to dust/ Since then holds many a secret yet for you/ And that of him, the radiant one, much now/ Has disappeared that you still call eternal." The poem "Böcklin," in which the Swiss painter is thanked for having kept the flame of beauty alive in dire times, has much the same tenor.

The death of the philosopher Friedrich Nietzsche on August 5, 1900, was the occasion for the poem which bears his name. The poem is a significant indication of George's attitude toward Nietzsche, particularly at this time, when, it is generally said, his influence on the poet becomes most apparent, beginning with *Der Siebente Ring*. In later years, George disavowed any central role Nietzsche might have played in his thinking:

> He said that Nietzsche had never had a constructive effect on him.... If he had heard anything impressive about [Nietzsche's] life, that he had disciples, for example, that would have impressed him more.... Already in 1892 he had esteemed Nietzsche as an orator and fighter whom one could use. But he was not interested in someone who still fought against Christianity. "When you're fighting against something, you're still very deeply involved in it. Not Nietzsche was beyond good and evil, but *Algabal*...." [Nietzsche] has neither a personality, nor a theory, nor direction....He saw the promised land, which he himself could not enter; he did see what was missing and that the Divine had to be re-created. The substance which he sought was no longer within him.[6]

These statements date from 1920. The core of many of these reservations concerning Nietzsche is already present in the poem, in spite of the admiration it expresses. Undoubtedly Nietzsche contributed much to crystallizing George's sense of his times, and reinforcing his conviction of what must be done, and even to the diction of the later poems. But this does not mean that George accepted all of the implications of Nietzsche's ideas. In his exaltation of Maximin there is a greater similarity to Dante's beatification of Beatrice than there is of Nietzsche's proclamation of the "Superman." In the poem, George describes mankind with truly Nietzschean scorn: "The herd trots stupidly below, disturb it not!/ What's a stab to a jellyfish, cutting to weeds?" (I, 231). Nietzsche was a martyr to his times: "Let the beast that smirched him with praise,/ And that still battens on decay's miasma expire;/ Then you will stand radiant for all times/ Like other leaders with the bloody crown" (I, 231). But his martyrdom is also self-imposed. George's verdict on Nietzsche is that he "killed that which was most precious" in himself, "only to passionately desire it anew and to cry out in pain of loneliness" (I, 231). For George, what Nietzsche had killed in himself was his faith in the divine and compassion for his fellow men. By a curious coincidence, George was in Turin in 1889, at the same time when Nietzsche's madness first burst forth there. This gives a particular poignancy to the last stanza, for he who would have come too late to Nietzsche is George himself.[7]

> Der kam zu spät der flehend zu dir sagte:
> Dort ist kein weg mehr über eisige felsen
> Und horste grauser vögel—nun ist not:
> Sich bannen in den kreis den liebe schliesst . .
> Und wenn die strenge und gequälte stimme
> Dann wie ein loblied tönt in blaue nacht
> Und helle flut—so klagt: sie hätte singen
> Nicht reden sollen diese neue seele! (I, 232)

> Too late would anyone have implored you:
> Your path no longer lies past cliffs of ice
> And eyries of fierce birds—your need is now
> To stay within the circle love defines . . .
> And when that stringent and tormented voice
> Reverberates in blue night like a hymn,
> And over the bright flood—let us mourn:
> It should have sung, not spoken, this new soul!

As the many echoes of Nietzsche's poems and writings in this stanza indicate, George knew Nietzsche's work well by this time. The metaphors of icy cliffs and the eyries of grim birds, used to describes Nietzsche's path, have a strong kinship with the landscape in the *Zarathustra* poems, and the *blaue nacht* is surely a reference to Zarathustra's "Nachtlied." That "this new soul" should have sung, not spoken, is a thought expressed by Nietzsche himself in his *Essay in Self-Criticism.*[8] By his reiteration of this thought in the last line of the poem, George means that, had Nietzsche's soul been able to "sing," as it could not through its torment, and had he been more of an artist and less a polemicist, he might have met with more understanding. If his life had been more exemplary and felicitous (a thought which George expressed in the later conversation quoted above), he would have had followers, among whom George would have included himself more unequivocally. In this poem, George sets himself apart from Nietzsche, knowing that unity must exist between the inward process and will of the *neue seele* and its outward expression.

The Porta Nigra in the German city of Trier on the Moselle River is a Roman gate built in the fourth century A.D., when the city bore the name Augusta Treverorum and was an important center of Germania Romana, of which George was proud as the region of his birth. The poem "Porta Nigra" bears the subtitle

"Ingenio Alf. Scolari" ("In the Spirit of Alfred Schuler") (I, 233), who saw in the heroic paganism of Imperial Rome the highest form of life. Accordingly, in this most outspoken and daring of the "Zeitgedichte," the inhabitants of present-day Germany are subjected to the pitiless gaze of the shade of an inhabitant of Trier during the Roman period. He laments that he should have to wake now, he who had known the Roman glories of the town, which is now disfigured by the barbaric houses of later times. Only his beloved gate remains and seems to look from its myriad windows with contempt on modern man: "Die fürsten priester knechte gleicher art/ Gedunsne larven mit erloschnen blicken/ Und frauen die ein sklav zu feil befände–" ("Princes, priests, servants–all alike/ Bloated masks with dead eyes/ And women which a slave would find too easy") (I, 234). What this race of men has lost is *blut* ("blood"), that is to say, the vitality of the primal worship of the pagan gods. "We shades breathe more strongly," says the speaker, identifying himself as "the youth Manlius," who would not want to rule over this people as a king–he who had plied a trade so lowly they cannot name it, for which they have no word. For he had gone perfumed round the gate and sold his body to the soldiers of the Caesars.

Of all the "Zeitgedichte," "Porta Nigra" is the most carefully constructed. Instead of summarizing the meaning of the poem, as is its function in the other poems of this cycle, the last line brings home the full humiliation of the modern age, over which the lowliest and most dishonorable personage of ancient Rome would disdain to rule. There is a darkly ironic intention in this device, in the springing of the carefully laid trap into which the reader has been led by listening so intently to the scornful and yet spellbinding voice from beyond the grave.

To the negation of the times expressed in "Porta Nigra," "Franken" and "Leo XIII" represent a response and a hope, both within the poet's own range of experience. In "Franken" (I, 235), the seventh poem of the cycle, George tells us how he had found solace from the cultural desolation of his homeland among his like-minded fellow poets in Paris, that is, in his personal rediscovery of the Carolingian cultural unity of the "Frankish lands" (See p. 22 in Chapter 1, above). "Leo XIII" (I, 236) is a tribute to the Pope who died in 1903, having done much to reassert the spiritual and moral authority of the Church after its ruinous temporal losses sustained during the unification of Italy. In the carefully arranged context of the "Zeitgedichte," Leo is that which Nietzsche could not be. He is shown as a man of unshakable majesty living in ascetic simplicity, his sleepless nights spent in composing hymns to the Virgin and her Child, from one of which a translated excerpt is included in the third stanza.

Pope Leo is both a poet and a seer: "So singt der dichter und der seher weiss:/ Das neue heil kommt nur aus neuer liebe" ("So sings the poet and the seer knows/ That new redemption comes only from new love") (I, 237). In his sacerdotal function, surrounded by clouds of incense and myriad candles, Leo is an exemplary image of "exalted pomp and divine governing." When he gives his blessing to the world, "So sinken wir als gläubige zu boden/ Verschmolzen mit der tausendköpfigen menge/ Die schön wird wenn das wunder sie ergreift" ("We kneel, believers, on the ground,/ One with the thousand-headed throng,/ Which is beautiful when touched by the miracle") (I, 237). George had ceased to be a practicing Catholic around the age of eighteen, but he still appreciated the Church as an expression of the human spirit, as a guarantor of order in the world, and as a counterweight against the spiritual poverty of modern man.[9] It is the personality of Leo himself, however, not the Church or the ideology he represents, that passes the "miracle" which is capable of transforming the *Menge*, so vehemently criticized in the earlier poems. The harmony and unity, the single-mindedness of his life as it is depicted in the poem, the blending of spiritual serenity and evident beauty strikingly contrast with the tormented soul of Nietzsche. Through such exemplary leaders, the multitude may yet be redeemed from its own debasement.

The four poems which follow "Leo XIII" also celebrate figures who have impressed the poet as being exemplary in their lives or in the manner of their deaths: the greatest of the medieval German emperors in "Die Gräber in Speier" ("The Graves in Speier") (I, 237); a young English friend of George killed while fighting for Greece against Turkey in 1897 in "Pente Pigadia" (I, 239); Sophie of Alençon and Empress Elizabeth of Austria in "Die Schwestern" ("The Sisters") (I, 240); and in "Carl August" (I, 241), Klein, George's earliest collaborator in publishing the *Blätter für die Kunst*. George attempts to elevate these personages from their immediate context of historical circumstance to the level of timeless, universally valid figures, almost mythical in their fatality. In "Pente Pigadia," he describes the death of Hugh Clement Gilbert Harris, the son of a British shipping magnate, in a manner which would have been just as fitting for a youth who had fallen in the Trojan War. Only the absolutely necessary timely circumstances are indicated, while, for the rest, the poem intentionally plays on ancient Greek reminiscences. Sophie, the duchess of Alençon, died in a fire in 1897 at a charity bazaar in Paris, refusing the opportunity to escape until all of the other guests had done so. In "Die Schwestern," this event is poetically transformed so that it displays almost classical qualities of majesty and tragedy:

> Ihr los erfüllte sich am fest des mitleids . .
> Schon gellte schrei· schon beizte rauch die augen·
> Man bot ihr rettung· doch sie sprach: "lasst erst
> Die gäste gehn!" and sank umhüllt von flammen. (I, 240)
>
> She met her fate at Pity's festival.
> Already cries rang out, smoke stung the eye,
> Offered rescue she said, "First let the guests
> Depart!" and sank enveloped by the flames.

George's ability to perceive mythic structures in the phenomena of his contemporary world is also manifested in "Die tote Stadt" ("The Dead City") (I, 243), inspired by a visit to the Italian port of Genoa. The poem is a parable of a rich, new harbor town which has grown up, a white crescent, at the base of a mountain on which is located the ancient "mother city," poverty-stricken and blackened by time. Its people live only in the silent preservation of the "consecrated images" (*weihebilder*) and in the certain knowledge that the day will come when the inhabitants of the city below will come, pleading for sanctuary. A nameless malady—possibly physical, possibly spiritual—will lay their city waste, and they will bring all that they hold most precious, gold and gems, in order to breathe the pure air of the heights and drink at the clean springs of the old city. A harsh answer awaits them from the *mutterstadt*, however. They are refused entry, their gifts spurned as rubbish and cast over the cliff into the sea by the youths of the old city. Only the seven who had come earlier and on whom the children had smiled will be saved. All the rest shall perish. The new city, which is doomed, is the modern mass civilization which George saw emerging in his time, the huge cities in which "the throngs haggle by day and rage after pleasure by night." By contrast, the old city is the repository of the values of spiritual dignity and individual worth impossible in a mass of people, where the will of the greatest number is considered the only valid criterion. This is what is meant by "In your numbers you are an abomination" ("Schon eure zahl ist frevel") (I, 244), which follows the sealing of their doom. The seven who are saved are those who have found their way back to the old values from which the culture once proceeded. They have come in genuine reverence and innocence, for the children have smiled on them. In this parable, George has made two stages of cultural development exist concretely side by side. They embody graphically the repeated warnings, expressed in the "Zeitgedichte" of a coming cataclysm which can be averted only, if at all, if men are led from their present path back to the ways of mutual reverence and self-restraint.

In "Zeitgedicht II" (I, 244), George returns to his initial concern: the relationship of the poet to the times in which he lives. He intends to be the "conscience," a "voice" penetrating the feckless apathy of his fellow men, whose plaintive cries George renders with mimetic sarcasm:

> "Nur niedre herrschen noch· die edlen starben:
> Verschwemmt ist glaube und verdorrt ist liebe.
> Wie flüchten wir aus dem verwesten ball?" (I, 244)
>
> "Only the base still rule, the noble are dead
> Faith has been washed away and love has withered.
> How can we flee from this corrupted globe?"

The purpose of the "Zeitgedichte" has been to disprove these propositions. If this is an age of decadence, then men have made it thus through their "overexcited senses and cloven hearts." Because they perversely wish to deny the existence of beauty and greatness, they turn their heads away from them in order not to see. They have built their philosophies, Babel-like structures "of smoke and dust and vapor," which are doomed to destruction. Realizing the transiency of this endeavor, men seek permanence (*dauer*) in a religion which demands the mortification of the flesh and the denial of the light of the sun. They have lost the rest of their vital substances by concocting an image of the soul composed of "poison and filth," that is to say, a belief in the inborn sinfulness and perversity of man's spirit. Like "Zeitgedicht I," this poem ends on a note of affirmation, in the knowledge that change is the only constant and the faith that there is a benevolent fatality at work in the world, which will yet see a better age than this one. The poet reads this message in the thousand-year-old eyes of statues of ancient kings, heavy with "our" dreams and "our" tears:

> sie wie wir wussten:
> Mit wüsten wechseln gärten· frost mit glut·
> Nacht kommt für helle—busse für das glück.
> Und schlingt das dunkel uns und unsre trauer:
> Eins das von je war (keiner kennt es) währet
> Und blum und jugend lacht und sang erklingt. (I, 245)

they knew like we:
Gardens alternate with deserts, frost with heat,
Night comes for brightness—atonement for joy
And if the dark should swallow us and our sadness
One that is always (no one knows it) lasts
And flowers and youth will laugh and songs ring out.

The representative human types of the cycle "Gestalten" move in a mythic dimension which combines elements of the heroic past of the component cultures of western European civilization: the Greek, the biblical, and the medieval Christian. This indefiniteness is intentional. George desired to emphasize the universality and immediacy of these figures, not their time-bound restriction to any one culture. Echoes and reminiscences of myths and historical occurrences of various cultures and epochs coexist and intersect in this cycle.

The poems present compressions of antithetical figures in dialectical relationships, which may be traced through the entire cycle. The ultimate poles of the dialectic, the Manichean struggle between darkness and light—a never-ending process—are indicated in the introductory poem, "Der Kampf" ("The Struggle") (I, 246), which describes the victory of a singing god of radiance over a brutal troglodyte bent on his destruction. Pairs of figures dominate the next four poems, which are all concerned with opposing aspects of the guidance of men and their destinies: active and contemplative leadership in "Die Führer" ("The Leaders") (I, 247); command and obedience in "Manuel und Menes" (I, 250); the torment of the ruler's servitude to time and the infinite and disembodied ecstasy of transcending religious devotion in "Algabal und der Lyder" ("Algabal and the Lydian") (I, 251); the burdensome guilt that comes with ruling and the free innocence of servitude in "König und Harfner" ("The King and the Harper") (I, 252).

The intent of "Der Fürst und der Minner" (I, 248) is less obvious than the representation of these polarities. Ernst Morwitz calls this poem a tribute to Maximin,[10] whose limitless compassion for those he loved is celebrated here. There is much in the words of the *Minner*, however, which anticipates the resignation to tragic loss which is dominant in the "Gezeiten." George took the concept of the *Minner* from the medieval courtly vocabulary to indicate a pure love that is the lover's total fate and that exists without hope of being requited. The "beloved ones" (*Geliebte*) of the *Minner* are far away. His love is a tribute joyfully rendered. Consenting to his fate, the *Minner* willingly suffers the reproaches of those "who pass below" that he does not participate in the "harvest" of life. An almost Christlike quality of self-sacrifice is attributed to this figure, who can do nothing but love, who pours his soul, his "life's blood" into the dusk for his "beloved–O all you beloved" (I, 249), even though his sacrifice cannot help "in the service of men." In the words of the Prince, the *Minner* has a priestly destiny, a unique function which is higher than the deeds of "the strong and the wise," who kneel before him to receive grace. In celebrating Maximin in this way, George perhaps comes closer to capturing the essence of the youth than do the poems of the actual "Maximin" cycle.

The following poems depict, often with vivid concreteness, the primal forces which men must acknowledge if they are to gain a new awareness of themselves and escape from the shallowness of life scourged in the "Zeitgedichte." "Sonnwendzug" ("Summer Solstice") (I, 253) celebrates Dionysian intoxication, complete abandonment to the senses, a passionate, violent fructification, reminiscent of choruses from Euripides' *Bacchae.* The sentence units are of varying lengths and are set within alternating five- and three-foot trochaic lines, resulting in a counterpoint of rhythm and meaning which gives the poem, in its uneven and gradual acceleration of movement, an impression of powerful, ineluctable dynamism leading to passionate exhaustion.

> Ruf von lust und grausen hallt im haine
> Vom beginnenden jagen·
> Zitternd tasten hände noch nach locken
> Da verdurstet schon manche
> Heiss von fang und flucht· bespriżt vom safte
> Ausgequollener früchte·
> Blut und speichel harter lippen trinken
> Und auf qualmigen garben
> Andre wechselnd beide blumen küssen
> Auf der brust den Gewählten. (I, 254)

> Cries of lust and terror echo in the vale
> Of the beginning chase,
> For locks of hair the trembling hands still reach,
> When many, thirsting,
> Hot with hunt and flight, sprayed with juice
> Of fruits overripe and flowing,
> Drink from hard lips blood and spittle.
> And on the sweet-smelling sheaves,
> Others kiss in turn the twin flowers
> On the bosom of the chosen one.

The witches in "Hexenreihen" ("Witches' Dance") almost seem to be commenting contemptuously on the previous poem. Familiar with the "thousand dark seeds" of the earth's secrets, they see man's life as a self-deceit. They see beauty only in the dark, pathological aspects of life, and harmony only in chaos:

> Uns ist der tanz im krampfe·
> In wülsten und gekrös
> Sind uns die leiber schön.
> Duft ist im moderdampfe.
> Im wirbelnden getös
> Vernehmen wir getön. (I, 254)

> We see a dance in writhing,
> In tumors and entrails,
> Bodies are lovely to us,
> Aroma's in musty decay,
> In the clangor of chaos
> We hear harmony.

This poem depicts dark, mystical forces beyond the immediate grasp of reason—but also the limitation of these forces—for the witches can see only that which is most common and elementary in man when they strip him of all other properties: "a shape of stone, like a beast's testicles," symbolizing only his lust. The witches see everything else in man, the result of his higher powers, as a delusion.

Beginning with his youth, George had a firm faith in the ability of a communal group of idealistic and disciplined young men to change the world. His conviction that the self-sacrificing, stoic spirit of such groups is ever-present in history as a militant force is manifested in "Templer" ("Knights Templar") (I, 255). The Order of Knights Templar was formed around 1100 to garrison the Christian kingdom of Jerusalem and was dissolved during the late Middle Ages. The Templars in the poem, however, speak in the present tense, in their own time, but also, by implication, in all time. As they describe themselves, they arouse the conscience of mankind in lax and cowardly epochs, compelling the peoples and their rulers to right action. Except for the rare "golden ages" of history, when the will of all men is identical with their own, the Templars lead austere lives remote from the world, almost as a secret order, because, by virtue of their selflessness and the high ethos by which they live, they are regarded with great suspicion. Warlike and devout at once, the Templars' way of life is expressed in two emblems: the rose, symbol of youth's warmth of spirit; and the cross, symbol of suffering proudly borne. Their order despises material gain, and its members are free from the restrictions of ordinary society and family. By consciously living according to a severe and ascetic code, they are able to carry out their redemptive historical function: to compel nature, grown sluggish and stubborn, to bring forth a new generation of better men, in whom the earthly and the divine will be felicitously blended, to make physical man godly and to make God's presence in man visibly incarnate:

Und wenn die grosse Nährerin im zorne
Nicht mehr sich mischend neigt am untern borne·
In einer weltnacht starr und müde pocht:
So kann nur einer der sie stets befocht

Und zwang und nie verfuhr nach ihrem rechte
Die hand ihr pressen· packen ihre flechte·
Dass sie ihr werk willfährig wieder treibt:
Den leib vergottet und den gott verleibt. (I, 256)

And when in wrath the Mighty Mother scorns
To lean and couple at the lower bourns,
Some world-night when her pulses scarcely stir,
Then only one who always strove with her,

Ignored her wishes and denied her will,
Can crush her hand and grip her hair until
Submissively she plies her work afresh:
Turns flesh to god, embodies god in flesh.[11]

For George, the Templars represent the spiritual and physical ancestors of the leading minds in all ages. He hoped that their spirit of selfless service and discipline would infuse his circle, the "hidden Germany" celebrated in the poem "Geheimes Deutschland" (I, 425), which has a strong kinship with "Templer." In "Die Hüter des Vorhofs" ("The Guardians of the Forecourt") (I, 257), the speaker explains his education of a group embodying the spirit of the Templars. The title indicates that the subjects of the poem are still young and entrusted as yet only with the guardianship of the forecourt of the unnamed sanctuary. They are thus placed within a distinct hierarchy of command and obedience, a *sine qua non* of George's pedagogical ideas. Inured to hardship and longing and inspired by hope, the "guardians," like the Templars, are to reawaken the latent primal energies of earth, healing the wounds inflicted by madness and greed. Again, at the conclusion of the poem, the divine provenience of man is stressed, the young men being seen as living testimony to this fact:

Ihr seid des zeichens dass von haft behindert
In rauhen mauern· dass in gleiss und sammet–
Wenn auch bei allen–nie bei euch vermindert
Erinnerung wie ihr von göttern stammet. (I, 257)

You are the sign that even in chains
Midst rough-hewn walls–in riches splendid–
If for all others–never for you wanes
Remembrance that you are from gods descended.

In the latter "Gestalten," the poet treats aspects of the historical primacy of dedicated ascetic groups in determining the fates of men and nations. More than any of the other poems in *Der Siebente Ring,* these prefigure the themes that are to be fully developed in *Der Stern des Bundes* (*The Star of the Covenant*), for what is sounded here is a note of prophetic urgency, an ominously cryptic warning of impending cataclysm. This is particularly suggested by the demonic figure of "Der Widerchrist" ("The Antichrist") (I, 258), whose coming, according to legend, will initiate the events leading to the Day of Judgment. The fatigue of nature described in "Templer"–her inability to bring forth new heroic generations–is echoed by descriptions of a ravaged, infertile earth, the terrestrial reflection of the state of men's souls. Drought, waste, and famine are the symbolic concomitants of evil, of delusions and false goals. A healing of the earth, a fresh flowing of the sources of fertility, and the resolution of the contradictions in man, is the task of the representatives of the heroic spirit in these poems. Especially in "Der Eid" ("The Oath") (I, 260) and "Einzug" ("Processional") (I, 261), are set forth intimations of a coming struggle of these heroic youths against an unnamed "foe," of the coming of a new age in which the spiritual barrenness of the present will yield to new fertility. As it began, the cycle thus ends on a note of struggle: the combat between darkness and light.

The poems contained in "Gezeiten" ("Tides") are far more personal than the hortatory and exemplary first two cycles of *Der Siebente Ring.* George wrote most of them for Friedrich Gundolf and Robert Boehringer. The placement of these poems, immediately preceding the central cycle devoted to Maximin, suggests that the ebb and flow of the relationships reflected here is only an approximation of the transcending, timeless significance of Maximin for George. These poems are passionate and poignant at once. Initially, we encounter the sense of the unseasonableness of the attachment of an older man to one much younger. This is resolved by their intellectual and emotional communion and by their mutual surrender to a friendship which is not lacking in strong sensual aspects.

The kiss and the embrace and the poet's esthetic pleasure at the sight of his friend—these are the outward manifestations of their all-too-brief spiritual rapport. For a time, the poet is elated at the understanding he finds in his younger friend, in the way the world is fresher and more beautiful through his eyes. Soon, however, the sense of the disparity of the friends' vision of the world and each other becomes apparent, and a parting of their ways becomes inevitable. The central metaphor is the rhythm of nature, of the seasons of the year. Its ineluctable course is unified in these poems with the poet's painful knowledge that the relationships celebrated in "Gezeiten" are subject to the same kind of flowering, maturation, and fading away that governs all earthly things:

Wieviel noch fehlte dass das fest sich jähre
Als schon aus einer gelben wolke frost
In spitzen körnern niederfiel! . . So sprosst
Denn keine unsrer saaten ohne zähre?

Für allen heftigen drang und zarten zwist·
So gilt für alle lust die uns erhöhte
Für alle klagen und beweinten nöte
Der eine sonnenumlauf nur als frist.

Herüberhingen schwellend und geklärt
Die traubenbündel an den stöcken gestern·
Die nun zu most der lang im dunkel gärt
Zerstossen werden und zu schaalen trestern.

Muss mit den ernten auch dies glück verfalben·
Verlieren zier um zier mit halm und strauch
Und unaufhaltsam ziehen mit den schwalben·
Verwehen spurlos mit dem sommerrauch? (I, 274)

Our feast day in the year had not recurred,
When early from a yellow cloud the frost
In pointed hailstones fell! . . . Can then
No seed of ours sprout without a tear?

For all our urgent passion, soft dispute,
For all desire exalting us in joy,
For all our plaints and all our many tears,
The term is but a turn around the sun.

The grapes which yesterday hung overhead,
Plump and full of sweetness on the vine,
Will now be bruised to juice that long ferments
In darkness and to mutilated husks.

Must this joy with the harvest too grow pale,
Lose grace and charm as stalk and kernel fall,
And with the swallows wing away in flight,
Ascend without a trace in summer's haze?

It is characteristic for George that he closes the groups of poems which touch most closely upon his personal experiences with an expression of his having overcome the travails he has described, of a new commitment to his chosen life, to his art. This affirmation is rendered by "Lobgesang" ("Song of Praise") (I, 276), in which a naked god, bearing the features of both Dionysus and the Angel of the "Vorspiel," is praised and the poet's dedication to him reaffirmed. The acute pain both of love and poetic creation is intermingled with the praise of the god:

Du rührest an—ein duftiger taumeltrank
Befängt den sinn der deinen odem spürt
Und jede fiber zuckt von deinem schlag.
Der früher nur den Sänftiger dich hiess
Gedachte nicht dass deine rosige ferse
Dein schlanker finger so zermalmen könne. (I, 276)

You touch me—a sweet-smelling elixir
Holds fast the soul which feels your swelling breath
And every fiber trembles at your blow.
Whoever once called you the Comforter
Did not consider that your rosy heel,
Your slender finger could inflict such wounds.

The god himself bears the marks of luxuriance and fertility, and the beasts which follow him the smell and dust of wildness, of ominous destruction. But the poet surrenders to this god of love and creation willingly, for through him a redemption, a triumph over the world, allowing him to endure, is possible:

Kein ding das webt in deinem kreis ist schnöd.
Du reinigst die befleckung· heilst die risse
Und wischst die tränen durch dein süsses wehn.
In fahr und fron· wenn wir nur überdauern·
Hat jeder tag mit einem sieg sein ende—
So auch dein dienst: erneute huldigung
Vergessnes lächeln ins gestirnte blau. (I, 277)

No thing that in your circle moves is base.
You purify defilement, heal the wounds
And dry the tears through your breath sweet and light.
In exile and enslaved—if we survive

Then every day will end in victory—
So too your service—renewed devotion,
A joyous smiling in the starry blue.

In the second edition of his collected prose writings, *Tage und Taten,* published in 1925, Stefan George included a brief paragraph entitled "Kunst und menschliches Urbild" ("Art and the Human Archetype"): "Our flow of life (rhythm) demands, beyond ourselves, an ideal archetype which expresses itself, in many persons, in individual and isolated characteristics, but may also achieve total incarnation approximately and for a time [*zeit- und näherungsweise*]. There is no other explanation for Dante's beloved or for Shakespeare's friend. To seek for a single real Beatrice and the single real W. H. is an idle pastime of the interpreters" (I, 532). This is also implicitly true of the youth celebrated by George as "Maximin" in the fourth and central cycle of *Der Siebente Ring,* and it should be taken as an indication of the irrelevance of concentrating on Maximilian Kronberger in a positivistic fashion. In the "Maximin" poems we find, once more, the concerns of the first three cycles: the spiritual poverty of the times, the attempt to overcome this poverty through the depiction of exemplary mythic prototypes, and the evanescence and insufficiency of human relationships. In Maximin, George's search for the heroic spirituality lacking in his age, and present only fleetingly in other youths, reaches its fulfillment.

In an age tacitly or explicitly atheistic, in which men seek salvation from their lot through the "miraculous" achievements of science and technology, Stefan George was a god-seeker in the most immediate sense. From his early youth onward, he had been unable to accept the teachings of the Catholic Church into which he had been born. Like Klopstock and Hölderlin, the German poets of the "vatic" tradition before him, George sought intimations of the divine presence in the immediate world of his experience, refusing to acknowledge that man's innate sinfulness denied him such knowledge until after death. For him, it was the function of the poet to make manifest the symbolic expressions of the divine spirit wherever he encountered them and to seek the realization of the *Urbild.* It is the essential intent of the "Zeitgedichte" and the "Gestalten," to show a divinity perceivable in its manifestations in man here and now. George once said: "Writing poetry is an un-Christian act,"[12] unchristian because it affirms, celebrates, and interprets the presence of a numinous spirit that is immanently present in the world. For George, poetry in its essence cannot point to a world beyond but must work with the symbolic phenomena of the world men know or have experienced. The proofs of God's being are perhaps evident in history ("There was only one thing, which ever made [God's] existence seem plausible to me: the existence of the Greeks")[13] but even more immediately in man's soul and in man's approximations to godliness. The question is poignantly and tellingly put in the second of the "Gebete" ("Prayers") from "Maximin":

Ist uns dies nur amt: mit schauern
Zu vernehmen dein gedröhn
Und im staub vernichtet kauern
Vor dir Furchtbarer der Höhn?

Warum schickst du dann die sommer
Wo wir schnellen frei und nackt?
Wo sich nachbar nennt dein frommer·
Helle raserei ihn packt?

Was erlaubst du uns die räusche
Wo der stolz allmächtig pocht·
Uns in Deine nähe täusche·
All dein tosen in uns kocht–

Wirbel uns aus niedrer zelle
Sternenan entführt geschwind:
Deinesgleichen in der welle
In der wolke in dem wind? (I, 289)

Is but this our lot: with terror
To receive your thunder
And in the dust distraught to cower
Before you, God of awesome heights?

Why then do you send the summers,
When naked we exult and free?
When our brethren with devotion
Are gripped by radiant ecstasy?

Why do you intoxicate us,
So that pride overpowering throbs,
Make us seem to feel your nearness,
All your raging in us boils,

From our lowly cells the whirlwind,
Starwards swiftly raises us,
Are we like you in the wave,
In the cloud and in the wind?

If God is the distant Thunderer of the Old Testament and the equally far-off Father of the New Testament, to whom the only path lies through his Son, the Redeemer, how can man have such an exalted sense of his own godliness in moments of Dionysian ecstasy, of harmony with nature? The question is left unanswered, but in its asking the faith that knowledge of a higher life is accessible to men is implicit; and this is the central concept of George's celebration of Maximin. There is no question of the creation of a "new god" or the establishment of a cult. What George has rediscovered for himself is the "incarnation of the divine" as expressed in "Templer" (I, 256), a valid revelation that what he had always hoped and believed is true and that divine power is actively present in the world and strives for its own physical realization in man. For George, this striving was, if only momentarily, achieved in the youth Maximin, whose physical and spiritual state at the time George knew him seemed miraculously to agree with the poet's long-cherished spiritual and esthetic *urbild*.

The "Maximin" cycle consists of twenty-one poems arranged in six groups. The first three poems of the central group of six, entitled "Auf das Leben und den Tod Maximins" ("On the Life and Death of Maximin"), were published in the memorial volume *Maximin: ein Gedenkbuch* in 1906, together with poetic tributes from Karl Wolfskehl, Friedrich Gundolf, and other friends of George, and a selection of poems by Maximin himself. It is in the central cycle of *Der Siebente Ring* that the meaning which Maximin had for George reaches its fullest expression, elucidating the new urgency of the "Zeitgedichte," the hermetic symbols of the "new life" set forth in "Gestalten" and in the passionately personal "Gezeiten."

The first three groups of poems—"Kunfttag" ("Advent") I, II, III; "Erwiderungen" ("Responses"); "Trauer" ("Mourning") I, II, III (I, 279-83)—express the existential significance of the encounter with Maximin for the poet. The full cycle of joy and anguish, from the coming of the youth to his death and the poet's desolation, runs its course in these nine poems. George's vision of Maximin is stated in the first poem with almost provocative frankness:

> Dem bist du kind· dem freund.
> Ich seh in dir den Gott
> Den schauernd ich erkannt
> Dem meine andacht gilt. (I, 279)
>
> To some you are child, friend to some.
> I see in you the God

Whom trembling I saw,
Who is my worship's goal.

George believed that the divine had taken, and could still take, many forms in the world, the Dionysian god celebrated at the end of "Gezeiten" and Christ being only two of many possibilities. The *urbild* in each man represents the striving for this divinity, and for George the realization of this *urbild* was Maximin. Contained in the assertion "Ich seh in dir den Gott," however, is its own self-restriction as the poet's subjective vision. The poet's self is the mediating link between his vision of the godly as embodied in Maximin and the expression of this vision in the poem. The presence of *ich, meine* in the third and fourth lines, reinforces the personal nature of the statement. The concentration on the poet's self is maintained throughout the poem:

Du kamst am lezten tag
Da ich von harren siech
Da ich des betens müd
Mich in die nacht verlor:

Du an dem strahl mir kund
Der durch mein dunkel floss·
Am tritte der die saat
Sogleich erblühen liess. (I, 279)

You came on that last day
When I of waiting sick
When I from prayer fatigued
Lost myself in the night:

You known to me by the ray
Which through my darkness flowed,
By the step 'neath which the seed
At once began to sprout.

In all of the "Kunfttag" poems, the "I-Thou" relationship, the personal communion of the poet with Maximin, is primary. It is the fulfillment of the relationships described in "Gezeiten," which approximated but did not achieve this epiphany, in which the world seems transformed and newly fertile as seen by the purified vision of the poet, whose heart is sanctified through his perception of the divine force. Thus, "Kunfttag III" concludes:

Eh blöd der menschen sinn
Ihm ansann wort und tat
Hat schon des schöpfers hauch
Jed ding im raum beseelt.

Wenn solch ein auge glüht
Gedeiht der trockne stamm·
Die starre erde pocht
Neu durch ein heilig herz. (I, 280)

Ere the dull mortal sense
Conceived his word and deed
Each thing's inspired with soul
From the Creator's breath.

When such an eye does glow
The driest branch will thrive,
The barren earth will throb
Anew through a holy heart.

The three "Erwiderungen" affirm the personal validity of the redemptive confrontation. The *du* addressed in "Das Wunder" ("The Miracle") (I, 280) and "Einführung" ("Introit") (I, 281)—the poet's self—is one who has searched for the divine presence and vainly implored that "He" might reveal himself. In his quest, he has touched forbidden regions, has descended from his former heights and has been "lost in a dark valley." In "Das Wunder," the poet admonishes himself to understand the "miracle" of "His" ways, in this case the fusion of the poet's dream with that of the "Messenger" sent by "Him," who has sought out the poet by virtue of the dignity of his art. In "Einführung," this "Messenger" is compared to an angel whose kiss "burns to purity" and sanctifies the earth, redeeming the soul from its despair and setting the poet in a sacred grove of fertility and warmth: "You have drunken from the source:/ Enter the open fields!/ Through violet-meadows the yellow wheat-stalk shows,/ In the grove the altars glow/ With roses wreathed..." (I, 281). The encounter with the Angel-Messenger is an intensification of the transformation described in so many guises in "Gezeiten," where the poet's view of an arid and cold world is suddenly transformed to the vision of a glowing, fertile landscape through the words and the proximity of the friend. The metamorphosis is now a sacred act, and the world is magically sanctified. Spring (the violets) and the harvest (the ears of grain) co-exist, and time, so tormenting in "Gezeiten," is miraculously suspended.

The third of the "Erwiderungen," "Die Verkennung" ("The Mistaking") (I, 281), is a parabolic variation on the failure of Mary Magdalene and the disciples to recognize Jesus after the Resurrection (John, 20:14 and 21:4). The despairing disciple complains to a stranger that his Lord, who has "risen to Heaven," has forgotten him in his new glory. The stranger attempts to soothe the disciple's suffering, but is rebuffed. Only by the celestial radiance which lingers after the stranger disappears does the disciple realize what his "blind pain and sick longing" had not let him see: it was the Lord who had come and gone. Neither the biblical events on which the parable is based nor Maximin are directly alluded to. The poem is clearly a self-admonition, however, against failing to recognize the presence of divinity, no matter how modest its guise, or how deep the despair of being apparently abandoned by its sustaining force. The voice of Maximin gives a similar admonition in the first of the poems entitled "Trauer" (I, 282), when the poet is racked with remorse and pain at the loss of Maximin, at not having been allowed to die in his stead: "Let me to the Heavens ascend!/ Arise now as one who is healed!/ Witness and praise my grace/ And wait with the living below!" (I, 282).

In the poems "On the Life and Death of Maximin," George's recognition of this "grace" takes on its most intense form. He exhorts his friends to take courage and to despair no longer in expectation of a coming doom, for a god, whose mediation George saw in the being of Maximin, had signaled their salvation. Thus, in the first poem of the group, there appear the words:

Vereint euch froh da ihr nicht mehr beklommen
Vor lang verwichner pracht erröten müsst:
Auch ihr habt eines gottes ruf vernommen
Und eines gottes mund hat euch geküsst.

Nun klagt nicht mehr—denn auch ihr wart erkoren—
Dass eure tage unerfüllt entschwebt . . .
Preist eure stadt die einen gott geboren!
Preist eure zeit in der ein gott gelebt! (I, 284)

Unite in joy since you no more in shame
Must blush before a splendor long since gone.
You too have heard the call of a god's voice,
And a god's kiss has touched upon your lips.

You have been chosen—now complain no more
That unfulfilled your days do drift away.
Your city praise which to a god gave birth,
And praise your age in which a god has lived.

George celebrates the coming of the incarnate god in Maximin as a recurrence of the "Hellenic miracle," the perfect union of spirit and flesh in the *leib,* the human form, which is the symbol of this unity, of which Maximin is the highest expression. George exhorts his hearers no longer to stand shamed by the perfection of the "splendor long-since gone" of Grecian statues, which captured the unity of matter and spirit implicit in the culture of ancient Greece for George, as they had for the German classical tradition. As an example of the incarnation of the divine, Christ is evoked in the second poem of the group, "Wallfahrt" ("Pilgrimage"), in which the dreary urban landscape of Berlin, where Maximilian Kronberger was born, is described, the hospital being compared, by implication, to the Manger: "This house so like all others is our goal./ With bared heads we see the barren hall/ From which you went into the world. . . . Did not three wise men/ Once follow a star to a stable?" (I, 285). The departed Maximin has undergone an apotheosis, but is still watching over men "in unapproachable majesty," assumed into higher realms in answer to a summons of which he had been aware in life. He is "one with the Word that spoke from above" ("eins/ mit dem Wort das von oben uns sprach") (I, 285), at one with God, whom George evokes in his manifestation of *logos*, as in the Gospel according to Saint John (1:1).

Maximin is regarded purely from the standpoint of his validity as a manifestation of transcendent spirituality, as evidenced by his exceptional physical beauty and the sensitivity of his poetic perception of the world. He is "the angel," the "glorious one," the "fire in the thornbush." To George, the highest imperative is now to make manifest his memory in order to regenerate out of longing and his recollection of the living Maximin the full beauty of his transcendent essence:

Was du zu deines erdentags begehung
Gespendet licht und stark
Das biete jeder dar zur auferstehung
Bis du aus unsrem mark

Aus aller schöne der wir uns entsonnen
Die ständig in uns blizt
Und aus des sehnens zuruf leib gewonnen
Und lächelnd vor uns trittst. (I, 287)

What you in deeds within your earthly day,
Poured forth so bright and strong,
Of that let each one now his offering make
Until, from our very marrow, you

From all the beauty which we ever dreamed,
Which always gleams within us,
And from the call of longing win new form,
And smiling stand before us.

Maximin's "command" to the circle of mourners is now to contain their pain, to "strew so many flowers, that we cannot see the grave." In the final poem of this group, the poet, having been shown the "far-off land" of purity and wholeness by the "messenger of joy" (*Du freudenbote*), becomes the medium of his praise: "Now your name rings out through endless spheres/ To purify our heart and mind/ On the dark ground of eternity/ Through me your star now rises" (I, 288). In "Einverleibung" ("Incarnation") (I, 291), a poem strongly reminiscent in meter and mood of Goethe's "Selige Sehnsucht," George seems to fulfill the exhortation to create out of the memory of Maximin and his intimations of Maximin's continued spiritual presence and unity with him, a new spiritual entity. George feels that Maximin has bound him in a new covenant, that he is reborn through the fact of Maximin's having lived and having been revealed to him. Paradoxically, George is "Ich geschöpf nun eignen sohnes" (I, creation of my son"). Maximin's spirit in the poet is the seed of a new creation of the poet's desire and memory:

Mein verlangen hingekauert
Labest du mit deinem seime.
Ich empfange von dem keime
Von dem hauch der mich umdauert:

Dass aus schein und dunklem schaume
Dass aus freudenruf und zähre
Unzertrennbar sich gebäre
Bild aus dir und mir im traume. (I, 291)

With your nectar you still nourish
All my longing cowering here
From the seed which I receive,
From your aura which surrounds me:

That from brightness and dark foaming,
That from cries of joy and weeping,
Inseparably is born an image
Out of you and me in dreams.

The merging of *traum und traum*, described as taking place during Maximin's life in "Das Wunder" (I, 280), the evocation of his spiritual perfection to obliterate the knowledge of his mortality, is here realized in the generation of a new *Bild*, a new archetype in the poet and a fulfillment of the *Denkbild*, the *Urbild* whose realization he had always been seeking in the highest human expression of physical and spiritual beauty.

The frequent occurrence of the term *Traum* in significant contexts of the poems leading to and embracing the phenomenon of Maximin indicates that, ultimately, this encounter has its pro-foundest meaning for George on a subjective level beyond the world of forms in a realm of magical ideality. The composite image engendered in his spiritual unity with Maximin exists *im traume*. In "Gezeiten," the supreme realization of the personal encounter was described as a commingling of dreams. The group of poems immediately following "Maximin" is entitled "Traumdunkel" ("Dream Darkness"), in which an inner world of memory and myth is explored. Throughout the Maximin poems, there is apparent a strong emphasis on the subjective experience, whose intensity is measured in esthetic and erotic terms rather than as a morally normative regeneration. Maximin seems to emerge as a personal "savior," a redeemer of George's faith in the existence of a divine will in the world, of powers of supernatural strength and capable of astonishing beauty. At first glance, there appears to be little relationship between the esthetic adulation of these poems and the declaration of war against a decadent and materialistic society sounded so fiercely in the "Zeitgedichte." For George, however, this involved no contradiction. He believed that moral goodness and, therefore, the social good, would arise out of each man's realization and manifestation of his own human dignity and beauty, out of a re-established wholeness of the material and spiritual aspects of existence. It was precisely in the perpetuation of the dichotomy between matter and spirit that George saw the major ills of Western civilization. Maximin represented for him an exhortation to reconcile this division in the Greek sense of the *kalokagathia*, "the good and beautiful."

The ethical meaning of the figure of Maximin is only adumbrated in the poems of *Der Siebente Ring;* it is more clearly set forth in the *Gedenkbuch für Maximin*. There, in the foreword, George describes how Maximin changed his view of the present and made reality correspond to a new standard of ideality. The appearance of this "savior" made all social and political questions seem illusory in the light of the great possible renewal which his coming seemed to promise. The renewal must begin in the soul of each individual, since help cannot come from the outside to ameliorate his condition. Rather, the individual, in his constant progression toward perfection of soul and body inspired by the archetype of Maximin, will, in his turn, make the world around him better in every way. "Then no one will any longer shake his head in reproaching a selfish isolation which is not concerned with the sufferings of fellow men; for the greatest benefactor of all is he, who fulfills his own beauty to the point of the miraculous" (I, 526).

A new sense for the worth of each individual, his transcendence of all social and biological determinism into a higher form of physical and spiritual being, then, represented for George the temporal solution of the moral depravity of mankind excoriated in the "Zeitgedichte." It is a reassertion of the Platonic ideal of the individual living according to the dictates of his own spirit, thus benefiting the entire *polis,* because the intimations of this spirit cannot be other than good. In his opposition to Naturalism, the artistic expression of the doctrines of social, economic, and biological determinism, George is entirely consistent with his optimism concerning the human soul, which must be confronted with visible proof of its worth and beauty in human incarnation to master the ills of man's existence.

The final poem of the "Maximin" cycle bears the title "Entrükkung," which can be understood either as "withdrawal" or "enchantment." George sees the world in which he has just lived so intensely fade away as he grows more and more distant from it in time and space. He senses the air from other realms, calling him forth from his celebration of Maximin, showing him new lands of clarity and freedom from heights of supreme knowledge above the "clouds" of human perception. His unity with the divine forces evoked in "Maximin" makes him only a part of a cosmic whole: "I am a mere spark of the holy fire/ I am a mere throbbing of the holy voice" (I, 293). The poetic vocation, autonomous and living beyond the poet's own will, uses him as a vessel, withdraws him from his prophetic stance, and does with him what it will.

George returns to the craft of poetry, to a realm of symbolic reality, in "Traumdunkel" ("Dream Darkness"). In this cycle, individual poems and smaller groupings have their own expressive integrity. The earlier sense of dialectic interrelation, in which poems seemed to comment on or intensify each other's meaning, is no longer evident. While the "Lieder" and "Tafeln" are loosely linked by a commonalty of intention, the poems in "Traumdunkel" range widely in their form and content, thus exhibiting the full scope of George's poetic practice. At times, they show the brilliant atmospheric lyricism of *Das Jahr der Seele;* at other times the esthetic objectivity of *Der Teppich des Lebens* and various aspects found in the earlier cycles of *Der Siebente Ring.*

In the first poem, "Eingang" ("Entry") (I, 294), George briefly bids farewell to the "world of forms," that is, to objective reality, in favor of an imaginative inner world, a symbolic autumnal forest of white trunks, whose pristine color is relieved only by the blue of the sky and rare glimpses of gold and carnelian of the foliage and fruits of fall. In the midst of this austere nature, and emblematic of the poet's sense of the approaching autumn of his life, stands a marble fountain, from which the water flows drop by drop, like grains falling into a silver bowl. The fountain symbolizes the poet's artistic impulse, ineluctable but ebbing. It stands in a cool twilight realm of enchanted anticipation, awaiting the quickening forces of inspiration, whose coming is implored with the words "Traumfittich rausche! Traumharfe kling!" ("Wing of dreams rustle! Harp of dreams, sound!") (I, 294). Through the explicit departure from one realm of experience into another, George is at pains to separate the plane of the mythico-religious, on which the "Maximin" poems moved, from that of artistic inspiration and integration of objective reality into a higher form, the plane of "Traumdunkel." It is the dark dream world of poetry itself, of the poetic experience and imagination, into which we are guided. Here, elemental human experiences, such as love, loss, inspiration, and death, coexist with intimations of otherworldly cosmic powers, the pageant of the history of George's native Rhineland with mythic descriptions of Dionysian rites for a terrifying god.

"Ursprünge" ("Origins") (I, 294) is said to have been written to fill the empty pages of the seventh volume of the *Blätter*, which was published in 1904; it appeared at the end of the volume without George's name.[14] The "origins" celebrated here are George's own—the landscape of the Rhine—in which he felt the surviving Germanic and Roman paganism underlying the stern Catholicism of the region, which had subjected the free, naked bodies of pagan men to its discipline, substituting for the healthy mean of Roman philosophy the dichotomy between spiritual ecstasy and despairing negation of man's fleshly existence. But children still hear the voices of the past, making them rulers of their universe, and speaking to them in a mystical language: "Sweet and inspiring as Attica's chorus/ Over the hills and the islands rang:/ Co besoso pasoje ptoros/ Co es on hama pasoje boañ" (I, 295). This is the only remaining example of George's personal secret language to appear in his poetry. This language was a development beyond the secret language "Imri" he had invented in his childhood. Although, assuming that the language is analogous to Romance languages, it would be possible to decipher this passage, its intention here is primarily musical, its actual meaning adding little to the understanding of the poem. The children involved presumably have no intellectual cognition of it either, but merely an indistinct intimation of its meaningfulness, which is the effect George wishes to convey to the reader.[15]

In the following poems—the three collectively entitled "Landschaft" ("Landscape") (I, 296-98) and "Nacht" ("Night") (I, 299)

—inward experience is inextricably integrated with a glowingly depicted landscape, modulated precisely to the mood which the poem conveys. In "Landschaft I" the "darkened mind" (*der trübe sinn*) of the protagonist has lost its way in autumnal woods fraught with the red shadings of suffering, the foliage taking on the connotative value of blood:

> Des jahres wilde glorie durchläuft
> Der trübe sinn der mittags sich verlor
> In einem walde wo aus spätem flor
> Von safran rost und purpur leiden träuft.
>
> Und blatt um blatt in breiten flecken fällt
> Auf schwarze glätte eines trägen bronns
> Wo schon des dunkels grausamer gespons
> Ein knabe kühlen auges wache hält . . (I, 296)
>
> The sad soul that at midday lost its way
> Roams through the late wild glory of the year
> In a wood where the foliage last to stay
> Drops suffering in saffron, rust, and scarlet tears.
>
> And leaf on leaf in patches broad does fall
> On inky smoothness of a quiet pool
> Where now the fearful mate of dark,
> A youth with cool eyes stands on guard . . .

Objectively, this youth is a statue in the park landscape. As the landscape simultaneously represents a terrain of the soul, he is the "fearful mate of night," the angel of death, whose power seems to grow as the sun sets, heavy and bright yellow, in the silent loneliness of the darkening wood. The "soul" stumbles forward to a wall covered with thorny plants, to which flowering nightshades cling. He thinks, "would slumber only come to this thicket," leaving undecided whether the tangled confusion of the physical thicket or that of his mind is meant. At this point, where the surrender seems imminent to physical exhaustion, to the longing for darkness and death, a new vista opens to the eye, a light reflected from the blue of a lake. A new hope of freedom becomes apparent, and the agonizing tension of the poem, the sense of imprisonment in a maze, is resolved with the falling "of blossoms upon open water," blue and silver, cool and pure, in contrast to the tortured reds and yellows of suffering found in the poem's beginning. Kurt Hildebrandt justly calls this poem dreamlike in its interchange of the external and the internal levels of perception, its ambiguity of discourse, which lend to it its compelling force and artistic perfection.[16]

In the "Landschaft" poems, George pursues the attempt to create landscapes which are at once tangibly natural and immanently symbolic. The phenomena depicted are to have an innate transcendent expressiveness without further interpretation by the poet through simile or other rhetorical devices. It is almost as if George were trying to create in these poems an impression of the universe so intense that Goethe's dictum in the poem "Epirrhema" would be manifested in its truth:

> Müsset im Naturbetrachten
> Immer eins wie alles achten;
> Nichts ist drinnen, nichts ist draußen:
> Denn was innen, das ist außen.
> So ergreifet ohne Säumnis
> Heilig öffentlich Geheimnis.[17]
>
> Viewing Nature you must see
> Each thing as the totality;
> Nothing is inner, nothing outer,
> For the inner *is* the outer.
> So now grasp without delay,
> The sacred secret–clear as day.

More succinctly, Goethe said: "Do not look behind the phenomena; they themselves are the truth." Precisely such expressive phenomena, revealed by the sensibility and skill of the poet, are presented in these poems. The woods in which the lovers in "Landschaft II" (I, 297) lose their way, experiencing "our wayward wandering, our joyous thrall," seem to encompass only an anecdotal occurrence in a warmly colorful October atmosphere. By the middle of the poem, however, it is clear that the brook, which they have followed to the point where they can no longer hear its beckoning, assumes the archetypal significance of the stream of Fate itself, leading the lovers to where "the path" and "the light" elude them. In this context, suddenly turned allegorical through the productive ambiguity of "stream," "way," and "light," "a child, still picking berries late" shows the lovers "the right way" (*die rechte richtung*) through the thickets. They who have, "in tender quarrel," pursued differing but parallel paths, take this path together and finally emerge into an open vista of flowery fields leading them to the "lovely goal" (*zum schönen ziele*). The child, relatively innocuous on the narrative level of the poem, on the allegorical level takes on the function of Eros in the complex of attributes characteristic of the god Dionysus, whose Bacchic identity is hinted at by the fact that the child is picking berries. Parallel to the matter of the poem, the walk through the woods, a merging of two human lives through the confrontation with love is represented in such a way that the narrative and symbolic levels of experience are unitary, almost inaccessible to analysis.

This integrative technique is also employed in the last poem of this group, in which the poet, preparing for a long, difficult journey through rough mountain passes, bids farewell to his sleeping younger companion, who has come this far with him, but will go no further. He will return to the fertile lowlands, while the poet will go on alone:

> In narrow clefts of everlasting ice,
> Past snow-decked craggy mountain cliffs,
> I reach the threatening giant blocks,
> Where frozen waters stand in barren veins.
>
> The winds already blow through last scant pines,
> Midst stony rubble the ascent is rougher, harder,
> Where every trail is quickly lost in darkness,
> I hear the dark harps of the abyss throb. (I, 298)

The forbidding landscape of the mountains simultaneously becomes symbolic of the awesome isolation and peril of the artist's path in areas of experience where few can follow him.

"Der verwunschene Garten" ("The Enchanted Garden") (I, 300f.) is an attempt to endow an idyllic legend with an other-worldly magical atmosphere through the skillful use of metrical and auditory qualities. The events of this *Märchen* present themselves to the poet at sunset in a formal park, a vision of a prince and princess, wedded but doomed to live apart and in sadness. For all of her delicate loveliness, the princess is unable to express her love for the prince, who, in turn, by virtue of the diadem weighing heavily on his brow, cannot subject himself to the bond of love. They meet only once a year in a melancholy, yet tender ritual, whose meaning is comprehensible only to those who feel the "nobility and grace of all that is fragile and shy" (I, 301). A strong pictorial quality pervades the poem, a decorativeness congruous with the art of *Jugendstil* so evident in the stress on color and line, which is reminiscent of the stained-glass tableaux of George's friend, Melchior Lechter. The colors associated with the princess are sea-green and silver, while the prince, pale as alabaster, lives in a scarlet-and-gold chamber and raises his arms in sadness into the dark blue of the evening sky. The restrained pathos and opulent decorum of the encounter and parting of the prince and princess demonstrates the interest in texture and color expressed in similes referring to precious stones:

Wonne durchrieselt der schauenden kreis der sich kniet
Der seiner höchsten entzückung so lange entriet:
Spitzen opalener finger zu küssen und kaum
Dieser sandalen und mäntel juwelenen saum—
Also erhebt sich in tränen manch stummes gebet. (I, 301)

Ecstasy thrills through the circle of watchers who kneel,
Who too long the rapture supreme could not feel:
Tips of fingers of opal to kiss: less to them
Are the slippers so fine, the jeweled garments hem—
Thus there comes forth with their tears a mute prayer.

The flowing dactylic meter of "Der verwunschene Garten"—the artful use of vowel quality and occasional alliteration to lend musical shading—supports the melancholy grace of the figures of George's fable. According to Ernst Morwitz, George intended, beyond the exploration of metrical and musical possibilities, to depict in this poem "the fate of modern persons," the inability to surrender to love because of an estranging sense of individual autonomy and a decay of the primeval strength of passion. These persons are shown in a setting of haunting beauty and melancholy, the garment of an imaginary past for a modern problem.[18] In its tone, the poem is similar to many found in the early *Buch der Hängenden Gärten.* Several of the remaining poems of "Traumdunkel" are also reminiscent of earlier volumes and of previous cycles of *Der Siebente Ring* itself. Some of them, like "Feier" (I, 303), "Litanei" (I, 305), and "Ellora" (I, 306), celebrate essential religiosity, by turns pagan and Christian, in a manner similar to some of the "Gestalten." Two poems reflect the central concern of "Traumdunkel," the foundations and limits of the dream realm of poetry. "Stimmen der Wolken-Töchter" ("Voices of the Cloud Children") (I, 302) posits the existence of supernatural forces, embodied in analogy to a Celtic myth,[19] in legendary "Cloud-Children," who love men and wish to commune with them but who are regarded by them as insubstantial, an unfulfilled dream and figment of the imagination. The only medium through which they can manifest themselves is, by implication, the poet. But he himself is a man "from the wooded valleys, of the weightier blood," who must tame his desires for the sake of communion with these evanescent but beautiful beings, who promise rich harvests in return for patience and self-discipline. A comparison of this poem with "Gespräch" (I, 20) shows the constancy of George's thematic concerns.

In marked contrast with this gentle view of artistic inspiration and communion with higher, unseen powers, "Empfängnis" ("Conception") (I, 304) depicts the visitation of "the god" with men as a violent event. A total conquest of the poet's being occurs, an immersion in the heaving storm which has entered his soul in a way strongly suggestive of the act of love. The poem ends with a plea to the unnamed *du* which has possessed him: "So that no sound in me throbs/ Other than fitting to you/ Subject me to your yoke./ Blanket me in embracing clouds/ Consecrate me as your vessel!/ Fill me: I lie and listen!" (I, 305). We have encountered this idea of an act of spiritual "conception," from which the birth of a new being of the spirit or *Bild* goes forth, in "Einverleibung" in the "Maximin" poems. Similar motifs are found in the "Vorspiel" of *Der Teppich des Lebens.* In "Empfängnis" and "Einverleibung," the similarity between inspiration and the act of love is expressed through the use of the term "conception" to describe the violence and all-encompassing love and tenderness of the event. The *du,* whose identity is not further specified, fills the *ich* with new light and multiplies his vision a hundredfold. The "secret" flows out of the violent storm into the poet's self, which is warmed by the "grace," scourged by the "greatness." This poem foreshadows a more explicit statement in the third book of *Der Stern des Bundes.* In "Ein wissen gleich für alle heisst betrug," George describes the third and highest level of ecstatic true wisdom beyond instinct and intellect as in the sole possession of those "with whom the god has lain" ("nur wen der gott beschlief") (I, 387). Ernst Morwitz points out that the intimate union of mortals with gods is a primeval symbol of the supreme infusion of the soul with the divine essence.[20]

"Traumdunkel" concludes with the poem "Hehre Harfe" ("Sublime Harp") (I, 307), in which the meaning of the entire cycle is compressed. Man must seek the answers to the evils which beset him in the world within himself, where the roots of these evils are. Relationships of reverence and love are the goals of man's inmost feelings and longings; he must not seek remedies outside himself. These elemental inward impulses must be hearkened to and followed:

> Alles seid ihr selbst und drinne:
> Des gebets entzückter laut
> Schmilzt in eins mit jeder minne·
> Nennt sie Gott und freund und braut! (I, 307)

> You yourselves are all—within you:
> The ecstatic sound of prayer
> With every love merges in union,
> Call it God and friend and bride!

Man must not seek to learn more of the "truth" of life than he can see and experience in his allotted span or sense in the phenomena surrounding him of the glory of the world. The poem closes in an advocacy of ecstatic praise, of *rühmen,* which seems to anticipate Rilke's existential conclusions concerning the meaning of life. Nature itself holds the secret, is the secret: the flowers and the stars are not merely symbols of a higher will but its manifestations. One of these manifestations, held back from this realization by his reason, by his mad compulsion to analyze and learn, is man himself, whose highest moment of union with the cosmic forces in the world is in the act of astonished admiration and unstinting praise:

> Hegt den wahn nicht: mehr zu lernen
> Als aus staunen überschwang
> Holden blumen hohen sternen
> EINEN sonnigen lobgesang. (I, 307)
>
> Cast out the mad wish to learn more
> Than to sing from wonder's excess
> To gracious blooms and far-off stars
> A *single* sunny song of praise.

The group of twenty-eight "Lieder" ("Songs") constitutes a transition between the symbolic domain of "Traumdunkel" and the poet's direct involvement with his contemporaries and their world in "Tafeln" ("Tablets"). As the next-to-last cycle in *Der Siebente Ring,* they are structurally in a symmetrical relationship with the second cycle, "Gestalten." Some of these "songs" are distinctly lyrical, particularly in "Lieder I-VI" (I, 308-11), where the eloquently simple statement of medieval German lyrics or the delicate indirection of Japanese *haiku* is often achieved. For the most part, however, the poems are no more songlike or musical than those of "Gezeiten" or "Traumdunkel." The distinction is one of intention rather than form. "Traumdunkel" was concerned primarily with the shifting dialogue between the artist and reality, with problems of perception and depiction, of creating a poetic reality which is both concrete and transcendingly symbolic. The "Lieder," on the other hand, are much closer to being *Erlebnisdichtung,* the concentrated experience of various stages of George's life and thought, now ready to be brought before the poet's circle of listeners. The song implies the singer and the audience. The three inner "rings" of *Der Siebente Ring*—"Gezeiten," "Maximin," and "Traumdunkel"—are, by their very nature, private, the product of the poet's innermost experiences, and are addressed to a single *du* or represent an interior dialogue. The four "peripheral" groups—"Zeitgedichte,"

"Gestalten," "Lieder," and "Tafeln"—are, as their titles imply, more public.

Many of the "Lieder" reflect personal relationships at various stages of George's life, some of them reaching back into the last decade of the nineteenth century. Kurt Hildebrandt asserts that the group "Lieder I-VI" is the document of George's problematic relationship with the painter Sabine Lepsius during the years 1903-6.[21] The following group of three poems reflects the poet's resigned affection for a twelve-year-old Argentinian boy of German parentage, Hugo Zernik, who is also the subject of the "Tafel," "Ugolino."[22] The most remarkable poems, from the biographical standpoint, however, are "Fenster wo ich einst mit dir . . ." ("Windows where I once with you . . .") (I, 317) and "Wenn ich auf deiner brücke steh . . ." ("When I stand upon your bridge . . .") (I, 319). Both poems are reminiscences of George's friendship with Ida Coblenz, which ended in 1896. In both, the sense of the poet as one desolated and alone, experiencing a sense of irreparable loss —very much like the death of a loved one—is strikingly expressed.

Yet another poem, "Darfst du bei nacht und bei tag" ("May you by night and day . . .") (I, 319), the so-called Vampire Poem, like the "Last Letter" in *Tage und Taten,* is a source of disagreement between Ernst Morwitz and Kurt Hildebrandt. In the poem, a *du* is addressed, a "shade" which haunts the poet, demanding its part of his living substance, intermingling pain in all of his joys. The plaint is ambivalent, however, for the victim admits that he derives a strange pleasure from being thus haunted and can only pose a possible determination to exorcise the spirit in terms of a question: "Sated with torment, will I/ Now stint in my tribute to you?/ Force you down into your casket/ And into your heart drive the stake?" (I, 319). Ernst Morwitz[23] believes that both the poem and the letter refer to Hugo von Hofmannsthal, with whom George had broken in 1906, whereas Hildebrandt[24] sees Ida Coblenz as the object of the love-hate expressed in these pieces. Internal evidence does not shed any light on this question. Whatever the answer, the very evocation of these central personalities of George's earlier life is significant, indicating that, in the "Lieder," George is coming to terms with the past and is drawing a personal balance of his life's experience at this crucial time, preparing to turn with determination to the world of the present and to whatever tasks the future and his new, self-elected role as a teacher might bring.

Even the last three "Lieder," which relate directly to Maximin, are restrained and resigned in their tone. The human encounter belongs as much to the past as do the earlier experiences evoked in this group. The god, whose embodiment the youth had been, is now "distant and on high" (I, 322), the poet in a desolate landscape, long out of the "zones of light" in which he had "reigned and loved." Only the whispering of twigs, like a voice, accompanies him, giving direction to his aimless existence; it is the voice of a *Du,* perhaps God, perhaps the poet's own ideal, his *Denkbild*:

> Nirgends weiss ich ziel und steg
> Wem zu freude wem zu nutze
> Und ich weiss mich nur im schutze:
> Bin auch hier auf Deinem weg. (I, 323)
>
> End and way I nowhere find,
> For whose joy or good I live,
> I only know I am protected,
> Here too I am on your path.

As Michael Winkler points out,[25] the last of the "Lieder," in which the poet bids farewell to his friends, who have shared his vigil of mourning and adoration for Maximin, betrays a sense of bitterness and disappointment. The friends, in their gestures and their expressions, now beg to be released; the poet needs his peace from them. The "stronger flood" of Fate, of death, has closed over the longing, the "surging flame" of the memory of the mortal Maximin. Only the *Du,* the inner essence of the experience, once more unified with the poet's ideal, remains; with it he must commune in isolation, freed from the outward accidents of remembered form, the distortions of the recollections of others. The "Lieder" not connected with a specific personal encounter also share the theme of leave-taking, of a resigned reckoning with the past, and of setting out for new heights, more lonely, but more promising of fulfillment. In the poem "Wir blieben gern bei eurem reigen drunten" ("Gladly we'd stay in your circle below") (I, 318), George is speaking as a poet, a wandering being on a special quest, very much in the sense of Novalis' sublime depiction of the poet's nature in *Heinrich von Ofterdingen.* The poet is drawn to the joys of this world and participates in them fleetingly and celebrates them, but ultimately must move on to sparser, colder landscapes.

> Auf dass für unser fährdevolles wallen
> Einmal uns lohnt des reinsten glückes kost:
> Uns nah am abgrund azurn und kristallen
> Die wunderblume sprosst. (I, 318)
>
> So that, for our perilous journey,
> The taste of purest joy will once reward us,

And near the abyss crystal and azure,
The wonder-flower blooms for us.

The final cycle of poems of *Der Siebente Ring*, "Tafeln," is composed of seventy epigrams from four to eight lines in length. As their name indicates, these "Tablets" are commemorative in nature, frequently "occasional" pieces, in that they were written to record George's thoughts in relation to specific events in the lives of friends or acquaintances, of places visited in his travels, or contemporary history. Like the "Zeitgedichte," whose counterpart in the structure of *Der Siebente Ring* they represent, the "Tafeln" more often than not carry a strong note of admonition, of warning, and of prophecy of impending catastrophe. In his three earlier collections—*Die Bücher der Hirten- und Preisgedichte, Das Jahr der Seele,* and *Der Teppich des Lebens*—George had dedicated individual groups of poems to his contemporaries. Similarly, the first twenty-seven "Tafeln" speak directly to such friends as Melchior Lechter, Karl and Hanna Wolfskehl, Friedrich Gundolf, and Albert Verwey. The second group of twenty-seven poems celebrates historic personalities or events connected with various localities in Germany. The last sixteen of the "Tafeln" are aphorisms, "Sprüche," directly expressing George's reflections on his times, but with more specific reference than was the case in the "Zeitgedichte," for the Boer War ("An Verwey"), the Russo-Japanese War, and the Russian revolution of 1905 ("Östliche Wirren") are directly alluded to.[20] The tenets of the "Zeitgedichte" are repeated, but now more urgently, more sharply. What has been lost to the spirits of men, what once bound them to each other and to their faith, cannot be regained or replaced by the nostrums favored by governments, politicians, and social thinkers around the turn of the century.

George's aphorisms speak for themselves. In relation to the Boer War, in which Great Britain defeated the rebellious Dutch settlers of South Africa for the sake of the empire, George said "No hope! masses today are rubble—No more/ Through ways and weapons of this world shall come salvation!" (I, 328). Modern science and technology, promising untold multiplication of wealth, seem to be the objects of George's scorn in the two poems entitled "Verführer" ("Seducers"), which are clearly related to the terrifying "Der Widerchrist." The fourth of the "Rhein" poems and "Quedlinburg" reflect his mistrust of the "Kleindeutschland" created by the unification of Germany under the aegis of Prussia. That the bustling capital of the new *Reich*, Berlin, filled him with contempt and sorrow over the prevalence of false values is evident from "Stadtplatz" ("City Plaza"): "Both high and low, you pursue the false god/ Who mints a tinsel coinage hollow, flat and mean/ From your heavy ore. I weep, my people,/ Lest this must be repented in poverty, hunger, and shame" (I, 338).

In a poem addressed to a Jesuit priest, George asserts that even the Jesuits' reputed conspiracies and assassinations are a better custom than those of "betrayers promising equality." George closes the poem: "Kein schlimmrer feind der völker als DIE mitte!" ("No worse foe of nations than *that* mean!") (I, 327). Thus, George also mistrusted social revolution for its own sake, since it would subject men to a fictitious and spiritually pernicious notion of equality, the lowest possible denominator. George could see hope for the ills of modern mankind, with whose fate he was vitally concerned—even if not with the same immediacy as other poets—in a renewal of the spirit, in a turning away from false gods, in a renewed reverence for the divine essence innate in man's temporal being.

In the "Jahrhundertsprüche" ("Aphorisms for the New Century"), George voices his sense of foreboding that terrible catastrophes will overtake the world before his hope for a new day for mankind can be realized. These aphorisms are peculiar in that they place cultural and historical categories on the same plane of discourse, through which an interrelationship is daringly posited. The first of these "Sprüche" proclaims that the new god of each age is revealed by the poets, who speak in the appropriate measure: "für zehntausend münder/ Hält einer nur das maass. In jeder ewe/ Ist nur ein gott und einer nur sein künder" (I, 338). Yet in this word *maass,* which implies that the measured speech of the poet is most appropriate to prophesy the new god of the age, there is also evoked the "measure" of judgment, the high norm of the "new life." The third aphorism infers that the "deed" of renewal might be done not by a man known and trusted by the people but perhaps by one "who has sat among your murderers for years/ Slept in your cells" (I, 339), a man rejected and reviled by the society of men. The nature of the deed, whether it be one of artistic or political significance, is mysterious. In this context no definite interpretation is possible, for the next "Spruch" is clearly a reference to a coming battle, in which the poet alone sees a small, gallant band defending its banner (I, 339). Morwitz says that this poem contains a prophecy of World War I, which many felt was imminent in the tense international atmosphere of the turn of the century.[27] The "battle" might be of another kind, however: a struggle of the proponents of the Hellenic unity of body and soul against the debased and degenerated values of the time. The use of the term *kleine schar* is certainly an echo of the seventh poem of the "Vorspiel" of *Der Teppich des Lebens,* in which George sees a similar "small band" bearing a banner with the motto "Hellas ewig unsre liebe" (I, 176). The association of struggle with spiritual renewal was to become a dominant theme in *Der Stern des Bundes.*

CHAPTER 5

The Poet in Times of Chaos

In haltung die uns werk und traum gegeben
Und aller küsse aller tränen mal
Zusammengehn von licht- zu schattental! . .
Ums andre sorgt nicht viel das Neue Leben. (I, 329)

I Der Stern des Bundes

DER *Stern des Bundes,* appearing in 1914, bears the same relationship to the totality of George's later work which a cycle of *Der Siebente Ring* has to the whole of that book. It is the essence of George's didactic *praxis,* intentionally separated from his more variously textured works written after *Der Siebente Ring,* most of which are contained in his last collection, *Das Neue Reich* (1928).

As Claude David has pointed out, George was relatively isolated following his break with Klages and Schuler in 1904. Only Wolfskehl, Gundolf, and, for a time, Lechter remained his close friends.[1] Aside from purely intellectual and literary relationships, George was not again to seek friends within his own generation. He had found the objective expression of his ideal—a new birth of the Hellenic unity of mortal flesh and divine spirit—in a youth, Maximin. Increasingly, he saw the young men of his time as the only hope for the future. In *Der Stern des Bundes,* this hope is expressed in all of its implications. Through the example of Maximin, George wished to re-create in the modern mind a sense of the mythic unity and greatness of the Hellenic ideal. He firmly believed that the remedy for the cultural ills of his age and nation lay in the realization of the actuality of such a synthesis, the way to a "new life." His own generation, now middle-aged and pursuing other goals, was, to George's mind, beyond his reach and open only to reproach for not having understood his meaning, as the first "Zeitgedicht" makes clear.

The affinity of Stefan George's poems to classical forms and themes and his esoteric allusion to mythic and poetic traditions appreciated fully only by the highly educated, created an enthusiastic response to his works among university students and young academics, particularly among those interested in philology and philosophy as avocations. George's intellectually demanding idealism, his teaching that the world can be re-created through the spirit and the word, gave their pursuits, which had become ever more questionable in a materialistic age, an intense and urgent new meaning. A significant part of George's appeal undoubtedly also lay in his insistence that man's spiritual attitudes must be altered in order for his life to improve. George was "conservative" in relation to political institutions and existing material circumstances, critical as he might be on the whole. Thus he also found a following among those who sought a meaningful response to the materialist social revolutionaries of the time, whose ideas they could not accept.

Friedrich Gundolf was George's first and closest younger friend and coworker. Between 1900 and 1910, the group of young men who saw in George the expression of their own ideas of what a man could be and achieve, grew to include, among others, Friedrich Wolters, Kurt Hildebrandt, and Berthold Vallentin. Together with Gundolf, they initiated the publication of the *Jahrbuch für die geistige Bewegung* (*Yearbook for the Renewal of the Spirit*), three volumes of which appeared in 1910 and 1911. The *Jahrbuch* was to be the vehicle of the ideas of the younger friends, many of them restricted to literary matters. Some of their articles, however, also touched upon larger cultural and historical questions, often with political implications. It is significant that George prohibited the publication of further volumes of the *Jahrbuch*, lest the polemical trend it early exhibited compromise, by association, his own essentially artistic and poetic intent.[2] These years also saw the beginning of George's long relationship with Ernst Morwitz. After Friedrich Gundolf became a professor at the University of Heidelberg, several of his best students came under George's influence. Among them was Norbert von Hellingrath, whose definitive editorial work on Hölderlin contributed to the "rediscovery" of that poet. Another member of Gundolf's circle was Edgar Salin, who later became a distinguished political economist and authority on Plato. It was to this small group of friends and those like them that *Der Stern des Bundes* was originally addressed.

Several of the poems of *Der Stern des Bundes*, written between 1909 and 1913, were published prior to the appearance of the book in January, 1914. George had read some of them to his closest friends, but the final form of the volume, the number and arrangement of the poems, was not revealed until George presented ten specially printed copies to Morwitz, Ludwig Thormaehlen, Robert Boehringer, Friedrich Wolters, and other friends shortly before

Christmas, 1913. Originally this collection was to have had the title *Lieder für die heilige Schar* (*Songs for the Sacred Throng*), which would have emphasized the significance of the circle of younger friends. The final title, however, stresses the centrality of Maximin, the unnamed inspiration of the *Bund*, the "star" exemplifying the divinity of man's spirit. The members of the *Bund*, participants in a covenant binding them together in loyalty to the ideals of the "New Life," were, in the first instance, George's younger friends. Less than a year after the first printing of *Der Stern des Bundes*, however, World War I broke out—an event which seemed to give new relevance to George's forebodings of a catastrophe for European culture and civilization. In the foreword to *Der Stern des Bundes* for the collected works of 1928, George was at pains to distinguish between the original intent of the book and its apparent impact:

About this work there exists a misunderstanding as incorrect as it is comprehensible, namely that the poet had concerned himself with immediate events instead of [remaining] remotely distant; indeed that he had wanted to create a breviary of national significance . . . particularly for the youth on the battlefields. . . . *Der Stern des Bundes* was first conceived for the closest circle of friends, and only the consideration that it is no longer possible to keep secret that which has once been said, made publication seem preferable as the most secure safeguard. Then the world events which occurred immediately after its appearance made minds in other circles receptive for a book which could have remained a secret many years longer. (I, 347)

Der Stern des Bundes contains 100 poems between seven and fourteen lines in length. They are divided into five sections: "Eingang" ("Introit"), containing nine poems; three "Books" of thirty poems each; and a single "Schlusschor" ("Chorale"). Each of the three Books is in turn divided into three groups of ten poems. Every tenth poem of each Book is rhymed, indicating the conclusion of a section. Similarly, the final poem of "Eingang" and the four closing lines of the "Schlusschor" are rhymed. The other poems of *Der Stern des Bundes* are not rhymed, indicating the primacy of content over form and message over music. Again, a complex interplay of numerological values—3, 7, 9 (3 x 3), and 10 (3 + 7)— defines the outward form.

Just as the *Vorspiel* of *Der Teppich des Lebens* had established the experiential and spiritual frame within which that book was to be understood, so "Eingang" celebrates the redemption of the poet through the revelation of Maximin, which makes possible and comprehensible the idea of the "New Life" in *Der Stern des Bundes*. The unity of being and action is a central concept. As Gundolf says:

This ethical imperative [*Sollen*] is an action of Being in the Platonic sense for [George], not, in the modern sense, a part, an opposite, a cause, or a result of Being. It is not an isolated imperative of reason or will, but rather—as effect—as much [a result of] contemplation as the subjectively perceived universe [*Ordnung*] and, like this view [*Schau*] made radiant for him through god-seeking Eros, and manifested through the divine Mean [*die göttliche Mitte*]. For him [the ethical imperative], precisely because it is carried out by a being, is never abstract theory. Just as the laws of natural necessity [*Mussgesetze der Natur*] appear only in real objects and processes, so the ethical laws of man [*Sollgesetze des Menschen*] only appear in human actions and attitudes.[3]

In its most essential aspect, this "New Life" is conceived by Stefan George as an attitude toward experience through which men would live more fully and felicitously, not determined by outside factors but by man's own will and vision of his ideal potential. Ultimately, it is a stoic posture toward existence, in which joy and sorrow, life and death, are faced with equanimity. This is stated most concisely in *Der Siebente Ring*, in the second of the "tablets," "For Robert" (I, 329):

> With bearing given us by deed and dream,
> And all the traces of our tears and kisses,
> To go from light to shadow's vale together . . .
> With more than this the New Life's not concerned.

The poet's integral view of the world and of man's place in it, which Maximin had affirmed for George, is celebrated in "Eingang." In the first poem, God is addressed as "Thou always our beginning, end, and middle," present everywhere and always, but revealing himself on earth only rarely—and then at a turning point in history or in a man's life. It is his "path down here," among mortals, which is to be praised, and, more precisely, in his manifestation to George in the form of Maximin. Before this event, darkness had lain over the land the poet had seen. The best energies were being sapped for questionable causes, and he could view the future only with despair:

> Then you came as a bud from our own bough,
> Fair as no image and real as no dream,
> Toward us in the god's own naked splendor:
> Then fulfillment flowed from sacred hands,
> Then there was light, and silent was all longing. (I, 350)

The "Maximin" poems in *Der Siebente Ring* had described the coming of Maximin as renewing the natural world for the poet. Here, however, reinforcing an element apparent earlier, motifs traditionally associated with religious concepts are used to convey the epochal significance of Maximin for Stefan George. Maximin's hands, from which "fulfillment flows," are "sanctified," an analogy to Jesus' state in baptism. "Then there was light" is an equally clear allusion to the Creation as described in Genesis. The godly nakedness of Maximin, finally, adds a Dionysian allusion to this syncretistic evocation of a new revelation of the divine will. Maximin is no longer seen as a godlike mortal but rather as a godly power which has only incidentally taken mortal form, which was, from the very outset, more than human:

> You know not who I am . . . hear only this:
> Not yet have I done word and deed of earth
> Which would make me mortal . . . now there nears
> The year in which I must choose my new form,
> I am transformed, but keep a constant essence,
> Like you I ne'er shall be: that choice is made. (I, 351)

It is Maximin's earthly form (*erdenleib*) which redeems the poet from despair over his own transitoriness, his inability to pour forth the "thousand-year-old fire" which burns within him, the longing of mankind through the ages for transcendent revelation:

> Thy earthly form, this slender, sacred shrine,
> Barely the span for mortal arm's embrace,
> All thoughts which to the stars would flee does catch
> And binds me in the day for which I live. (I, 351)

The fact that the divine power manifests itself to men in human form, whether in the person of Christ, Dionysus, or, for Stefan George, Maximin, is celebrated as the central mystery of life. The "deepest root" of the mystery "rests in eternal night" (I, 353): why the divine spirit should become "earthly matter" (*erdenstoff*), fulfill itself through a sacrificial death, which, in turn, inspires the deeds of men. The impenetrability of this secret is expressed as a paradox similar to that stated in the "Maximin" poems (I, 291): as Maximin, the manifestation of the divine spirit is the poet's "child," in the sense that he is human. So, too, the poet is Maximin's "child," through the spiritual rebirth inspired by him. The poet tells his followers: "Inquire no more! you have me but through him!/ I was lost and now I am redeemed" (I, 353). In the "spirit of the sacred youth of our people" (I, 353), George sees yet another primal manifestation of the spiritual inspiration of man.

The closing poem of the "Eingang" (I, 354) is the closest approach to a definition of what George means when he speaks of God or evokes the divine power. In *Der Teppich des Lebens* only very indistinct hints were given. In *Der Siebente Ring,* a timeless force, similar to the Hegelian *Geist* manifesting its will in history, was extolled ("Zeitgedicht II"). In *Der Stern des Bundes,* however, the elements of the personal ideal and the concept of an eternal force operative in the destinies of peoples and individuals are merged. For the individual, this "power" makes itself known through intimations of the soul's higher ideality, such as the angel of the *Vorspiel*:

> Who is thy God? All of my dream's desire,
> My ideal's near fulfillment, fair, sublime,
> The gift of the dark power of our loins,
> What to us e'er has given worth and greatness. (I, 354)

In the noblest deeds and thoughts of men, God is present. It is only through man and his continuity that God's will can be done. His power is derived from the "dark power of our loins." Thus, there exists an intimate relationship between man's fate and the unfolding of God's will. His nature is and must remain a mystery, but man's knowledge of, and faith in, His being makes meaningful all religious creeds and gives new life to "long-dead words the world has long forgot." God reveals Himself directly to men through human beings who symbolize or "re-present" (*darstellen*) His spiritual ideality to such an extent that they seem to be "begot by the stars," born out of a "New Mean" of the extremes of spirit and matter. This new synthesis has originated from *Geist,* the divine intellect, which is reflected in man's recognition of his own ideal potential. Such an individual is Maximin who, for George, has been reunited with the divine power whose living symbol he was.

The first book of *Der Stern des Bundes* deals with the relationship of Stefan George to his vocation in the world, to his own time, and to his closest friends before the revelation which Maximin brought to him. Just as he had realized in the *Vorspiel* that he had been doing the will of the angel in all of his earlier striving, the poet understands that even the angel had only been an aspect of God's will and has been transcended. It is "the Thunderer," God Himself, who speaks in these poems and whom George acknowledges as the goal of all his striving:

> Day and night I only this have done,
> Since I of my own life have feeling known,
> Sought but you on every path I've trod. (I, 356)

The priestly office of the poet in his time is now unshakable certainty for George. He asks whether, in a time of premonitions of impending catastrophe, it is not "sacrilege" to "seek harmonies" in verse. The "Thunderer" replies:

> The harp sublime and even the supple lyre
> Speak out my will in the rise and fall of the ages,
> Tell what's ordained in the stars' ineluctable order.
> And keep this truth to yourself alone—that on earth,
> No ruler, no savior can be who, in his first breath,
> Has not breathed an air filled with the music of prophets,
> Around whose cradle no hymn praising heroes has sounded.
> (I, 356)

The poet's suffering, his cry "which rose to the stars" for help, evokes, as in the *Vorspiel*, a special mercy (I, 357). "From the stars," he hears what no mortal has heard:

> . . Remain!
> You must pursue your path without a guide,
> Succor for you is but in what you've borne,
> Blame not your grief, for you yourself are grief.
> Turn into image, turn into tone!

The poet must bear the seed of his own salvation from despair, must make his redeeming dream tangible, for the very nature of his earthly existence is suffering. Any help must come from the dream within himself.

Just as the bard of antiquity inspired his city to victory (I, 359) by the power of his song, thus putting "words before deeds," the poet's dream, his longing for a tangible symbol of God's love, "became flesh" and sent forth into the world "a child of sublime joy and sublime devotion." The poet is a medium of God's word, which displaces every other thought but the will to express it and to lead men in his vision of the right path. Whether it be regarded rationally, psychologically, or mystically, the nature of the poet's sense of divine inspiration is inexpressible. He can only know what it commands his will to do:

> Call it a bolt that struck, a sign that beckoned,
> The thing that came into me at my time . . .
> Like a seed it is intangible, yet real.
> Call it a spark that came out of the void,
> Call it the ever circling thought's return:
> Words cannot grasp it: as a force and flame
> It flows in images, in worlds of men and gods!
> I am not come to preach a new Tomorrow:
> Out of the arrow-straight will of the age,
> I wrest you to the round path of a ring. (I, 358)

The "arrow-straight will of the age," the faith of men in continuous progress, whether through an unfolding of the dialectic of *Geist* or through man's own rational powers, is here countered by the poet's sense that he must restore the knowledge of a cyclical movement of the fate of the world, and of his premonition that progress is not indefinitely continuous. The recurrence of certain events through the will of God,[4] such as a "reincarnation," is here postulated.

Momme Mommsen has most recently pointed out the importance for the "vatic" poet of priestly silence, of the preservation of the inmost secrets of the divine power, lest he betray himself as a "false priest."[5] Several times in *Der Stern des Bundes,* Stefan George stressed the importance of guarding the "holy secrets" (I, 357) and withholding them from the knowledge of the many. In his heightened concern for this question, George was quite likely under the influence of his interest in Hölderlin during this period of his life. In a poem which contains an acrostic of Hölderlin's name (I, 389),[6] knowledge of the ultimate secrets of the divine power is termed "deadly for him who does not comprehend." Only through "image, tone, and the round-dance," that is, in the raiment of art, can these secrets be preserved, made safe for men to know, and are passed on "from mouth to mouth" from one age to the next. What George now regards as a perilous secret is his conclusion regarding the problem that has oppressed him, ever-changing in its guise, since the beginning of his creative life: the relationship of man to God, to a power greater than himself, all-knowing and eternal.

By the middle of his life, George had evidently come to the conclusion that there was more of this power in man himself than his contemporaries realized, that it, and not the material forces in which they were increasingly placing their faith, controlled man's destiny. *Der Siebente Ring* and, to a far greater extent, *Der Stern des Bundes* partially reveal this "secret." Its potentially destructive aspect for George is that man might be led to believe that God dwells *solely* within him, that man is not merely a *symbol* of the divine power, but its totality. What George regarded as the central belief of the ancient Greeks, namely that the "body *is* the God" (*Der Leib SEI der Gott*), could, correctly understood, bring about a spiritual reawakening in men, calling forth their higher moral judgment and redressing the balance of the material and spiritual to create a "New Mean," thereby freeing man's soul from the bondage in which material forces seemed to hold it. If this truth is misused, it could lead to a solipsistic *hybris,* under which man would fail to recognize that the divine power also exists beyond him. The "New Mean," then, represents a delicate balance between ethical responsiveness to higher imperatives—the positive aspect—and the negative aspect, the delusion that man, by virtue of his divinely endowed powers of reason and judgment, is a God unto himself, a moral free agent.

In *Der Stern des Bundes,* George's vision of this volatile secret, the nature of God, the order of the universe and man's place in it, are presented as revelation in terse, oracular, syntactically often enigmatic poems. *What* must be done is stated, rather than *why* it must be done. God's reasons for ordering the universe as He does are the deepest heart of the secret for the poet. Clues to these reasons are revealed in history. The poet must be content to do "the modest labor of [his] day" (I, 358) and "wed [himself] to the dream of Tomorrow," for he himself cannot hope to experience the fulfillment of the "New Life," which must evolve gradually. The "word," the statement of God's will to mankind, once stated, loses its power after a time, and a "new awakener" must come. Thus, the coming of Maximin and George's proclamation of him as a symbolization of God's power is not a chiliastic event, but only one segment of the cycle of the manifestation of God's will to men. The poet, even if he would, could not and should not tell all he knows and believes, for others will come after him, perhaps in more propitious moments, to bring the word anew.

The second group of ten poems in the First Book has a function similar to that of the "Zeitgedichte" in *Der Siebente Ring,* namely the description of the spiritual and cultural decay of the times, which make a new assertion of God's will vitally necessary. The tone of these poems is far more reproachful, scornful, and urgent than that of the "Zeitgedichte." God has "turned [His] countenance from this people" (I, 360) and follows with benevolence only the steps of those who serve Him through their pursuit of the ideal, who live in a state of longing for a spiritual revelation and serve God in their lives and in their art. As for the greater part of this people, "Their spirit is sick! dead is the deed!" Modern man, who knows and has "all," finds life bare and empty of meaning. He does not see the "grain, wine, and gold" all around him, that is, the force of man's primal imagination, his relationship to God and his fellow men, and the hope embodied in the youth: "Tons of pure gold scattered in the dust:/ The people in rags touch it with their hems—/ No one sees" (I, 360). The poet accuses his "enlightened" contemporaries of being more cruel than the men of the so-called Dark Ages in creating the false image of a merciful, reasonable god, whom they can endow with endearing names, a God who affirms all they do and does not judge or punish. The people of medieval times, for all of their murderous errors, at least strove for a recognition of an absolute force beyond themselves, while the men of the present only reduce God and His mind to their own dimensions, sacrificing the best things they have to this idol (I, 361). They ignore the urgent warnings of such "warners" as Nietzsche, who had attempted to arouse an awareness of a higher destiny for mankind in them:

> And you? if dull or clever, false or true
> You acted as though nothing had occurred . . .
> You go on dealing, talking, laughing, breeding.
> The warner went . . no hand is there to grasp
> Spokes of the wheel that rolls down to the void. (I, 362)

The civilization of the poet's time is a wheel careening into the void of nihilism created by the loss of the God-centered vision of the universe of past ages. Man's faith in his reason and ability to control the material world will also bring nothing but disaster:

> Destroyers of proportion and limit, you build:
> "What is high can go higher!" No foundation,
> No brace, no patch can help . . the building totters.
> And at your wits' end you cry up to Heaven:
> "What can we do ere we are smothered in debris
> We made, ere illusion we made destroys our brain?"
> And Heaven laughs: too late for remedies!
> Ten thousand must the sacred madness fell,
> Ten thousand must the sacred plague undo,
> Ten thousands yet the sacred war. (I, 361)

All too often, the term "the sacred war" (*der heilige krieg*) is taken to be an idealization of actual warfare and particularly of Germany's cause in the events leading to World War I, which was considered imminent years before its outbreak. Such an interpretation, implying a *jihad,* a "holy war" willed by God and fought for the "true faith" or in the name of the "true nation," is not supportable in terms of the context of the poem itself and those among which it appears. Rather, the "madness," the "plague," and the war are the result of Man's *hybris,* his insistence on erecting Babel-like towers, both physical and conceptual, by force of his technology and philosophic reasoning, from which to assert his supposedly godlike power. This overweening pride and the resulting moral irresponsibility of men will ultimately bring about plague and want, which in turn will precipitate war. These self-inflicted catastrophes are "sacred" only in the sense that they ultimately visit justly deserved punishment upon those who have blindly challenged God's omnipotence. It is only through atonement, a reinstatement of self-discipline in men and awe for the authority of superior beings, that the essential concepts of man's civilization and culture—God, love, and society—can become meaningful and vital once more (I, 362). Thus, there is an implication that it might still not be too late to avoid the threefold calamity George saw approaching, which many took as a prophecy, not only of World War I, but of its historic aftermath.

Stefan George tempers scorn with pity in addressing the friends of his own age who have not understood the significance of Maximin for him. He has achieved a new insight into the nature of God's will in the world which they cannot share: "We have crossed over, and you stayed behind" (I, 364). Any sympathy he might have had with the irrational spiritualism of the "Cosmics" is now behind him. He sees the desperate emptiness of their séancelike gatherings (I, 364) and views with objective irony the archetypal principles they cherish: the demonic paganism and glorification of the Nordic races. In Ludwig Klages in particular, George felt the frenetic activity and aimless longing of these *Nordgermanen.*[7] In describing this state of mind, however, he also seems acutely to portray the existential dilemma of a whole age which has lost sight of its ultimate reason for being:

> You roam in rash abandon without goal,
> You roam in storm, you roam through sea and land,
> You roam among men longing to be grasped,
> You are ungraspable. For fulfillment
> You long, the unfulfillable. You fear
> Repose in which you find yourselves alone.
> Yourselves you dread more direly than a foe.
> Release you give yourselves in death alone. (I, 365)

In contrast to the supernatural fulfillment sought by the "Cosmics," it is God's revelation in the empirical and historical world, "the greater miracle of finitude" that the poet would have men probe. They are to regard themselves as symbols of the divine will in this world: "He who is noble fulfills himself solely as image" (I, 364).

At the center of *Der Stern des Bundes*, in the Second Book, the poet is concerned with the spiritual preparation of the youths who will be the exponents of the "New Life," with his relationship to them as friend and teacher. Like the "Gezeiten," these poems reflect Stefan George's experiences with various friends.[8] The teacher demands a complete surrender of the being of the young men to the exalted passions and ideals he espouses. His spiritual union with them excludes their worldly concerns, their social inhibitions, and the cynicism of the age. They are to be instilled with the knowledge of the striving of their souls toward ideality, of the mission which is theirs to fulfill as living symbols of the higher knowledge of the "New Life." The personal relationship of teacher and disciple has strong erotic overtones (Cf. I, 372), and the god who is evoked (I, 377-78) is more reminiscent of the young Dionysus or Eros than of the Jehovah-like "Thunderer" of the Old Testament who spoke in the First Book. But the love and reverence which exists between teacher and disciple must serve a higher goal and cannot be its own fulfillment. This would only be possible in an idyllic time of "gracious freedom and gracious peace" (I, 378). By giving completely of himself, the disciple "gains himself completely" (I, 375). The poet experiences the physical and spiritual grace of his friends and, through his spirit, manifested in his art, in a way analogous to his concept of the total interrelationship of matter and spirit, makes their essence endure in his image of them. A poem which appears toward the end of the Second Book is one of the rare documents of Stefan George's sense of the poetic process, which is here seen to be classical and Apollonian. The form of the poem itself seems to emphasize this intention:

Some teach: earthly here—there eternal...
And some: you are abundance, I privation.
Here be it told: how the earthly is eternal,
And how abundance can absolve privation.
Itself not knowing blooms and withers Beauty,
Eternal Spirit seizes what is mortal,
It thinks, enhances, and it preserves Beauty;
With power supreme it renders it immortal.
A body which is fair inspires my blood,
Spirit I am grasps it in a rapture,
It is reborn of spirit and of blood,
Thus it is mine, enduring source of rapture. (I, 380)

The Third Book of *Der Stern des Bundes* is devoted to the spiritual state of the "New Life," which began for George after the revelation of Maximin, just as, for Dante, the beginning of his love for Beatrice signified a *vita nuova.* The knowledge that the world is infused with God's spirit makes the natural universe seem transformed and spiritual, like a reflection of the poet's own abstract contemplation:

Dies ist reich des Geistes: abglanz
Meines reiches· hof und hain.
Neugestaltet umgeboren
Wird hier jeder: ort der wiege

Heimat bleibt ein märchenklang.
Durch die sendung durch den segen
Tauscht ihr sippe stand und namen
Väter mütter sind nicht mehr . .
Aus der sohnschaft· der erlosten·
Kür ich meine herrn der welt. (I, 382)

This is a realm of Spirit: image
Of my realm, field and forest.
Newly formed and reborn
Is each one here: his place of birth,
Homeland's but a fable now.
Through the call and through the blessing,
You change tribe and class and name,
Fathers, mothers are no more . . .
Among the sons, among the chosen,
I elect my masters of the world.

Through their adherence to the "New Mean," their entry into the "New Life," those chosen by the poet have attained mastery of the world, not in the sense of domination over other men, but in their intellectual ability to appraise their relationship to reality, to know what is essential to their lives and what is accidental. Conventional categories of family, class, and especially nation are rejected. The obligations toward these institutions may still be binding, but they are transcended by those to the "New Life," which is borne by an "aristocracy" in the sense of "the best, the most meritorious." In warning against seeking the "new nobility" among the hereditary aristocracy or royalty (I, 383), George says:

Holders of each rank alike
Have the same sordid, sensual glance,
Have the same brutal glance of hunting.

The "new nobility"—a social entity unto itself in the first instance —has its "own ranking" and is "without ancestral tradition" (*stammlos*) and thus beyond categories of social classification or national identity. Although at this point Stefan George was primarily concerned with the youth of Germany, there is every indication in these poems that he explicitly rejected nationalism or chauvinism in any guise. Those living the "New Life" constitute a "New Estate" (*Stand*) (I, 386), which despises the materialistic and philistine values of the existing culture. Old men who affirm these values may be excused, but youths who devote themselves to the decadent pursuits of this world are condemned as "slaves." The coming cataclysm demands that young men strive ceaselessly for the propagation of the "New Mean."

The place George assigns to Woman in his scheme of things is distinctly conservative. His justification of a subordinate role for the feminine principle is philosophically schematic:

> This era of the world Spirit created,
> Which is always Man: revere in Matter
> Woman . . . No less sacred she. Woman
> Bears the beast, Man creates Woman and Man. (I, 387)

George shared the basic premise of this poem with the "Cosmics,"[9] namely that the prehistoric matriarchal worship of chthonic powers posited by Bachofen was succeeded by the patriarchal, idealistic era which has existed since the beginning of historic time. Thus, there exists an apparently necessary polarity between Man/Spirit and Woman/Matter. Although the feminine principle is as important to life and culture as the masculine, and its mysteries are to be equally revered, it must play a subservient role. Just as men must, ideally, symbolize the totality of the spiritual aspect of humanity, women must live in such a way as to represent the material principle and create the emotional and physical "order" in which men live. George exhorts his followers to shun women whose lives deny this principle (I, 383). He quotes an apocryphal saying of Christ to support his contention that a new balance between the material and spiritual aspects of life must be achieved, that the material/feminine principle dominates the present to an unwholesome extent: "I have come to undo the works of Woman" (I, 387).

The tone of *Der Stern des Bundes* is predominantly didactic and imperative. The poet attempts to mold his followers to the form he feels necessary to the "New Life." They must not give way to elegiac moods or romantic illusions (I, 384). They must have the courage to espouse their convictions without compromise or apology (I, 386). Their lives are to have the exaltedly earnest quality (*heilig nüchtern*) (I, 384), which Hölderlin[10] had denoted as the elemental property endowed by contact with the divine spirit. Despite this certainty in the ethical realm, *Der Stern des Bundes* is a book of religious questing in that it emphasizes time and again the unknowable and incommunicable Highest Good–God, as the source of all Being, from whom man's spirit comes and must owe its final allegiance. George's experience in seeking to know this God as He manifests Himself in the world is ultimately personal and mystical. Its expression is syncretistic, partaking of the symbolic language of the Bible and of Greek and Germanic mythology, as well as of concepts of medieval mysticism. Only he "with whom the God has lain" (I, 387) can attain the inmost vision of His nature, the highest degree of intuitive knowledge possible for man.

George is not espousing a new faith on the basis of the insights he communicates but is trying to make man newly aware that the decisive factor of his existence is his spirit, his soul, rather than his intellect or his material circumstances. George was by no means alone in his conviction that the traditional religions of the West were no longer capable of doing this. Therefore it is necessary for each man to arrive at these insights for himself, compelled by the power of the poet's word. A reconsecration to God whom man has perceived in the world is the new imperative, and action in the spirit of this belief, for without action, faith is meaningless. *Der Stern des Bundes,* perhaps one of the most remarkable religious books of our century, closes with a "Chorale" (I, 394) affirming the centrality not of Maximin or any cult, but of the place of God in the lives of men:

Path of God is open to us,
Land of God our destiny,
Strife of God's commanded for us,
Wreath of God our just reward.
Peace of God is in our hearts now,
Strength of God is in our breasts,
Wrath of God upon our foreheads,
Love of God upon our lips.
Bond of God has now embraced us,
Light of God has us illumed,
Grace of God has poured forth for us,
Joy of God for us has bloomed.

II Das Neue Reich

In 1928, the year of Stefan George's sixtieth birthday, *Das Neue Reich* (*The New Realm*) appeared as the ninth volume of his Collected Works. Except for the miscellaneous pieces contained in the final volume (*Schlussband*), which appeared posthumously, this was to be his last book of poems. *Das Neue Reich* embraces the period from 1908, when "Goethes lezte Nacht in Italien" ("Goethe's Last Night in Italy") was written, until shortly after World War I. Almost all of these poems had been published in the *Blätter für die Kunst* or, in the case of "Der Krieg" ("The War") and the *Drei Gesänge* (*Three Hymns*), in separate editions. The title, *Das Neue Reich,* has no political or geographic connotations, difficult though it may be in German to distinguish between the primary meaning of *Reich* as "Kingdom" or "Empire," and its more abstract connotation as "realm." The "New Realm" is the state of humane balance between body and soul envisioned in *Der Stern des*

Bundes as the "New Mean" (I, 354), which would make possible the "New Life" for the "New Estate" (I, 386). It is a dream, yet to be realized, of a world in which will prevail the values of spiritual strength and insight, of human courage and dignity.

In respect to Stefan George's art, too, *Das Neue Reich* presents formal aspects not apparent in the earlier collections. Parallel to the terse, oracular poems typical of *Der Stern des Bundes,* George developed a more expansive, metrically freer form, most readily comparable to the ode, which first appears in "Goethes lezte Nacht in Italien." Its immediate predecessors are the "Zeitgedichte" of *Der Siebente Ring,* which also combine critical introspection with visionary narrative breadth. The other formal innovation of *Das Neue Reich* is the dramatic dialogue. In George's earliest works, the dramatic element was evident, insofar as many *personae* expressed dialectically the various points of view he wished to synthesize. This was especially apparent in the "Zeitgedichte" and the "Gestalten" and, earlier yet, in the poetic drama, *Manuel* (II, 523-50).

George called "Goethes lezte Nacht in Italien" the "beginning of a new sequence [*reihe*]." This is true of the form of the piece, an elegiac ode consisting of seven twelve-line stanzas in an unrhymed, irregular dactylic metric scheme. Considering its nearness to the searing condemnation of Germany's decadent materialism in *Der Siebente Ring,* however, this poem also represents a new thematic departure. Goethe is no longer shown as the misunderstood, suffering genius of "Goethe-Tag" (I, 229f.) but as a harbinger of hope for a spiritual and cultural rebirth of the German nation under the aegis of the civilizations of Greece and Rome. On the eve of his return to his native land, Goethe has a vision of two young men swearing eternal friendship in the name of "lordship and light" (I, 401), their ideals of self-mastery and the striving for perfection. This "shimmer which struck [him] from the southern sea" makes Goethe reflect on his crucial experience in Italy. He had come, "the heart of his people, their truest heir," and realized his own impoverishment. Only by "beginning again as a child," could he become a whole, balanced man. Unlike more fortunate peoples, Germany did not have a seer and poet to pass on the all-important knowledge of the divinity of man's spirit, one who was a "son and not a grandson" of Gaia, the mother of the Olympians (I, 402).

Although Goethe had known the Promethean and the Faustian compulsion to harness the secrets of the universe for mankind, he denies having the power of such a seer as the Greeks had in Homer, Rome in Virgil, the Italians in Dante, England in Shakespeare: "Such a one came not to you, and I am not he" (I, 402).[11] In his native Rhineland, the area formerly within the Roman *Limes,* with its many pagan reminiscences, Goethe had had the first hint of his "secret homeland," Italy, and the classical civilization of Rome. Later, in despair over the apparent dichotomy of matter and spirit, symbolized in the relentlessly vertical aspiration of Gothic architecture, he had fled to Italy and found himself anew. He will bring to his people his vision of classical Apollonian serenity, preserving for himself the secret of its roots in Dionysian passion until such a time as they are sufficiently enlightened:

> Homeward I bring you a ray of the life-giving sun,
> Deep in my heart I conceal its darker fires,
> A danger to you as long as your minds are confused.
> Take up this ray in your souls—O call it not coldness!
> And I will scatter before you in brightest profusion,
> Stones and flowers and precious ores, all and nothing,
> Until the scales fall from your eyes and you see
> The magic of Things, of the Body, the God-given norm (I, 402-3)

Goethe knew of the organic interrelationship between all forms of being, of the morphological progression discernible in all matter. For him, the world is the expression of a single "striving to be," which determines the rhythm of life and finds expression in ever higher levels of being, ultimately to reach the most perfect form possible for each variety of life, the "God-given norm." This is George's reading of Goethe's theories of natural history and morphology. In its pantheistic aspects, this view of the world no doubt was instrumental in forming George's own, discernible primarily in his later works, of the "greater miracle of finitude" (I, 365). This "striving," common to all being, is, for George's Goethe at least, divinely inspired. When men become conscious of this central fact, a new age of reverence for life and the spirit and of harmony in the striving for perfection will begin.

In the period between the completion of *Der Siebente Ring* and World War I, George's works show the optimistic conviction that the poet's word, his awareness of his nation's broader spiritual and cultural heritage, could still play a normative role in its life. The dark prophecy in "Goethes lezte Nacht in Italien," that millennia might yet be necessary for this hope to be realized, does not detract from the strength of this conviction.

Throughout his life, Stefan George was keenly aware of the German and European poetic tradition of earlier times and of his own, a fact to which his anthologies of German poetry, *Deutsche Dichtung,* and of contemporary poets of the early twentieth century bear witness, as well as do his translations of Shakespeare and Dante. In George's poems, besides the influence of the Symbolists, that of nineteenth-century poets such as Heine, Platen, Annette von Droste-Hülshoff, and Conrad Ferdinand Meyer can be discerned.[12] In his own works, however, up to and including *Der Teppich des Lebens,* George chooses to see himself as *sui generis,* expressing feelings and thoughts he alone has known in a form only he can give them. After *Der Teppich des Lebens,* however, his concern with the spiritual crisis of the West and his assumption of an essentially religious world view aroused in George an urgent sense of mission. From this time on, he sought and acknowledged in his works the German poets of the past who had anticipated his vision. He found only two: Goethe and Hölderlin.

George had included poems by Friedrich Hölderlin in the third volume of *Deutsche Dichtung, Das Jahrhundert Goethes,* in 1902, predating by a decade the reawakening of interest in the poet, which occurred after the appearance of Wilhelm Michel's biography of Hölderlin in 1912. It is no coincidence that Norbert von Hellingrath, one of the most gifted of George's younger friends, was asked by Michel to undertake the task of preparing the critical edition of Hölderlin's works.[13] For George, Goethe had chosen to reveal only the Apollonian aspect of the existential polarity which Nietzsche had seen in its tragic entirety. Hölderlin, however, had discovered the Dionysian antipode before Nietzsche and was accordingly celebrated in George's eulogy, *Hölderlin,* which appeared in the *Blätter* in 1919:

> The masters of the Classical period, who could not properly esteem [Hölderlin's] best qualities, had the difficult task of purifying themselves and their contemporaries out of barbaric confusion and instinctive tempestuousness to the point of Hellenic clarity. In art, they recognized only Apollo, or, rather, they had to sense intimations of him in smoothed-over imitative works. . . . Dionysus and Orpheus were still buried and [Hölderlin] alone was the discoverer. He needed no hints from without: his inner vision came to his aid. Like a lightning bolt he tore open the heavens and showed us deeply moving images [opposed to our conceptions of the gods], such as Hercules-Christ. (I, 520)

George shared with Hölderlin the belief that all of the gods revered in the history of mankind are in reality manifestations of the same divine spirit and are thus "brothers," as Hölderlin called Hercules, Christ, and Dionysus in his ode "Der Einzige" ("One Alone").[14]

Stefan George wrote the three poems entitled "Hyperion" and the eulogy on Hölderlin during the same period, just before World War I, when his preoccupation with Hölderlin was strongest through his contact with Norbert von Hellingrath. "Hyperion" is

Hölderlin himself, here given the name of the hero of his novel. In these poems, George captures the essence of Hölderlin's sense of alienation from his own countrymen and his age, his reverence for ancient Greece and its gods, his hopes for a new synthesis of man's comprehension of the divine spirit. It is the "terrible doing" of Fate that "life must die through life," that the glories of the Greek gods and the art and civilization they had inspired were eclipsed by the coming of Christianity, with whose teachings their being could not be reconciled: "Woe, at the Syrian's command, the light-world plunged into the night" (I, 405). Hölderlin's apotheosis culminates in the third "Hyperion" poem with the enunciation of hope for a spiritual and, hence, an empiric renascence. This will come about through men's love for the transcendent divinity of all being and through their awe of both the Dionysian and the Apollonian principles, united in a new incarnation of the God. Through men capable of such understanding, a new age, the second great era of man's culture, will be ushered in:

> MIT DIESEN KOMMT DAS ZWEITE ALTER· LIEBE
> GEBAR DIE WELT· LIEBE GEBIERT SIE NEU.
> Ich sprach den spruch· der zirkel ist gezogen . .
> Eh mich das dunkel überholt entrückt
> Mich hohe schau: bald geht mit leichten sohlen
> Durch teure flur greifbar im glanz der Gott. (I, 406)

> WITH THESE COMES THE SECOND AGE—LOVE
> GAVE BIRTH TO THE WORLD—LOVE WILL BEAR IT ANEW.
> I have spoken the word, the circle is closed . . .
> Ere darkness overtakes me the high vision
> Raises me up: soon on gentle soles will pace
> Through meadows dear, tangible in glory, the God.

The first two lines of the poem are a paraphrase of a central concept of the novel *Hyperion*: "Love gave birth to the world, Friendship will bear it anew."[15] George sees Hölderlin about to enter the long night of his madness transfigured by the vision of a promised land he can never enter.

The didactic optimism which pervades George's works between 1908 and 1914, the hope that his idealism would be understood and carried to ever wider circles, was abruptly dashed by the outbreak of World War I. This catastrophe, which George, like most of his contemporaries, had seen approaching in the countless international crises of the previous fifteen years, reawakened in the poet the cold fury and vatic pathos which had characterized the "Zeitgedichte." Almost all of George's younger friends—the circle to which *Der Stern des Bundes* had been addressed—were called to the army, some, like Norbert von Hellingrath, never to return. In *Der Stern des Bundes,* George had written of a "sacred war" (I, 361) which men would inflict upon themselves through their denial of the imperatives of the spirit. From the very beginning of World War I, however, George made it clear that he did not see any chiliastic meaning or a national mission in a war of this kind. His attitude toward the often chauvinistic martial enthusiasm of his younger friends was skeptical, indeed negative. There can be no doubt, however, that George was deeply concerned by the events of the war, aloof as he seemed to be. As a German, he was loyal to his nation, but he did not feel that Germany's cause was juster than that of the other nations. George saw that the concerted rapacity and ignorance of Europe's politicians had brought things to this pass. In October, 1914, he wrote to Gundolf: "The enormous stupidity of German statesmanship has made this war so dangerous, and if nothing is done, this stupidity will thrive. . . . When the war is over [humanitarian-sentimental narrowmindedness] will lead to the same foolish errors and tragic results before many more [wars] have passed. The world which is yet to come and which will conquer the real enemy and Anti-Spirit [*widerdämon*]—to that world no one today belongs who is now opening his mouth."[16] George condemns as "humanitarian-sentimental narrowmindedness" the attempt to end wars on the basis of rational, material self-interest, which in George's opinion can only lead to still fiercer conflicts, anticipating and rejecting the hopes of those who believed that this could be "the war to end all wars."

The poem "Der Krieg" dramatically reveals George's attitude toward the war, his assumption of a lonely pessimism which strikingly contrasts with the patriotic fervor shared by even the most reserved German intellectuals during this time. How important it was for George to make clear exactly where he stood after almost three years of apparent silence is indicated by the fact that "Der Krieg" was first published in July, 1917, as a separate brochure. It was written between 1914 and 1917, and although its diction is generalized, its poetic attitude oracular and hortatory, the poem chronicles the elements of the war which moved Stefan George during its first three years: the initial attempts at national cohesion between the various classes, which had been in conflict before the national emergency; the victory of Hindenburg at Tannenberg the constantly increasing horror of the war of attrition on the western front; and the first phases of the Russian Revolution.

Throughout "Der Krieg" it is the poet, here depicted as the hermit (I, 410), the "seer," who speaks. His office it is to "praise and condemn, pray and repent" for his people, who ridicule his warnings of catastrophe and vent their rage on him when it occurs. He tells those who come to him for an omen:

> What moves you now has long been known to me,
> Long have I sweated the red sweat of fear
> While you played with fire, wept my tears
> Long ago. Now I can find no more.
> The most had happened, and yet no one saw,
> The worst is yet to come, and no one sees. (I, 410)

"The most," which had already occurred, and of which the war is only a symptom, was the decay of the human spirit, the assent of men to purely mechanical laws of necessity and purely material concepts of felicity:

> Wantonness heaped high,
> Called by all necessity and fortune,
> Lying decay from Man to Mask, demand
> Repentance . . . (I, 411)

For the poet, life itself has been murdered through man's failure to acknowledge the sanctity of his divine provenience. The mythic powers which infuse and are embodied in all of man's acts are not "fable" but real and ever-present to the "seer," who implores them not to let men come to facile conclusions about the crisis, which cannot be viewed only as a political event open to merely rational analysis. Men must see its transcendent implications, its consequences for their souls. On the other hand, the poet warns of the "worst" of disgraces, the continuation of slaughter for its own sake, out of bloodthirstiness and the desire to obliterate the enemy totally. George calls this the "blood disgrace" (*Blutschmach*) (I, 411) and says that nations which are guilty of the senseless slaughter of others, denying the honor which prevails even in war, would deserve to be obliterated themselves, for in their brutality, they are casting off their "best treasure," their humanity.

In this war, which men have brought upon themselves, the categories of historic conquest—like the wars of the great migration, the "Völkerwanderung," and the honorableness of combat for the sake of the people—which had once given war a necessary place in the lives of men and nations, no longer exist. George sees the war in its eerie, dehumanized brutal reality:

> Zu jubeln ziemt nicht: kein triumf wird sein·
> Nur viele untergänge ohne würde . .
> Des schöpfers hand entwischt rast eigenmächtig
> Unform von blei und blech· gestäng und rohr.

Der selbst lacht grimm wenn falsche heldenreden
Von vormals klingen der als brei und klumpen
Den bruder sinken sah· der in der schandbar
Zerwühlten erde hauste wie geziefer . .
Der alte Gott der schlachten ist nicht mehr. (I, 412)

No cause for joy. No triumph will there be,
Only much dishonor and decline . . .
Monstrosities of lead and steel fly free,
Barrel and rod, escaped from maker's hands.
He must laugh grimly when he hears resound,
False heroic speeches of the past,
He, whose brother fell as pulp and clumps,
Has dwelt, an insect, in the ravaged earth.
The ancient god of battle is no more.

Military victories, such as Hindenburg's rout of the Russian armies at Tannenberg in East Prussia, cannot save the people from the "worse enemy," their own blindness. Vanity, egoism, and opportunism characterize the leadership of the nation. The masses, the "substance" of the nation, though potentially strong, have no higher goal, create no ideal which they can follow, and have no memory of a meaningful heritage. The war will not generate a new political or intellectual awareness: "He who yesterday was old/ Will not now return renewed" (I, 413). For the trials to come, the present holds few lessons: "For them/ Only fullest change will arm: seeing and inward sense" (I, 413). "It is less amazing that so many die/ Than that so much dares to live," says the poet, scourging the delusions of his fellow men that "surely the rule of Eternal peace will now begin." He knows that after a time, the hypocrisy and rapacity of men will precipitate another bloodbath. His only hope is a new generation "that has no liar's eye" (I, 413) and that is able to regard the paralyzing Gorgon of the terror of fate without fear. "A people is dead when its gods are dead" (I, 414), when it has let its ideals die by betraying them, killed its gods by turning away from them. This is the truth that the combatants on both sides, whose common homeland is Europe, do not choose to see, preferring to follow their own selfish and shortsighted ends. They do not understand that the way of life that has been destroyed by the war, the dynasties which are toppling, were ripe for destruction. They will not acknowledge that, perhaps, none of their pragmatic solutions for the problems of the world can be realized, that perhaps a new "abomination of mankind," as Tacitus called the early Christians in his *Annals*,[17] with as radical a view of man's perversity and need for spiritual salvation as theirs was, might yet bring a new redemption.

Yet, the song does not end with a curse. The poet knows that his teaching of the interdependence of matter and spirit goes not entirely unheeded, for many reach out to him. Europe, "where the dream still lives/ Indestructible in the often disloyal heirs" (I, 414), the "land which still holds much promise," will survive for the sake of that hope. Western civilization must revive the idealism of its beginnings and realize the essential unity of all of mankind's gods:

> Apollo lehnt geheim
> An Baldur: "Eine weile währt noch nacht·
> Doch diesmal kommt von Osten nicht das licht."
> Der kampf entschied sich schon auf sternen: Sieger
> Bleibt wer das schutzbild birgt in seinen marken
> Und Herr der zukunft wer sich wandeln kann. (I, 415)

> Apollo leans in secret
> On Baldur. "For a time night will prevail,
> But this time light will not come from the East."
> On stars this struggle was resolved. Who shields
> The guardian image in his lands is victor,
> And future's master who transforms himself.

As Hölderlin had proclaimed the "brotherhood" of Christ, Hercules, and Dionysus in "Der Einzige," so George recalls the affinity between Apollo, the Greek god of light, and Baldur, his counterpart in Germanic mythology. Instead of from the East as at the coming of Christ, it is from the cultural and intellectual unity of the West—the entity whose extremes Apollo and Baldur represent—that the "new light" of salvation will come. That the "light" will not come from the East also reflects George's pessimism about events in Russia and his mistrust in the fatalism of Asiatic philosophy. Like the poverty-stricken inhabitants of the "mother-city" in "Die tote Stadt" in *Der Siebente Ring,* those who will prevail after the holocaust of war nurture in austerity and discipline the ideals of their cultural traditions in their homelands and live according to them, striving for new forms as the times and circumstances demand, but retaining these ideals as the lodestone of all of their actions.

In 1921, three years after Germany's capitulation and the Treaty of Versailles, Stefan George published another brochure, *Drei Gesänge,* which contained the poems "An die Toten" ("To the Dead"), the first poem of the "Sprüche an die Toten" ("Words for the Dead") in *Das Neue Reich,* "Der Dichter in Zeiten der Wirren" ("The Poet in Times of Chaos"), and "Einem jungen Führer im Ersten Weltkrieg" ("To a Young Officer in the First World War").

"Der Dichter in Zeiten der Wirren" shares with "Der Krieg" the conception of the poet as a seer and prophet, tolerated in quiet times as a dreamer who lends charm and beauty to the lives of other men. In times of danger, however, when, like a biblical prophet or Cassandra, he attempts to warn of the impending catastrophe which he has seen in visions, he is ignored, even incarcerated. Only when all is lost do men turn to him for counsel, and then he can only mourn and scourge them. It is senseless to talk of the spirit when even the counsels of reason go unheeded. The "entire tribe of the living":

> Has now forgot its being's highest law,
> On which its continuity was founded,
> Trusts in no Guide, needs no Penitent,
> Would with a clever ruse outwit its fate.
> Still harder plowshares must break through the sod,
> Still denser fogs must darken our air. (I, 417)

The worst consequences of the unnamed new catastrophes which the poet foresees can only be avoided if "all who speak the same language"—all of those, whatever their nationality or political conviction, who believe, as the poet does, in salvation through the spirit—shake off the tattered rags of their various banners and unite to take counsel together. In dark times, the poet forms the link of tradition between the wisdom of the past and the despair of the present. He envisions a new generation which will, by force of its high ideals, its "hallowed dreams, deeds, and trials," bring forth the man who will cleanse the defiled world and make a reality of the dream of the "New Realm," where long-disregarded or misunderstood values assume their true meaning, "where the great is great once more, lord once more lord, discipline once more discipline" (I, 418). When the right relationships are re-established in human society—the leadership of the best and the willing discipleship of the less gifted—then the "true device" will be affixed to each nation's banner, its existence as a nation made meaningful, and the "New Realm" founded. Again, this visionary view bears a close similarity to the idealistic concept of an aristocratic order developed in *Der Stern des Bundes.*

"Geheimes Deutschland" ("Secret Germany") is one of the few poems of *Das Neue Reich* not to be published previously. This circumstance seems to indicate that it was completed after the appearance of the last volume of the *Blätter* in 1919 and of the *Drei Gesänge* in 1921. The preceding poem, "Burg Falkenstein," was written in 1922.[18] Thus, "Geheimes Deutschland" can be regarded as the latest of Stefan George's major poems and warrants special attention as the last document of his cultural criticism and his poetic art.

"Geheimes Deutschland," perhaps more than any other poem of Stefan George, approximates the classical ode. At significant junctures, the poet invokes the abyss, the wing of his dream, and the peak of his hope, which bear his inspiration. The initial image of the world is a foreboding of the terrible violation of earth by man's "conquest" of nature through his intellect and technology:

Wo unersättliche gierde
Von dem pol bis zum gleicher
Schon jeden zoll breit bestapft hat
Mit unerbittlicher grelle
Ohne scham überblitzend
Alle poren der welt:

Wo hinter maassloser wände
Hässlichen zellen ein irrsinn
Grad erfand was schon morgen
Weitste weite vergiftet
Bis in wüsten die reitschar
Bis in jurten den senn: (I, 425)

When insatiable greed,
From pole to equator,
Has now paced off every inch,
With ruthless brightness,
Without shame flashing over
All the pores of the world:

When behind enormous walls,
In ugly cells a madness
Has just invented what tomorrow
Will poison furthest reaches,
In the desert the riders,
In the yurtas the cowherds:

When man has completely defiled earth by tampering with the order of nature, the dark chthonic powers and the "Heavenly Ones" will "change the laws of matter" and create "new space within the space." The new "dimension" in which positive change is still possible after all physical space has been exhausted is the dimension of the spirit, still open to the power of the inspiring word. This realization comes to the poet on a southern shore, as he is contemplating man's lot, deeply grieved, like Nietzsche, when the vision of Zarathustra came to him.[19] He returns to his homeland, where "untouched earth," "sleeping abundance" await him, "as in the darkest primeval forest" (I, 426). The "secret Germany," which the poet discovers, "the space within space," is the capacity of certain of the poet's contemporaries, amidst the deadened world of man's civilization, to feel and live life with mythic immediacy, on an experiential level that is supposed to have long disappeared.

The figures that are apostrophized as representatives of this "secret Germany," the still-hidden seed from which the poet hopes a spiritual renewal will arise, were encountered by Stefan George at various periods of his life. The godlike beauty of Maximin is celebrated, as is the demonic atmosphere radiated by Alfred Schuler, and the cataclysmic, all-encompassing twilight of an age in World War I. The attitudes exhibited by most of the persons depicted in "Geheimes Deutschland" are "heroic" chiefly in their acknowledgement of their limitations, their ability to resign themselves to ordinary lives in the face of the greater abilities of others, or their capacity for self-sacrifice for the sake of their friends.[20] This is quite characteristic of Stefan George's assessment of the world, for he believed, as we have seen earlier, especially in the "Gestalten," that the ability to follow, to take the second rank, is at least as significant a part of the origin and survival· of a true culture as the ability to lead. This is perhaps most clearly expressed in the aphorism "R . . ." of the "Words for the Living," which—"R . . ." being a place name—[21] may be a late reproach to Hugo von Hofmannsthal, who resided at Rodaun near Vienna:

> The highest place has he whom God on earth,
> Has lifted o'er the threshold of the senses,
> Not much lower he who knowing this,
> Content serves at the place the law demands. (I, 448)

The hope George has for his nation is that these qualities of selfless insight, an ethic based on reverence for the mutual humanity and nobility of the mind of others, will let the "Secret Germany," the realm of the spirit, survive the depraved present, and determine a better future, a time, however, which the poet no longer hopes to experience:

> Wer denn· wer von euch brüdern
> Zweifelt· schrickt nicht beim mahnwort
> Dass was meist ihr emporhebt
> Dass was meist heut euch wert dünkt
> Faules laub ist im herbstwind
> Endes- und todesbereich:
>
> Nur was im schützenden schlaf
> Wo noch kein taster es spürt
> Lang in tiefinnerstem schacht

Weihlicher erde noch ruht–
Wunder undeutbar für heut
Geschick wird des kommenden tages. (I, 428)

For who, who of you, brothers–
Start not at my warning–can doubt
That what you praise most highly,
That what you now think most worthy,
Is sodden foliage in fall wind,
Realm of the end and of death.

Only that which in safeguarding sleep,
There where no seeker will find it,
Long in the deepest cavern,
Of hallowed earth does rest–
Inexplicable wonder today,
Is the destiny of tomorrow.

The forces evoked in "Geheimes Deutschland," from which George expects a reversal of the fate of mankind in a distant future, become increasingly prominent in his later works. In their name, he expressed the warnings of *Der Siebente Ring* and *Der Stern des Bundes,* hoping through the power of his words to effect a wider awareness that man's faith in his reason and his technology, in an indefinite progress, might, in the light of the religious and philosophic insights of the past, be more questionable than generally supposed. In *Das Neue Reich*, there is a sense of resignation and doubt that the reversal George hoped for would come in the immediate future, although his faith in his insights and his art certainly never waned. In the foreword to the final volume of the *Blätter*, George expressed confidence that his ideas and the principles of art he propounded would live on in the younger members of his circle, the "grandchildren," as he called them–"the expectation of a single human life can hardly reach further." In the arts and sciences, he saw only

chaos . . . here rodent-like pedantry and baffling divisions and distinctions, there dissolution and distortion to the point of jabbering, smearing, and grotesque grimace. We can only be concerned with what lies beyond the great swamp [of the present]. . . . In this general confusion, in which sides which are essentially the same are furiously in conflict, it hardly makes sense to call out words of dignity, of noble feeling, or even of reason. . . . Only very few can see that the ultimate fate of a people reveals itself in its poetry.[22]

George's resignation about the immediate impact of his works is apparent in the greater degree of literary distance he interposed between himself and his audience. In his later works, he eschewed the immediacy of the first-person lyrical statement used in *Der Siebente Ring* and *Der Stern des Bundes* in favor of their expression through dramatic masks, *personae*. In *Algabal* and the "three books," he had used this technique to communicate the extremes of his personal, existential situation. Now it is merged with the urgency of his religious conviction, to which he wishes to give a form beyond his lyrical personality. The use of Goethe and Hölderlin as such *personae*, the consistent reference to the "seer" and "poet" in the third person in "Der Krieg" and "Der Dichter in Zeiten der Wirren," are significant examples of the withdrawal of the lyrical self from the polemic aspect of George's work in favor of the search for a more universally valid epic or dramatic presentation.

In the four brief dramatic episodes which close the first section of *Das Neue Reich*, this literary distance becomes unmistakable. According to Morwitz, "The four dialogues treat powers opposed to present-day attitudes and actions, which, in the opinion of the poet, are not acknowledged today but are vitally necessary to complete the cycle of life and thereby preserve its vitality. 'Der Gehenkte' ('The Hanged Man') embodies the 'anti-deed,' the 'Faun' [in "Der Mensch und der Drud" ("Man and Faun")] embodies 'anti-magic,' Christ [in "Gespräch des Herrn mit dem römischen Hauptmann" ("The Lord and the Roman Captain")] here the 'anti-faith,' and the Conqueror [in "Der Brand des Tempels" ("The Burning of the Temple")] the anti-world."[23] "Der Gehenkte" (I, 429) insists that men must understand the force of evil in order to be able to understand virtue, with which evil is in an inextricably intimate relationship in the dynamism of life. In "Der Mensch und der Drud" (I, 430-32), a hunter meets a faun, the half-animal, half-human representative of a realm of magic and myth which the hunter had long believed banished by human progress. The faun tells him that the chthonic powers of nature, which man does not choose to understand, are the essential links in the chain of being, which give life its proportion, its rhythm, and its meaning. The faun tells the hunter, who is sufficiently infuriated to kill him, but relents:

> Had but your mind been at work, long since
> Would your race be destroyed and all its deeds,
> Your wood would all be dry, barren your fields . . .
> Only through magic does life arise. (I, 432)

Despite the similarity of the position of the faun to that of the witches in "Hexenreihen" (I, 254-55), he is distinctly the party of this dialogue to "have the last word." Contrary to the witches, he subsumes in his arguments the position of human rationality and its ideals and does not have the same restriction of viewpoint which casts an ironic light on the insights of the witches.

"Gespräch des Herrn mit dem römischen Hauptmann" (I, 433-34) is a dialogue between Christ and a Roman captain, Philippos, who comes to Him for counsel in his spiritual need. Stefan George invented this situation, and although the dialogue obviously reflects elements from the New Testament and Christian apocryphal writings, it is not based on any specific chronicle. In answering Philippos' questions, Jesus explains that the miracles he performed—"Child he who needs them, child whom they offend" (I, 433)—were acts of faith for Him and those they benefited, not mere demonstrations of His power. Without faith they would not be. Christ preaches to the poor, to fishers and publicans, rather than to the wise, because the highest degree of rational knowledge of the present is "rubble and chaff." Only through the "inflamed blood" of the faithful, the inspiration of the souls of the common people, can come the salvation of the world.

The central question which Philippos puts to Jesus is whether He has "led the round-dance," the ritual dance in whose ecstatic frenzy the God is united with the leader of the round, as all of the religions Philippos knows—the Eleusinian mysteries, Mithraism, the asceticism of the Gymnosophists[24]—teach is necessary for the epiphany. Christ answers that He had indeed led this round, although the main body of the Christian teaching does not mention this, and Christ speaks no words about it, preferring to reveal only part of His nature, namely the fire of his faith. For George, Christ's relationship to God encompasses a greater whole than tradition, except for the apocryphal "dance hymns" of Christ and His disciples, makes known.[25] For George, Christ is thus far closer to "brotherhood" with Dionysus than is acknowledged in the sharp rejection of pagan analogues by Christian theology; but the time is not yet ripe for this truth to be understood, except by very few. Jesus says to Philippos:

> Des Sohnes banner mag im erdrund siegend wehn
> Äonenlang sein sinnbild ob den völkern stehn
> Eh wer des bundes fülle schaut: den Christ im tanz. (I, 434)
>
> The Son's victorious banner in the world
> Must wave for eons, symbol for the peoples,
> Ere the bond's fullness is revealed: Dancing Christ.

Christ dismisses Philippos, whose blood is "too thin" to bear this truth.

The longest and most portentous of the four dialogues is "Der Brand des Tempels" (I, 435-41), which was published in the final volume of *Die Blätter für die Kunst* in 1919. For many of its readers, this poetic drama seemed to symbolize the end of Western civilization, which had begun with the savage combat among the members of the European cultural community and the outbreak of the Russian Revolution. It accorded with the cultural pessimism of Oswald Spengler's *Decline of the West* (1918-22), which was, as Hildebrandt says, "in everybody's minds at the time."[26] The sense that the end of an eon had come when Last Judgment should rightfully take place is expressed in a poem by George entitled "Nova Apocalypsis" ("New Apocalypse"), which he published in the section devoted to Wolfskehl's poems in the last volume of the *Blätter*. Instead of Christ triumphant come to judge the world after the reign of Antichrist, it is Beelzebub, the god of the flies, who reigns in the form of the barbarous masses which overrun the world, destroying everything:

End-Christ, End-Christ, mocked with foul lies,
Instead of You comes the Lord of the Flies,

Larva crawled out of rotting brains rife
Have now broken forth, have come to life,

In all streets they strut like conquering lords,
"Ours is the kingdom, we're coming in hordes.

One man's standing straight, knock him down,
THAT one's fair face we'll distort to a frown.
. . .
Away with souls, with heights and heaven,
We creep and we swarm; dust is our leaven."[27]

That this mordant pessimism was only regarded by George as a momentary mood of despair is attested by the fact that he did not choose to have this poem appear under his own name. It also does not appear in his *Collected Works.* The truer indication of George's thinking is the end of "Der Brand des Tempels," at which the temple, the repository of all the religious and cultural traditions of the conquered civilization, which have no binding power anymore, are destroyed, and it will take another "half-a-thousand years" for the cultural height to be achieved at which such a temple can be built once more out of the fresh energy of a new civilization and culture which will arise from the ashes of the old.

The entire action of "Der Brand des Tempels" is reported by the priests, who await the momentary destruction of the sacred shrine or word of its salvation through the intercession of the princess of the conquered city, Pamfilia. In a final attempt to move the leader of the Huns, who have conquered this older, more urbane, but exhausted culture, to spare the temple, she has gone to him to plead for mercy. The leader of the Huns, called Ili by the priests, terms himself the "scourge of God," as Attila styled himself. Although he does not appear in the play, he is its dominating personality, the most fully developed and rounded of the warrior-kings who have appeared in George's works since the *Pilgerfahrten*: the ruler in "Mahnung"; Algabal; the oriental king of *Das Buch der Hängenden Gärten*; and the various kings and conquerors of the "Gestalten" in *Der Siebente Ring*. It has been pointed out earlier (Cf. p. 52, above) that George felt a strong affinity to this kind of figure, rejecting ultimately the course of action such a nature implied. This affinity emerges more strongly than ever in "Der Brand des Tempels," where episodes from the reported life of Ili even correspond to events of George's own.[28] The enigmatic ruler is harsh but just, as the priests admit, and thus wins the confidence of the conquered people. He regards himself less as a conqueror than as a deliverer from the weakness and slackness that have made this city fall before him. He says to the priests:

> "You cannot heal the rot that plagues your land,
> What good are gods that render you no help?
> Or books or pictures that no more exalt?
> Thank him who frees you from this chaos." (I, 436)

His own integrity, his sense of rightness and necessity will not let him do otherwise than destroy the temple, for it is merely a relic, symbolic of a cultural heritage that has lost its meaning in the present. To the princess, "the choicest and fullest flower of her clan," who exhorts him to spare the temple, he answers:

> "Mildness suits majesty
> In face of every frailty but never
> When principle must suffer. So 'tis here.
> Must I pay THAT price to show you my mercy?
> What bends me now will break me on the morrow." (I, 440-41)

Pamfilia, seeing the relentlessness of his logic, takes her own life, fleeing from "a world grown poor." As the flames begin to break out at all corners of the temple, the priests follow her example:

> The temple burns. Half a thousand years
> Must roll on ere it stands anew. (I, 441)

Stefan George shares the sadness and despair of the priests over the loss and destruction of the wisdom and beauty of the cultural tradition, as much, if not more, than he does the ruthless knowledge of the conqueror that it is necessary, an ineluctable law of history, of new growth and development. That which is overripe must rot and disappear, making room for the new. "Der Brand des Tempels" is the most eloquent and balanced expression of Stefan George's cultural despair.

The closing section of *Das Neue Reich,* following the more personal statements of the "Words for the Living" and "Words for the Dead" (I, 442-60), is entitled "Das Lied" ("The Song"). These twelve poems, together with the odes "An die Kinder des Meeres" ("To the Children of the Sea") (I, 406-9) and the three "Gebete" ("Prayers") (I, 421-22), are the sectors of the subjective lyrical impulse in *Das Neue Reich,* which is otherwise dominated by the vatic and didactic function of the poet. Ranging from the balladesque tribute to the magic of poetry and the imagination, "Das Lied" ("The Song") (I, 461-62), to the exquisite intensity of the closing poem, "Du schlank und rein wie eine flamme" ("Thou pure and slender as a flame") (I, 469), these poems show the lyrical art of Stefan George at its apex. At the close of his creative life, the poet strove for the impersonal, universal validity of the *Volkslied.* One poem especially, "Das Wort" ("The Word") (I, 466-67), restates the conviction of the magical power of language to mediate men's understanding of the world, a conviction that underlies the entire work of Stefan George from the earliest *Hymnen* onward. The poet brings his treasured dreams to the "norn," the symbol of his poetic power, who gives them reality by finding their "names" in the spring she guards. For one dream, especially precious, she can find no name, and it is doomed to disappear. This drives home to the poet the ultimate truth of his art:

So lernt ich traurig den verzicht:
Kein ding sei wo das wort gebricht. (I, 467)

Sad resignation ends my tale,
No thing can be where words must fail.

CHAPTER 6

Conclusion

"I am an end and a beginning." These words from *Der Stern des Bundes* define the poet's capacity to embrace all extremes of earthly existence. As self-appraisal, they have also been aptly cited as an index of Stefan George's place in the development of lyrical poetry in Germany.[1] To accord with the sequence of George's career as a poet, however, this formulation would have to be reversed, for his role in influencing the main trends of this development precedes the time in which he perpetuated the tradition of the classical idealism of Goethe and Hölderlin. This apparent later "conservatism" of form on George's part, his attempt to express values alien to the disillusioned *Weltanschauung* of modern man, has led to his consistent exclusion, on the critics' part, from the ranks of truly "modern" poets, to a denial even of his relevance to the major literary movements of his time and ours. Thus, Hugo Friedrich groups George with "heirs and late classical authors of a centuries-old lyrical style,"[2] and Hans Magnus Enzensberger considers him too far removed from the "world language" (*Weltsprache*) of lyrical evolution in the past century for inclusion in his *Museum of Modern Poetry.*[3]

Especially in the light of Enzensberger's working definition of modern poetry as "poetry after Whitman and Baudelaire, after Rimbaud and Mallarmé,"[4] such judgments distort the truth, useful as they may be in defining their author's intentions. Choosing to see only the latest phase of Stefan George's creative life, such historians ignore the fact that the greater part of his activity as a poet, translator, and critic was devoted to the "renewal" of German poetry, to the creation of a modern, "spiritual" art which would continue the tradition which, as George himself acknowledged, was founded by Baudelaire and the "masters," Verlaine and Mallarmé. These opinions, still widely held, were pronounced almost a decade ago. Lately, a wider awareness of Stefan George's significance to the literary scene of his time outside his immediate circle is becoming apparent, as evidenced by Manfred Durzak's recent study of George's influence on Expressionist writers, such as Ernst Stadler, Georg Heym, Carl Sternheim, Ernst Blass, Gottfried Benn, Fritz von Unruh, and Reinhard Goering.[5]

Stefan George was a modern poet through more than an accident of birth. In his life and art he sought answers to the same questions which had occupied Baudelaire and Mallarmé: the existential problems of the creative spirit in an adversary relationship to the axioms of the empiric universe. This opposition is engendered by the individual's perception of another, transcendent dimension of reality which can only be expressed symbolically. Through the magic of words, the poet can create an esthetically, and ultimately morally, felicitous "antiuniverse." Because of the hermetic quality of the poet's relationship to language, the contours of this "anti-universe" are even more idiosyncratic and private than comparable writings of the German Romantics, which, for all their visionary nature, still had archetypal analogues in folk songs and legends. It is the tension between an intensely perceived subjective world and an apparently ephemeral objective reality, with the poet consciously opting for the former, which constitutes the watershed between the "traditional" and the "modern."

Stefan George's development as a poet can be seen in terms of a lifelong attempt to resolve this polarity. Conditioned, at least in part, by his upbringing in the Catholic faith and by a strong affinity for Platonic idealism, George was, from the very outset, at odds with the extremes of nihilism implicit in the poetry of Baudelaire and Rimbaud, for whom the synthetic order of the work of art represented the only rescue from the chaos of existence. This nihilism seemed to dictate the poet's flight into a solipsistic world of hermetic symbols. In *Hymnen, Pilgerfahrten* and especially in *Algabal,* the possible joys, but also the certainly present terrors, of such an escape from confrontation with existence are pondered, and the solipsistic alternative rejected.

The "three books" convey the insight that men in other and earlier cultures were better able to endure the trials of human existence through knowledge of their inclusion in a divinely ordained order, their unquestioning commitment to their fates. The rationalistically ordained alienation between perceiving mind and empiric matter had not yet been inflicted upon them. In *Das Jahr der Seele* and *Der Teppich des Lebens,* George's conviction emerges that this alienation, through which man has become, in his own eyes, merely a mechanically and biologically determined element of the universe, is not *necessarily* in the nature of things, is not an inescapable curse of modern existence. Rather, the individual can be reconciled in his existence to the universe of "objective reality." This can occur through his understanding of the transcendent interrelation of all phenomena, that the universe is the physical extension of a higher, spiritual realm, man's fate the symbolic expression of an ultimately inscrutable providence, analogous to divine will. Thus, George commits himself to the essentially religious world view, theologically unorthodox as his synthesis of pantheistic ideas might be.

This new intellectual and spiritual constellation put Stefan George into opposition with the "modern" insights about human existence and the hopelessness of its alienation. In contrast to the esthetic, subjective order which the Symbolists had created in their poetry, George had seemingly found a moral, objective order, to which his art was thenceforth to be subordinated. Formal perfectionism, exciting variety of rhythms, rhymes, and moods, continued to characterize his poems; but in *Der Siebente Ring, Der Stern des Bundes,* and *Das Neue Reich,* these elements no longer served the search for a subjectively satisfying order, but the proclamation of a hopefully redemptive perception. A poet whose beginnings had associated him closely with the significant trends of contemporary European poetry, George now became a "vatic" poet, a "seer" and idealistic interpreter of a high principle of will in the world in the tradition of Goethe, Hölderlin, and Nietzsche.

To his mind, George had achieved the synthesizing harmony between the subjective and objective perception of reality which contemporary and younger poets were still seeking, either in an embrace of pure feeling, as with the Expressionists, or, in the case of later poets, in an attempt to integrate material reality, the language and concerns of the present, into their poetry. This certainty in the midst of uncertainty, this absoluteness in the face of a general insight into the relativity of all things, obviously served to isolate George in his time. These qualities explain much of the vehemence in the controversy his name is still capable of arousing. The apparent assurance he had in the rightness of his views, George's fatalism as to whether he would ever be understood is expressed in the last lines of a poem from *Das Neue Reich*:

> You had a vision fair and new,
> But time grew old, no man now lives,
> If e'er he'll come, you do not know,
>
> He who can see this vision too. (I, 463)

Whether or not we can see and share Stefan George's vision of the world and his times, his works bear witness to the unremitting striving of a man of unique poetic and intellectual powers to find a higher meaning in his existence and ours.

Notes and References

Chapter One

1. Novalis (Friedrich von Hardenberg), *Heinrich von Ofterdingen* (Frankfurt, Hamburg: Fischer, 1963), p. 77.

2. Stefan George, *Werke,* 2nd ed., 2 vols. (Munich, Düsseldorf: Küpper-Bondi, 1968), I, 479-80. Hereafter referred to as I, II within the text.

3. See Robert Boehringer, *Mein Bild von Stefan George,* 2nd ed., 2 vols. (Munich, Düsseldorf: Küpper-Bondi, 1968), I, 21-26. Hereafter referred to as *Mein Bild.*

4. Ulrich K. Goldsmith, "Stefan George and the Theatre," *PMLA,* LXVI (1951), 85-95.

5. Karl Wolfskehl, *Gesammelte Werke,* 2 vols. (Hamburg: Claassen, 1960), II, 351. For his description of the people of Darmstadt see *ibid.,* II, 347-50: "Darmstädter Nationalgesichter." Little has been written about George's early years. Again Robert Boehringer provides most of the information we possess. See also Friedrich Wolters, *Stefan George und die Blätter für die Kunst: Deutsche Geistesgeschichte seit 1890* (Berlin: Bondi, 1930), pp. 13-16. Wolters criticizes the system of German higher education which stressed accumulation of knowledge rather than the formation of personality: "traditions gradually decayed, and the way of teaching caused in him [George]—as in all richer minds—more resistance than love." See also Bernhard Zeller, ed., *Stefan George. 1868-1968. Der Dichter und sein Kreis* (Munich: Kösel, 1968), pp. 40-46. Another treatment of this early period can be found in the book by Ulrich K. Goldsmith, *Stefan George: A Study of his Early Work* (Boulder, Colo.: University of Colorado Press, 1959). See also the short English biography by Ernst Morwitz in Stefan George, *Poems,* tr. Carol North Valhope and Ernst Morwitz (New York: Pantheon, 1943), pp. 11-13. The most recent publication on George's early years is by Manfred Durzak, *Der junge Stefan George: Kunsttheorie und Dichtung* (Munich: Fink, 1968). This book in particular treats George's sense of crisis concerning poetic language before *Algabal.*

6. *Blätter für die Kunst,* founded by Stefan George, publ. by C. A. Klein, 12 vols. (Berlin, 1892-1919) [Reprint: Düsseldorf, Munich: Küpper-Bondi, 1967]. Hereafter referred to as *Blätter.*

7. U. K. Goldsmith, *Stefan George,* p. 27.

8. R. Boehringer, *Mein Bild,* I, 33.

9. *Blätter,* V, 2.

10. Ernst Robert Curtius, *Kritische Essays zur europäischen Literatur,* 3rd ed. (Bern, Munich: Francke, 1963), p. 112.

11. F. Wolters, *Blätter für die Kunst*, pp. 16-17.
12. R. Boehringer, *Mein Bild*, I, 28.
13. *Ibid.*, I, 29.
14. *Ibid.*, I, 28.
15. *Ibid.*, I, 30.
16. Karl Beckson, ed., *Aesthetes and Decadents of the 1890's* (New York: Random House, 1966), p. 141.
17. Albert Mockel, "Quelque Souvenirs sur Stefan George," *Revue d'Allemagne*, II (1928), 389.
18. P. Martino, *Parnasse et Symbolisme. 1850-1900*, 2nd ed. (Paris: Colin, 1928), p. 124. See also Robert Gibson, ed., *Modern French Poets on Poetry* (Cambridge: At the University Press, 1961), pp. 81-90; and Wallace Fowlie, *Mallarmé* (London: Dobson, 1953), pp. 18-21.
19. Hubert Arbogast, *Die Erneuerung der deutschen Dichtersprache in den Frühwerken Stefan Georges. Eine stilgeschichtliche Untersuchung* (Cologne, Graz: Böhlau, 1967), p. 57.
20. Angel Flores, ed., *An Anthology of French Poetry from Nerval to Valéry in English Translation* (Garden City, N. Y.: Doubleday, 1958), p. 100 and p. 348.
21. R. Boehringer, *Mein Bild*, I, 222: "Paris, le seul endroit où j'ai trouvé et possède encore de véritables amis."
22. See M. Durzak, *op. cit.*, pp. 113ff., especially the section "The discovery of language."
23. U. K. Goldsmith, *Stefan George*, p. 12. Goldsmith refers to R. M. Berry's thesis "The French Symbolist Poets in Germany," which "shows conclusively that the new poetry became known about 1890 through the efforts of critics and writers outside George's circle. . . . Hermann Bahr, who was, perhaps, the most sensitive of the group, . . . through his friendship with Hugo von Hofmannsthal, was later in indirect contact, although never associated, with the George circle." Bahr also visited France in 1889.
24. *Blätter*, I, 1-2.
25. Georg Peter Landmann, *Stefan George und sein Kreis. Eine Bibliographie* (Hamburg: Hauswedell, 1960), p. 129. This bibliography is the most complete collection of data on George to have appeared.
26. *Briefwechsel zwischen George und Hofmannsthal*, ed. Robert Boehringer, 2nd ed. (Munich, Düsseldorf: Küpper-Bondi, 1953), pp. 12-13.
27. *Ibid.*, p. 14.
28. *Ibid.*, p. 239.
29. R. Boehringer, *Mein Bild*, I, 49.
30. *Ibid.*, I, 62.
31. Edgar Salin, *Um Stefan George. Erinnerung und Zeugnis*, 2nd ed. (Munich, Düsseldorf: Küpper-Bondi, 1954), p. 165. Hereafter referred to as *Um Stefan George*.
32. Stefan George und Karl Wolfskehl, *Deutsche Dichtung. Zweiter Band: Goethe*, 2nd ed. (Berlin: Bondi, 1910), p. 7. See the unpublished M.A. thesis by Erika A. Metzger (-Hirt), "Klopstock and the Stefan George *Kreis*" (Cornell University, 1961); and, by the same author,

"Das Klopstockbild Stefan Georges und seines Kreises," *PMLA*, LXXIX (1964), 289-96.

33. *Stefan George, Friedrich Gundolf, Briefwechsel,* ed. Robert Boehringer and Georg Peter Landmann (Munich, Düsseldorf: Küpper-Bondi, 1962). Hereafter referred to as *Briefwechsel.*

34. For a biography and comprehensive treatment of Gundolf's life and work, see Victor A. Schmitz, *Gundolf. Eine Einführung in sein Werk* (Düsseldorf, Munich: Küpper-Bondi, 1965).

35. Goethe, *Werke,* ed. Erich Trunz, 14 vols. (Hamburg: Wegner, 1948ff.), XII, 487.

36. For example, Franz Schonauer, *Stefan George in Selbstzeugnissen und Bilddokumenten* (Hamburg: Rowohlt, 1960), p. 92.

37. St. George, F. Gundolf, *Briefwechsel,* p. 381

38. R. Boehringer, *Mein Bild,* I, 84.

39. E. Salin, *Um Stefan George,* p. 192.

40. *Blätter,* IX, 2.

41. Edward Jaime-Liebig, *Stefan George und die Weltliteratur* (Ulm: Aegis-Verlag, 1949), pp. 40 and 41.

42. E. Salin, *Um Stefan George,* p. 46.

43. Rudolf Pannwitz, *Albert Verwey und Stefan George* (Heidelberg, Darmstadt: Schneider, 1965), p. 48. Shakespeare quoted from the following edition: *The Complete Plays and Poems of William Shakespeare,* ed. W. A. Neilson and C. J. Hill (Cambridge, Mass.: Houghton Mifflin Co., 1942), p. 562.

44. *Briefwechsel zwischen George und Hofmannsthal,* p. 166.

Chapter Two

1. Claude David, *Von Richard Wagner zu Bertolt Brecht. Eine Geschichte der neueren deutschen Literatur,* tr. Hermann Stiehl (Frankfurt: S. Fischer, 1964), p. 17.

2. Friedrich Nietzsche, *Werke,* ed. Karl Schlechta, 3 vols. (Munich: Hanser, 1966), I, 776.

3. See the interpretation of *Hymnen* by H. Stefan Schultz, *Studien zur Dichtung Stefan Georges* (Heidelberg: Stiehm, 1967), pp. 11-32.

4. Edith Landmann, *Gespräche mit Stefan George* (Munich, Düsseldorf: Küpper-Bondi, 1963), pp. 153-54.

5. R. Boehringer, *Mein Bild,* I, 40-41. Also Ernst Morwitz, *Kommentar zu dem Werk Stefan Georges* (Munich, Düsseldorf: Küpper-Bondi, 1960), pp. 7ff. Hereafter referred to as *Kommentar.*

6. Friedrich Gundolf, *George* (Berlin: Bondi, 1920), pp. 61-62. Hereafter referred to as *George.* Also H. S. Schultz, *op. cit.,* pp. 12-17.

7. E. Morwitz, *Kommentar,* p. 29. In the second edition of *Mein Bild,* I, 277-78, Boehringer argues that George probably did not meet Ida Coblenz until the summer of 1892.

8. H. S. Schultz, *op. cit.,* p. 25, fn. 27.

9. E. Morwitz, *Kommentar,* p. 41. Also U. K. Goldsmith, *Stefan George,* p. 49.

10. Claude David, *Stefan George. Sein dichterisches Werk,* tr. A. Remmen and K. Thiemer (Munich: Hanser, 1967), pp. 63-64.

11. Claus Victor Bock, *Wort-Konkordanz zur Dichtung Stefan Georges* (Amsterdam: Castrum Peregrini Presse, 1964), pp. 318-20.

12. Carl August Klein, "Über Stefan George. Eine neue Kunst," *Blätter,* I, 49-50.

13. Victor A. Oswald, "The Historical Content of Stefan George's 'Algabal'," *GR,* XXIII (1948), 193-205. For the section on *Algabal* and the artificial kingdom as symbol of the modern poet and his realm, see Werner Vordtriede, *Novalis und die französischen Symbolisten* (Stuttgart: Kohlhammer, 1963), pp. 43-97. Also Manfred Durzak, *op. cit.,* pp. 190-202.

14. F. Gundolf, *George,* p. 77.

15. *Ibid.,* p. 81.

16. C. David, *Stefan George,* p. 76.

17. E. Landmann, *Gespräche,* p. 100.

18. C. David, *Stefan George,* pp. 77ff.

19. Professor H. Stefan Schultz made these remarks in a paper read at the Stefan George Symposium at Northwestern University in October, 1968.

20. Manfred Durzak, *op. cit.,* pp. 242-44, also intepretes *mal* in the sense of human feeling, but believes that Algabal rejects the priestess for having lost the individuality he himself has destroyed in her.

21. Hugo von Hofmannsthal, "Gedichte von Stefan George," *Ausgewählte Werke in zwei Bänden,* ed. Rudolf Hirsch, 2 vols. (Frankfurt: S. Fischer, 1957), II, 306-13.

22. *Ibid.,* p. 308.

23. *Ibid.,* p. 311.

24. E. Morwitz, *Kommentar,* pp. 63-64.

25. F. Gundolf, *George,* p. 94. See also U. K. Goldsmith, *Stefan George,* Chapter V: "The Search for a Companion," pp. 57-82.

26. Most of the identities of the recipients of the *Preisgedichte* are still tentative. "Damon" is almost certainly Albert Saint-Paul, "Menippa" Ida Coblenz, "Kallimachus" Waclaw Rolicz-Lieder, "Phaon" Paul Gérardy, "Luzilla" Luisa Brück, an acquaintance of George's during this time, "Isokrates" Ludwig Klages, "Kotytto" Frieda Zimmer-Zerny, a singer, "Antinous" Edmond Rassenfosse. The identities of "Sidonia" and "Apollonia" are still indefinite. See E. Morwitz, *Kommentar,* pp. 69-79.

27. H. von Hofmannsthal, *op. cit.,* p. 313.

28. Johann Wolfgang von Goethe, "Noten und Abhandlungen zu besserem Verständnis des *West-östlichen Divans,*" *Werke,* II, 169.

Chapter Three

1. F. Gundolf, *George,* p. 131.
2. R. Boehringer, *Mein Bild,* I, 206.
3. E. Morwitz, *Kommentar,* p. 125.
4. U. K. Goldsmith, *Stefan George,* p. 78.

5. E. Morwitz, *Kommentar,* p. 125.
6. *Ibid.,* p. 112.
7. *Ibid.,* p. 119.
8. F. Gundolf, *George,* p. 157.
9. C. David, *Stefan George,* p. 174.
10. *Ibid.,* pp. 188-89.
11. E. Morwitz, *Kommentar,* p. 175.
12. C. David, *Stefan George,* p. 168.
13. E. Morwitz, *Kommentar,* pp. 187-88.
14. *Ibid.,* pp. 192-97.

Chapter Four

1. St. George, F. Gundolf, *Briefwechsel,* p. 136.
2. Hereafter the following distinction will be made: "Ihr meiner zeit genossen" = "Das Zeitgedicht I" and "Ich euch gewissen. . ." = "Das Zeitgedicht II."
3. Jakob Grimm, Wilhelm Grimm, *Deutsches Wörterbuch* (Leipzig: Hirzel, 1956), XV, 585.
4. Heinrich Heine, *Sämtliche Werke,* ed. O. Walzel, 11 vols. (Leipzig: Insel, 1912), II, 127-52.
5. Dante Alighieri, *The Divine Comedy,* ed. C. H. Grandgent and E. H. Wilkins (New York: Random House, 1950), p. 606.
6. E. Landmann, *Gespräche,* pp. 100, 115.
7. E. Morwitz, *Kommentar,* p. 222.
8. *Ibid.,* p. 223.
9. F. W. L'Ormeau, *Die Christologie Stefan Georges* (Amsterdam: Castrum Peregrini Presse, 1953), p. 7.
10. E. Morwitz, *Kommentar,* pp. 239-40.
11. *The Works of Stefan George,* trans. Olga Marx and Ernst Morwitz (Chapel Hill, N. C.: The University of North Carolina Press, 1949) [Reprint: New York: AMS Press, 1966], p. 178.
12. E. Landmann, *Gespräche,* p. 42.
13. *Ibid.,* p. 46.
14. E. Morwitz, *Kommentar,* p. 288.
15. *Ibid.,* p. 290.
16. Kurt Hildebrandt, *Das Werk Stefan Georges* (Hamburg: Hauswedell, 1960), p. 289.
17. J. W. Goethe, *Werke,* I, 358.
18. E. Morwitz, *Kommentar,* p. 293.
19. *Ibid.,* p. 295.
20. *Ibid.,* p. 298.
21. K. Hildebrandt, *Das Werk Stefan Georges,* pp. 299-300.
22. E. Morwitz, *Kommentar,* pp. 303-4.
23. *Ibid.,* p. 310.
24. K. Hildebrandt, *Das Werk Stefan Georges,* pp. 303-4.
25. Michael Winkler, "Zu einigen Liedern im *Siebenten Ring* Stefan Georges," *GQ,* XXXVIII (1965), 298-309.

26. E. Morwitz, *Kommentar,* p. 334. Momme Mommsen has discovered the important influence of the *Centuries* by Nostradamus on the "Rhein-Tafeln": "Nostradamus-Anklänge in Stefan Georges 'Tafeln'," *Castrum Peregrini,* LXXXI (1968), 44-57.
27. E. Morwitz, *Kommentar,* pp. 333-34.

Chapter Five

1. C. David, *Stefan George,* p. 276.
2. E. Salin, *Um Stefan George,* pp. 236-37.
3. F. Gundolf, *George,* p. 244.
4. E. Morwitz, *Kommentar,* p. 352.
5. Momme Mommsen, "Die Problematik des Priestertums bei Hölderlin," *Hölderlin-Jahrbuch 1967/1968,* pp. 53-74. Cf. especially pp. 53ff.
6. The poem consists of nine lines. The first letter of the first line, the second letter of the second, etc., together spell the name *Hölderlin.*
7. E. Morwitz, *Kommentar,* p. 362.
8. *Ibid.,* pp. 365ff.
9. *Ibid.,* pp. 389f.
10. F. Hölderlin, "Hälfte des Lebens," *Friedrich Hölderlin, Werke in einem Band,* ed. F. Usinger (Hamburg: Hoffmann und Campe, n.d.), p. 97.
11. E. Morwitz, *Kommentar,* p. 408.
12. Cf. Hans Gerhard, *Stefan George und die deutsche Dichtung,* Gießener Beiträge zur deutschen Philologie, 53 (Giessen, 1937).
13. F. Hölderlin, *Werke,* p. 12.
14. *Ibid.,* p. 119.
15. *Ibid.,* p. 220.
16. St. George, F. Gundolf, *Briefwechsel,* pp. 263-64.
17. E. Morwitz, *Kommentar,* pp. 422-23.
18. *Ibid.,* p. 436.
19. *Ibid.,* p. 442.
20. *Ibid.,* pp. 443-45.
21. *Ibid.,* p. 463.
22. *Blätter,* XI/XII, 5.
23. E. Morwitz, *Kommentar,* p. 457.
24. *Ibid.,* p. 452.
25. Cf. also K. Hildebrandt, *Das Werk Stefan Georges,* pp. 425-34; and F. W. L'Ormeau, *Die Christologie Stefan Georges.*
26. K. Hildebrandt, *Das Werk Stefan Georges,* p. 439.
27. *Blätter,* XI/XII, 32.
28. Morwitz, *Kommentar,* pp. 455f. For example, it is reported how Ili's mother carried her son up to the mountain as a child so that the sun would shine upon him. George's mother is said to have done this with her children.

Chapter Six

1. Eckhard Heftrich, *Stefan George* (Frankfurt: Klostermann, 1968), p. 6.

2. Hugo Friedrich, *Die Struktur der modernen Lyrik* (Hamburg: Rowohlt, 1956), p. 8.

3. Hans Magnus Enzensberger, *Museum der modernen Poesie* (Munich: dtv, 1969), p. 24.

4. *Ibid.*, p. 9.

5. Manfred Durzak, "Nachwirkungen Stefan Georges im Expressionismus," *GQ*, XLII (1969), 393-417.

Selected Bibliography

Note: Since the volumes of the original edition of George's *Collected Works* have become collectors' items, the edition in two volumes, which appeared in 1958 and 1968, has become standard for scholarly purposes. The individual volumes of the original complete edition are being reprinted. These contain appendices in which earlier publication of poems is indicated with variants wherever appropriate. Thus, the individual volumes approximate most closely a critical edition. The two-volume edition should be used with constant reference to the newly reprinted *Blätter für die Kunst* for critical purposes. The two most complete bibliographies on George are those by Ulrich K. Goldsmith (1959) and Georg Peter Landmann (1960). The following bibliography is not intended to be complete, listing only the most important publications in German and as many titles as possible which the English-speaking reader would find helpful. Titles consulted which do not relate directly to George and his work are listed in the footnotes to the various chapters. All abbreviations of periodical names are in accordance with the "Master List and Table of Abbreviations" appearing in the *PMLA International Bibliography*.

PRIMARY SOURCES

STEFAN GEORGE. *Gesamt-Ausgabe der Werke: Endgültige Fassung*, 18 vols. in 15 (Berlin: Bondi, 1927-34).

------. *Werke. Ausgabe in zwei Bänden*, ed. R[OBERT] B[OEHRINGER]. 2nd ed., 2 vols. (Düsseldorf, Munich: Küpper-Bondi, 1968).

Blätter für die Kunst, founded by STEFAN GEORGE, publ. by CARL AUGUST KLEIN. 12 vols. (Berlin, 1892-1919) [Reprint; Düsseldorf, Munich: Küpper-Bondi, 1967].

Deutsche Dichtung, ed. STEFAN GEORGE and KARL WOLFSKEHL. 2nd ed., 3 vols. (Berlin: Bondi, 1910).

Briefwechsel, STEFAN GEORGE and FRIEDRICH GUNDOLF. Ed. ROBERT BOEHRINGER and GEORG PETER LANDMANN (Munich, Düsseldorf: Küpper-Bondi, 1962).

Briefwechsel zwischen George und Hofmannsthal, ed. ROBERT BOEHRINGER. 2nd ed. (Munich, Düsseldorf: Küpper-Bondi, 1953).

Translations of works by Stefan George into English can be found in the following:

BROICHER, DAISY. *German Lyrists of Today* (London: Mathews, 1909).

COXWELL, C. FILLINGHAM. *German Poetry* (London: Daniel, 1938).

Deutsch, Babette and Avraham Yarmolinsky. *Contemporary German Poetry* (New York: Harcourt-Brace, 1923).

Gee, Kenneth. "Seasong," *Translation* (London: Phoenix Press, 1945).

———. "Abend des Festes," "Die Fremde," *Translation* (London: Phoenix Press, 1947).

———. "Komm in den totgesagten park," *The Listener*. London, November 6, 1952.

Gross, Harvey. "The Tapestry, after Stefan George," *Poetry*, LXXXIII, 1 (1953), 18.

Kyler, Ingrid. "Days and Deeds. Notes and Sketches by Stefan George," *University of Kansas City Review*, XVIII (1951), 143-57.

Luke, F. D. "Poems by Stefan George," *GLL*, V (1952), 184-87.

Marx, Olga (Carol North Valhope). "Ten Poems by Stefan George," *Poet Lore*, XLV (1939), 343-47.

———. [Four poems by Stefan George], *GLL*, III (1939), 231f.

——— and Ernst Morwitz. *Stefan George. Poems* (New York: Pantheon, 1943).

———. "The Mirror," "Looking Back," *Translation* (London: Phoenix Press, 1945).

———. *The Works of Stefan George*, "Studies in the Germanic Languages and Literatures," II (Chapel Hill, N. C.: The University of North Carolina Press, 1949) [Reprint: New York: AMS Press, 1966].

Münsterberg, Margarete. "The Shepherd's Day," "The Vigil," *A Harvest of German Verse* (New York, London: Appleton, 1916).

Phelps, Reginald H. and E. B. Ashton. "Poems by Stefan George," *Decision*, II, 4 (1941).

Ponsonby, E. Talbot. "Poems by Stefan George," *GLL*, II (1938), 150-52.

Salinger, Herman. *Twentieth-Century German Verse* (Princeton, N.J.: Princeton University Press, 1952).

Scott, Cyril Meir. *Stefan George. Selection from His Works Translated into English* (London: Mathews, 1910).

———. *The Celestial Aftermath, a Springtide of the Heart and Faraway Songs* (London: Chatto and Windus, 1915), p. 67.

———. "Translations from Stefan George," *GLL*, XII (1959), 191-94.

Spender, Stephen. "Stefan George. My Boy Came Home," *Encounter* XII (April, 1959), 27.

Steinberg, Sigfrid Heinrich. *Fifteen German Poets* (London: Macmillan, 1945).

SECONDARY SOURCES

Arbogast, Hubert. *Die Erneuerung der deutschen Dichtersprache in den Frühwerken Stefan Georges. Eine stilgeschichtliche Untersuchung* (Cologne, Graz: Böhlau, 1967).

Bays, Gwendolyn. *The Orphic Vision: Seer Poets from Novalis to Rimbaud* (Lincoln: University of Nebraska Press, 1964).

BECKSON, KARL, ed. *Aesthetes and Decadents of the 1890's* (New York: Random House, 1966).

BENNETT, E[DWIN] K[EPPEL]. *Stefan George.* "Studies in Modern European Literature and Thought" (Cambridge: Bowes & Bowes, 1954).

BENTLEY, ERIC RUSSELL. "The Story of Stefan George," *Partisan Review,* IX (1942), 321-30.

BERRY, ROBERT MEYERS. "The French Symbolist Poets in Germany (Baudelaire, Verlaine, Rimbaud): Criticism and Translations, 1870-1914." Diss., Harvard, 1944.

BITHELL, JETHRO. "Stefan George and Ida Coblenz," *German Studies Presented to L. A. Willoughby* (Oxford, 1952), pp. 1-18.

———. "Stefan George–the Man," *GLL,* IX (1955), 47-55.

BOCK, CLAUS VICTOR. *Wort-Konkordanz zur Dichtung Stefan Georges* (Amsterdam: Castrum Peregrini Presse, 1964).

BOEHRINGER, ROBERT. *Ewiger Augenblick.* 2nd ed. (Düsseldorf, Munich: Küpper-Bondi, 1965).

———. *Mein Bild von Stefan George.* 2nd ed., 2 vols. (Düsseldorf, Munich: Küpper-Bondi, 1968).

BONDI, GEORG. *Erinnerungen an Stefan George* (Berlin: Bondi, 1934).

BÖSCHENSTEIN, BERNHARD. "Wirkungen des französischen Symbolismus auf die deutsche Lyrik der Jahrhundertwende," *Euphorion,* LVIII (1964), 375-95.

BOULBY, M. "Nietzsche's Problem of the Artist and George's 'Algabal'," *MLR,* LII (1957), 72-80.

BOWRA, C[ECIL] M[AURICE]. "Stefan George," *New Oxford Outlook,* V (1934), 316-31.

———. *The Heritage of Symbolism* (London: Macmillan, 1943).

BUTLER, E. M. *The Tyranny of Greece over Germany* (Boston: Beacon Press, 1958) [Reprint of the 1935 edition].

CLOSS, AUGUST. "Stefan George's 'Third Humanism'," *Medusa's Mirror: Studies in German Literature* (London: Cresset, 1957), pp. 185-201.

CURTIUS, ERNST ROBERT. *Kritische Essays zur europäischen Literatur.* 3rd ed. (Bern, Munich: Francke, 1963).

DAVID, CLAUDE. *Stefan George. Son œuvre poétique* (Lyons, Paris: I.A.C., 1952).

———. *Stefan George. Sein dichterisches Werk,* trans. Alexa Remmen and Karl Thiemer (Munich: Hanser Verlag, 1967).

———. *Von Richard Wagner zu Bertolt Brecht. Eine Geschichte der neueren deutschen Literatur,* trans. Hermann Stiehl (Frankfurt, Hamburg: Fischer, 1964).

DURZAK, MANFRED. *Der junge Stefan George. Kunsttheorie und Dichtung* (Munich: Fink, 1968).

———. "Nachwirkungen Stefan Georges im Expressionismus," *GQ,* XLII (1969), 393-417.

DUTHIE, ENID LOWRIE. *L'influence du symbolisme français dans le renouveau poétique de l'Allemagne: Les "Blätter für die Kunst" de 1892 à 1900* (Paris: Champion, 1933).

———. "Some References to the French Symbolist Movement in the Correspondence of Stefan George and Hugo von Hofmannsthal," *Comparative Literature Studies,* IX (1943), 15-18.

ENRIGHT, D. J. "Stefan George, Friedrich Gundolf, and the Maximin Myth," *GLL,* V (1952), 176-83.

FABER DU FAUR, CURT VON. "Stefan George et le symbolisme français," *Comparative Literature,* V (1953), 151-66.

FUERST, NORBERT. *The Victorian Age of German Literature* (University Park and London: The Pennsylvania State University Press, 1966).

GERHARD, HANS. *Stefan George und die deutsche Dichtung,* Gießener Beiträge zur deutschen Philologie, 53 (Giessen, 1937).

GOLDSMITH, ULRICH K. "Stefan George and the Theatre," *PMLA,* LXVI (1951), 85-95.

———. "The Renunciation of Woman in Stefan George's 'Das Jahr der Seele'," *Monatshefte,* XLVI (1954), 113-22.

———. *Stefan George: A Study of his Early Work.* University of Colorado Studies. "Series in Language and Literature," No. 7 (Boulder, Colo.: University of Colorado Press, 1959).

GRAY, RONALD. *The German Tradition in Literature. 1871-1945* (Cambridge: At the University Press, 1965).

GUNDOLF, FRIEDRICH. *Stefan George in unsrer Zeit.* 3rd ed. (Heidelberg: Weiss, 1913).

———. *George* (Berlin: Bondi, 1920).

HEFTRICH, ECKHARD. *Stefan George* (Frankfurt am Main: Klostermann, 1968).

HELLEINER, KARL F. "Stefan George: Poet and Prophet," *UTQ,* XXI (1952), 376-86.

HILDEBRANDT, KURT. *Das Werk Stefan Georges* (Hamburg: Hauswedell, 1960).

———. *Erinnerungen an Stefan George und seinen Kreis* (Bonn: Bouvier u. Co., 1965).

JAEGER, HANS. "Stefan Georges französische Gedichte und deutsche Übertragungen," *PMLA,* LI (1936), 563-93.

JAIME-LIEBIG, EDWARD. *Stefan George und die Weltliteratur* (Ulm: Aegis-Verlag, 1949).

JOST, DOMINIK. *Ludwig Derleth* (Stuttgart: Kohlhammer, 1965).

KAHLER, ERICH VON. *Stefan George* (Pfullingen: Neske, 1964).

KLUSSMANN, PAUL GERHARD. *Stefan George. Zum Selbstverständnis der Kunst und des Dichters in der Moderne. Mit einer George-Bibliographie,* Bonner Arbeiten zur deutschen Literatur, I (Bonn: Bouvier u. Co., 1961).

KOHN, HANS. *The Mind of Germany. The Education of a Nation* (New York: Harper & Row, 1960).

LANDMANN, EDITH. *Georgika* (Heidelberg: Weiss, 1920).

———. *Gespräche mit Stefan George* (Düsseldorf, Munich: Küpper-Bondi, 1963).

LANDMANN, GEORG PETER. *Stefan George und sein Kreis. Eine Bibliographie* (Hamburg: Hauswedell, 1960).

———, ed. *Der George-Kreis. Eine Auswahl aus seinen Schriften,* Neue Wissenschaftliche Bibliothek, 8 (Cologne, Berlin: Kiepenheuer-Witsch, 1965).

LEHMANN, PETER LUTZ. *Meditationen um Stefan George* (Düsseldorf, Munich: Küpper-Bondi, 1965).

LEPSIUS, SABINE. *Stefan George. Geschichte einer Freundschaft* (Berlin: Verlag die Runde, 1935).

LINKE, HANSJÜRGEN. *Das Kultische in der Dichtung Stefan Georges und seiner Schule.* 2 vols. (Munich, Düsseldorf: Küpper-Bondi, 1960).

L'ORMEAU, F. W. *Die Christologie Stefan Georges* (Amsterdam: Castrum Peregrini Presse, 1953).

MARX, OLGA. *Stefan George in seinen Übertragungen englischer Dichtung* (Amsterdam: Castrum Peregrini Presse, 1967).

METZGER, ERIKA ALMA. "Klopstock and the Stefan George-*Kreis,*" M.A. thesis, Cornell University, 1961.

———(-HIRT). "Das Klopstockbild Stefan Georges und seines Kreises," *PMLA,* LXXIX (1964), 289-96.

MICHELS, GERD. *Die Dante-Übertragungen Stefan Georges: Studien zur Übersetzungstechnik Stefan Georges* (Munich: Fink, 1967).

MOMMSEN, MOMME. "Der Rhein und das Rheinland in der Dichtung Stefan Georges," *Castrum Peregrini,* LXXXI (1968), 30-43.

———. "Nostradamus-Anklänge in Stefan Georges 'Tafeln'," *Castrum Peregrini,* LXXXI (1968), 44-57.

MORWITZ, ERNST. "George, Stefan," *Columbia Dictionary of Modern European Literature,* ed. Horatio Smith (New York: Columbia University Press, 1947).

———. *Kommentar zu dem Werk Stefan Georges* (Munich, Düsseldorf: Küpper-Bondi, 1960).

———. *Kommentar zu den Prosa- Drama- und Jugend-Dichtungen Stefan Georges* (Munich, Düsseldorf: Küpper-Bondi, 1962).

New York Times. "Stefan George, 65, German Poet Dies." December 5, 1933, p. 23, col. 1; December 6, 1933, p. 22, col. 4.

NORWOOD, EUGENE. "Stefan George's Translation of Shakespeare's Sonnets," *Monatshefte,* XLIV (1952), 217-24.

OSWALD, VICTOR A. JR. "The Historical Content of Stefan George's 'Algabal'," *GR,* XXIII (1948), 193-205.

———. "Oscar Wilde, Stefan George, Heliogabalus," *MLQ,* X (1949), 517-25.

PANNWITZ, RUDOLF. *Albert Verwey und Stefan George* (Heidelberg, Darmstadt: Schneider, 1965).

PERL, WALTER H., ed. *Leopold Andrian und die Blätter für die Kunst* (Hamburg: Hauswedell, 1960).

Revue d'Allemagne. II, No. 13-14 (November-December, 1928). The entire issue is devoted to George.

ROSTEUTSCHER, JOACHIM. *Das ästhetische Idol im Werke von Winckelmann, Novalis, Hoffmann, Goethe, George und Rilke* (Berne: Francke, 1956).

SALIN, EDGAR. *Um Stefan George. Erinnerung und Zeugnis.* 2nd ed. (Munich, Düsseldorf: Küpper-Bondi, 1954).

SCHLÖSSER, MANFRED, ed. *Kein ding sei wo das wort gebricht. Stefan George zum Gedenken.* 2nd ed. (= *Agora,* vol. 11) (Darmstadt: Agora, 1961).

SCHMITZ, VICTOR A. *Gundolf. Eine Einführung in sein Werk* (Düsseldorf, Munich: Küpper-Bondi, 1965).

SCHONAUER, FRANZ. *Stefan George in Selbstzeugnissen und Bilddokumenten* (Hamburg: Rowohlt, 1960).

SCHULTZ, H. STEFAN. *Studien zur Dichtung Stefan Georges* (Heidelberg: Stiehm, 1967).

———. *Stefan George. Rede zur Eröffnung der Stefan George Ausstellung in Marbach a.N. 25. Mai 1968.* (Heidelberg: Stiehm, 1968).

SOKEL, WALTER H. *The Writer in Extremis. Expressionism in Twentieth-Century German Literature* (Stanford, Calif.: Stanford University Press, 1959).

STARCK, TAYLOR. "Stefan George and the Reform of the German Lyric," *MLN,* XXXIV (1919), 1-7.

STAUFFENBERG, ALEXANDER. *Der Tod des Meisters* (Überlingen: Delfinverlag, 1948).

THORMAEHLEN, LUDWIG. *Erinnerungen an Stefan George* (Hamburg: Hauswedell, 1962).

URBAN, G. R. *Kinesis and Stasis. A Study in the Attitude of Stefan George and His Circle to the Musical Arts* (The Hague: Mouton, 1962).

VALLENTIN, BERTHOLD. *Gespräche mit Stefan George. 1902-1931* (Amsterdam: Castrum Peregrini Presse, 1961).

VERWEY, ALBERT. *Mein Verhältnis zu Stefan George. Erinnerungen aus den Jahren 1895-1928,* trans. from the Dutch by Antoinette Eggink (Strassburg: Heitz, 1936).

VORDTRIEDE, WERNER. "The Conception of the Poet in the Works of Stéphane Mallarmé and Stefan George." Diss., Northwestern University, 1944.

———. "Direct Echoes of French Poetry in Stefan George's Work," *MLN,* LX (1945), 461-68.

———. "The Mirror as Symbol and Theme in the Works of Stéphane Mallarmé and Stefan George," *Modern Language Forum,* XXXII (1947), 13-24.

———. *Novalis und die französischen Symbolisten* (Stuttgart: Kohlhammer, 1963).

WEIGAND, HERMANN J. "Stefan George Poems. Rendered into English by Valhope and Morwitz," *JEGP,* XLIII (1944), 141-49. (Review article.)

WINKLER, MICHAEL. "Zu einigen Liedern im *Siebenten Ring* Stefan Georges," *GQ,* XXXVIII (1965), 298-309.

———. "Über die Lieder im *Neuen Reich* Stefan Georges," *JEGP,* LXIV (1965), 505-22.

———. *Stefan George* (Stuttgart: Metzler, 1970).

WOLFSKEHL, KARL. *Gesammelte Werke,* 2 vols. (Hamburg: Claassen, 1960).

WOLTERS, FRIEDRICH. *Stefan George und die Blätter für die Kunst. Deutsche Geistesgeschichte seit 1890* (Berlin: Bondi, 1930).

ZELLER, BERNHARD, ed. *Stefan George. 1868-1968. Der Dichter und sein Kreis* (Munich: Kösel, 1968).

Index